D0383082

SRI DAYA MATA

Sanghamata ("Mother of the Society"), president and spiritual head of Self-Realization Fellowship/Yogoda Satsanga Society of India

Finding the Joy Within You

Personal Counsel for God-Centered Living

BY

SRI DAYA MATA

A publication of
SELF-REALIZATION FELLOWSHIP
Founded in 1920 by Paramahansa Yogananda

ABOUT THIS BOOK: *Finding the Joy Within You,* published in 1990, is the second anthology of talks by Sri Daya Mata, president and spiritual head of Self-Realization Fellowship. The first volume, *Only Love: Living the Spiritual Life in a Changing World,* was published in 1976. Since the mid-1950s monastics in the ashrams of Paramahansa Yogananda have been recording the talks given by Daya Mata during *satsangas* (gatherings of truth-seekers at which the leader speaks extemporaneously on inspirational subjects), in order to preserve her many personal stories about Paramahansa Yogananda and the wealth of spiritual counsel she had absorbed during her more than twenty years with him. The recordings were subsequently transcribed, and selections from the talks became a regular feature in *Self-Realization* (the magazine founded by Paramahansa Yogananda in 1925). Because people of all different faiths and walks of life found them to be a source of helpful and compassionate guidance, the material was compiled into book form. New talks appear in each issue of *Self-Realization,* and will be published in future volumes in this series.

Authorized by the International Publications Council of
SELF-REALIZATION FELLOWSHIP
3880 San Rafael Avenue • Los Angeles, CA 90065-3298

Self-Realization Fellowship was founded by Paramahansa Yogananda as the instrument for the worldwide dissemination of his teachings. The Self-Realization Fellowship name and emblem (shown above) appear on all SRF books, recordings, and other publications, assuring the reader that a work originates with the society established by Paramahansa Yogananda and faithfully conveys his teachings.

~First Edition, 1990. This Printing, 2008.~

Library of Congress Catalog Card Number: 90-63632
ISBN-13: 978-0-87612-288-4
ISBN-10: 0-87612-288-8

Printed in the United States of America
1813-J874

With eternal gratitude and devotion,
this volume is dedicated
to my revered Gurudeva

PARAMAHANSA YOGANANDA

for lovingly and unerringly
guiding this devotee to
the perfect joy

Contents

Illustrations

FOREWORD

By Dr. Binay Ranjan Sen

Former Ambassador of India to the United States and Director General of the Food and Agriculture Organization of the United Nations

Nearly forty years ago I had the great good fortune to meet Paramahansa Yogananda, that divine soul whose spirit and teachings are so beautifully conveyed in this volume of talks by his foremost living disciple, Sri Daya Mata. The experience of meeting Paramahansaji is etched in my memory as one of the unforgettable events of my life. It was in March of 1952. I had taken up my duties as India's Ambassador to the United States late in 1951, and was on an official tour visiting the different parts of the country. Upon my arrival in Los Angeles, the uppermost thought in my mind was to meet Paramahansaji, whose teaching of Self-Realization was exercising a great spiritual influence not only in the United States, but in many other countries of the world.

Even though I had heard much about Paramahansaji and his work, I was not really quite prepared for what I found at the Self-Realization Center on Mt. Washington. From the moment I arrived, I felt as if I had gone back three thousand years to one of the ancient ashrams we read about in our holy scriptures. Here was the great *rishi* (illumined sage) surrounded by his disciples, all clad in the saffron robes of the *sannyasi* (renunciant). It seemed an island of divine peace and love in a sea buffeted by the tumult of the modern age.

Paramahansaji was at the door to greet my wife and me. The impact of seeing him was incalculable. I felt uplifted in a way I had never known before. As I looked into his face, my eyes were almost dazzled by a radiance—a light of spirituality that literally shone from him. His infinite gentleness, his gracious kindliness, enveloped my wife and me like warm sunshine.

In the days that followed, the Master gave every minute he could spare to be with us. We spoke much about India's difficulties and about the plans our leaders were making to better the conditions of her people. I could see that his understanding and insight extended to the most mundane of problems, even though he was a man of Spirit. In him I found a true ambassador of India, carrying and spreading the essence of India's ancient wisdom to the world.

The last scene with him, at the banquet in the Biltmore Hotel, remains permanently engraved in my mind. Those events have been described elsewhere; it was truly a scene of *mahasamadhi*. It was immediately clear that a great spirit had passed in a way that only such a one could. I do not think that any of us felt like mourning. It was a feeling above all of exaltation, of having witnessed a divine event.

Since that day my work has taken me to many lands. In South America, Europe, and India, people who have been touched by Paramahansaji's divine light have approached me and asked for some words about this great man, having seen the widely published photographs of the final days of his life during which I was present. In all of those who came, I felt an urgency, a longing for some sense of direction to guide their lives in these troubled times. I began to see that, far from dying out with the Master's passing, the work he started was shedding its light on ever greater numbers of people around the world.

Nowhere does his legacy shine with more radiance than in his saintly disciple Sri Daya Mata, whom he prepared to carry on in his footsteps after he would be gone. Before his passing he told her, "When I am gone, only love can take my place." Those who, like myself, were privileged to have met Paramahansaji find reflected in Daya Mataji that same spirit of divine love and compassion that so impressed me on my first visit to the Self-Realization Center almost forty years ago. In her words recorded in this volume we have a priceless gift of the wisdom and love that radiated from the great Master into her life, and which indelibly touched my own.

As our world moves toward a new millennium, we are threatened by darkness and confusion as never before. The old ways of country versus country, religion versus religion, man versus nature, must be transcended in a new spirit of universal love, understanding, and concern for others. This is the eternal message of India's seers—the message brought by Paramahansa Yogananda for our own time and for generations to come. It is my hope that the torch he left, which is now in the hands of Sri Daya Mata, will light the way for millions who are seeking direction for their lives.

Calcutta
October 20, 1990

PREFACE

From 1931 until 1952, it was my privilege and duty to record stenographically Paramahansa Yogananda's teachings for posterity: his public lectures and classes, the Sunday and Thursday inspirational services he conducted at his Self-Realization Fellowship International Headquarters and temples, and much of his informal spiritual counsel to disciples.

The teachings presented in the Guru's classes and lectures around the nation—particularly the detailed instructions on yoga meditation techniques taught to those who enrolled for the private classes he held in each city—were compiled into the *Self-Realization Fellowship Lessons*. Of the inspirational talks he gave over the years to members and the interested public at Self-Realization temples and the international headquarters, over a hundred have been published in two anthologies, *Man's Eternal Quest* and *The Divine Romance;* others appear in each issue of *Self-Realization* magazine. The purpose of the present volume (and its predecessor, *Only Love*) is to convey the personal guidance and inspiration Paramahansaji gave to the close disciples who lived around him—those who received through day-to-day association with the great Master his in-depth spiritual training and discipline.

To those of us who came to him with the earnest desire to know God, Gurudeva* would speak very

* In referring to her guru, Paramahansa Yogananda, Sri Daya Mata uses the terms *Gurudeva* ("divine teacher"), *Guruji* ("*ji*" is a respectful suffix added to names and titles in India), and *Master* (the nearest English equivalent for the Sanskrit term *guru*—signifying one who, in his attainment of self-mastery, is uniquely qualified to lead others on the inner journey to God-realization). *(Publisher's Note)*

frankly about what we needed to do to change ourselves and to grow in awareness of God. Most of his guidance to us, however, was not in the form of long discourses or detailed explanations. When our thoughts or actions strayed from the goal of God-centered living, he had many subtle ways—and some that were not so subtle!—of refocusing our endeavors. A few pointed words, a significant glance, an encouraging remark about the qualities of an ideal devotee or some principle of truth, always wielded their full potential to bring about some change in us. Primarily, however, we learned through Gurudeva's example and through our efforts to emulate that life which so perfectly reflected the love and joy of God.

The counsel in this book is a gathering of the fruit of those twenty years at the feet of my Guru. It is the guidance he gave to all in whom he found not merely an intellectual curiosity about spiritual truths, but a genuine longing to draw nearer to God by anchoring their lives in Him.

Most of the material presented here has been taken from *satsangas*—informal gatherings at which the leader answers questions from those present, or speaks extemporaneously, on spiritual subjects. Over the years, Guruji's disciples have tape-recorded many of these talks and published them in *Self-Realization* magazine, as well as releasing some as recordings. In recent months I have been able to work with our editors in reviewing the previously printed material—clarifying certain points, adding further details here and there, and arranging the subject matter for publication in book form.

Looking back over the many years that my life has been guided by the counsel of Gurudeva, I feel deeply grateful. These have been years of complete satisfaction of heart and soul. No personal credit is due to me; it is the blessing of my Guru and his teachings. My humble hope is that the spiritual practices and ideals that had such a transforming effect on my life will prove of like blessing to others who find introduction to them through the pages of this book.

Los Angeles
November 19, 1990

INTRODUCTION

"What a vast world of love and joy is within the soul!
We don't have to acquire it; it is already ours."
—Sri Daya Mata

This collection of talks offers compelling testimony that every one of us—whatever our outer circumstances—can learn to live each day in the continual joy and security found at the deepest level of our being. *Finding the Joy Within You* is a compassionate and practical guide to a life of attunement with the Divine—the fruit of the author's sixty years of living for God and sharing His joy with others.

Sri Daya Mata was born on January 31, 1914, in Salt Lake City, Utah.* From her earliest years she had a deep longing to know God. At the age of eight, when she first heard about India in school, she felt a mysterious inner awakening, and with it a conviction that India held the key to the fulfillment of her life. That day, when school was over, she ran home and exclaimed jubilantly to her mother, "When I grow up I will never marry; I will go to India." Prophetic words from a child.

When Daya Mata was fifteen, she was given a copy of the Bhagavad Gita, "Song of the Lord." This scripture deeply moved her, for it revealed God's compassionate love for and understanding of His children. He was seen to be approachable, knowable; and His children were called divine beings, who through self-effort could realize their spiritual birthright, oneness with Him. Daya Mata resolved that somehow, in some way, she

* Born Faye Wright, she later became known by the monastic name Daya Mata, "Mother of Compassion." *Sri* is a title of respect.

would devote her life to seeking God. She went from one religious authority to another, yet always there remained in her heart an unsatisfied question: "But who *loves* God; who *knows* Him?"

In 1931, Paramahansa Yogananda came to Salt Lake City to give a series of classes.* Daya Mata, then seventeen, attended with her mother and sister. Recalling her first impressions, she has said, "As I stood at the back of the crowded auditorium, I became transfixed, unaware of anything around me except the speaker and his words. My whole being was absorbed in the wisdom and divine love that were pouring into my soul and flooding my heart and mind. I could only think, 'This man loves God as I have always longed to love Him. He *knows* God. Him I shall follow.'"

In an assemblage of thousands it seemed unlikely that the young girl would have any opportunity to meet the Guru. But it is said that adversity is sometimes a blessing in disguise. Daya Mata had long suffered from a severe blood disorder. The illness, which doctors had been unable to cure, had finally forced her to leave school. However, she was faithfully attending Paramahansaji's classes, and the bandages covering her swollen face apparently attracted the attention of the great Guru. Toward the end of the classes he gave her a divine healing, and predicted that within seven days no trace of her illness would remain, nor would it

* Paramahansa Yogananda, founder of Yogoda Satsanga Society of India in 1917, had been in the United States since 1920. At that time he had been invited as a delegate from India to the International Congress of Religious Liberals in Boston. During the intervening years, he had lectured throughout the country, and had established in Los Angeles an international headquarters for his work, Self-Realization Fellowship.

ever recur. And so it was.* But to Daya Mata, an even greater blessing than her remarkable cure was an opportunity to meet this man of God. She was extremely shy, and to this day wonders how she found the courage to speak her first words to him: "I want so much to enter your ashram and devote my life to seeking God." The Guru looked at her penetratingly for a moment before replying: "And you shall."

But it would require a miracle for that to come to pass, as family opposition was great. She was still a young girl, and her family—with the exception of her understanding mother—was firmly set against her leaving home to follow a religion wholly foreign to them. One evening, Paramahansa Yogananda said in his lecture that if a devotee called deeply enough to God, with determination to receive a response, His response would be forthcoming. Daya Mata made her resolve; and that night after the family had retired, she went into the living room, where she could be alone. Tears flowed as she poured out her heart to God. After several hours, a profound peace came over her whole being, and she could cry no longer: she knew that God had heard her prayer. Within two weeks all doors were opened, and on November 19, 1931, she was able to enter Paramahansa Yogananda's ashram in Los Angeles. The following year, she took her final vows of renunciation and consecration to God, becoming one of the first *sannyasinis* of the monastic Self-Realization Order.

Time sped by quickly at the feet of her Guru. Although she was deeply happy, those early years of ashram training were not without struggle. Paramahansaji was lovingly but firmly engaged in the task of

* Daya Mata describes this instance of divine healing in more detail on pages 3–4.

transforming the young nun into an exemplary disciple. From the beginning it was evident that Paramahansaji had singled out Daya Mata for a special role. He later told her that he had given to her the same intense spiritual discipline that his guru, Swami Sri Yukteswar, had given to him—a significant remark, since she was to inherit the spiritual and organizational mantle that Sri Yukteswar had bestowed on him.

For more than twenty years, Sri Daya Mata was part of the small circle of his closest disciples, who were with him almost constantly. As the years passed, he assigned more and more responsibility to her; and in the closing period of his life, he began to speak openly to the disciples of the worldwide role she was destined to play.

Wanting only to remain in the background, Daya Mata found the position of leadership that was being thrust upon her a tremendous test. She pleaded with the Master to let her serve instead under whomever else he would choose. But he remained adamant. Desiring above all else to do the will of God and her Guru, Daya Mata inwardly surrendered to what was being asked of her. "Now my work is finished," the Master told her. "Your work begins."

Paramahansaji entered *mahasamadhi** in 1952. In 1955, succeeding the late, saintly Rajarsi Janakananda, Sri Daya Mata became president of Self-Realization Fellowship/Yogoda Satsanga Society of India. As spiritual successor to Paramahansa Yogananda, she sees to the guidance of SRF/YSS members, the training of

* A God-realized soul's conscious exit from the body at the time of physical death. Paramahansa Yogananda entered *mahasamadhi* at the Biltmore Hotel in Los Angeles on March 7, 1952, just after giving a speech at a banquet in honor of Ambassador B. R. Sen.

monastic disciples who reside in the Self-Realization/Yogoda ashrams, and the faithful carrying out of Paramahansa Yogananda's ideals and wishes for the dissemination of his teachings and the expansion of his spiritual and humanitarian work worldwide.

On March 7, 1990, Los Angeles-area newspapers reported Sri Daya Mata's thirty-fifth anniversary as president of the society. One article read, in part: "As one of the first women in recent times to be appointed spiritual head of a worldwide religious movement, she has been a forerunner of today's increasing trend toward accepting women in positions of spiritual authority that have traditionally been reserved for men in most denominations. In the thirty-five years she has held that position, many have become acquainted with her through her global speaking tours, her writings, and the films and recordings of her talks on the universal ideals espoused by the great religions of both East and West."

Paramahansaji wrote to Daya Mata on her birthday in 1946: "May you be born in the Cosmic Mother, and inspire all with your spiritual motherliness only—only to bring others to God by the example of your life." Today, Self-Realization/Yogoda members around the world look to Sri Daya Mata as *Sanghamata* or "Mother of the Society." Many others, as well, have been touched by the great love and spiritual strength she inspires. A businessman who has rendered professional service to Self-Realization Fellowship over the years wrote to her: "Your personal serenity is very important to me and to others. You and the people around you are like bedrock—a foundation to cling to in a very precarious world. I know you claim no personal merit for this—you live out your convictions and the rest follows."

Though her life is given primarily to her Guru's work and to followers of the path of Self-Realization, she feels all seekers of God to be a part of her spiritual family, whatever their creed. A Catholic Sister of Charity, after meeting Daya Mata and hearing her speak on several occasions, remarked: "For me, as a member of a religious order, Daya Mata is a shining example of what a life committed to the service of God and neighbor ought to be. She makes me think of that great forerunner of Christ, John the Baptist, who said of himself, 'I am the voice of one crying in the wilderness. Make straight the way of the Lord.' In her presence there are no Catholics, Protestants, or Hindus, but only children of the one Father, God. And each one of them she receives graciously and has a place for them in her heart. I, a Catholic nun, have experienced so much her kindness and her interest and encouragement. I always felt that she treated me as one of her own. For me she will always be an ideal of what my life as a religious ought to be....She radiates God."

SELF-REALIZATION FELLOWSHIP

FINDING THE JOY WITHIN YOU

Yes, We Can Know God!

Opening talk at one of the Self-Realization Fellowship Convocations: a week of classes, meditation, and spiritual fellowship held annually in Los Angeles

Tomorrow the classes begin, and I am remembering the time in Salt Lake City, many years ago, when I first took such classes from our revered guru, Paramahansa Yogananda. What a tremendous impact he had on my life!

From my earliest years, I had an unceasing desire to find God in this lifetime. It was in my seventeenth year that I met Paramahansaji. My body was very ill at that time. I was suffering from blood poisoning throughout my system, and the doctors could find no cure for it. One eye was swollen closed, and I had three bandages on my face. Those bandages were actually a blessing, because I stood out rather like a sore thumb even in that large audience!

In those days Master would give several lectures, introducing his teachings, before the classes in which he dealt with the deeper aspects and methods of yoga. After the last of the public lectures, he would invite the congregation to come forward, and would greet them individually. I approached him with legs shaking; I was so very, very shy. When I stood before him, he looked at my disfigured face and asked, "What is the matter with you?" After my mother, with whom I had come to the lectures, explained my health problem, he said, "Come back tomorrow to the classes," (of course I was coming anyway!) "but remain afterward."

I spent the next day in eager anticipation of personally talking with the Guru again. That night he spoke on faith and will power. He so inspired me that as I sat and listened to him I felt it was definitely possible to move mountains with faith in God.

After the meeting, I waited to be the very last to greet him. During our conversation, out of the blue, he suddenly said to me, "Do you believe that God can heal you?" As he said that, his eyes were alight with divine power.

I replied, "I *know* God can heal me."

He touched me in blessing between the eyebrows, at what we call the Christ or *Kutastha* center.* Then he said, "From this day forward, you are healed. Inside one week the bandages will no longer be necessary; your scars will be gone." And that is exactly what happened. Within one week the condition cleared, and has never returned.

Harmonious Development of Body, Mind, and Soul

The teachings of Self-Realization Fellowship are based on harmonious development of body, mind, and soul. If we are wholly engrossed in the problems of this body, if physical pain absorbs all of our concentration, it is impossible to know God. It is also impossible to know God if the mind is filled with worry, fear, doubt, emotional problems—because we cannot then give to Him the attention necessary to find Him. Therefore the yogis of India say that an important adjunct to seeking

* The subtle center (*ajna chakra*) at the point between the eyebrows; seat of the all-perceiving spiritual eye and the universal Christ Consciousness in man; and center of will and concentration.

God-realization is to follow certain methods whereby you can keep the body strong through simple, daily care; and learn to develop your powers of concentration so that the mind, made restless by the ups and downs of this world, will not be able to disturb you when you sit to meditate.

The "how-to-live" guidance of Paramahansa Yogananda and the techniques* that you will receive over the next week are based on these principles. They will help you in the development and control of the body and the mind, and will enable your consciousness to go beyond physical and mental limitations to the realization that you are made in the image of the One Cosmic Beloved.

You will be given a key; but, as Guruji used to say to us, it is up to you to use it. If you come, take these teachings, are temporarily inspired by them, go back to your homes saying, "That was a very refreshing week," and forget them—then, my dears, they are of no permanent value to you. One must practice diligently and regularly, with concentration and enthusiasm, in order to achieve success with the *Raja Yoga*† we teach.

The Divine Purpose of Life

We are on this earth for a definite purpose—to reclaim, as Christ taught, our lost divine heritage as children of God. "Know ye not that ye are the temple of God, and that the Spirit of God dwelleth in you?"‡

* Reference to the Kriya Yoga science of concentration, meditation, and life-energy control taught by Paramahansa Yogananda in the *Self-Realization Fellowship Lessons.*

† The "royal" or highest path to God-union, *Raja Yoga* includes the essentials of all other forms of yoga. It stresses scientific meditation techniques, such as Kriya Yoga, as the ultimate means of attaining God-realization.

‡ I Corinthians 3:16.

We have all heard this before, but who among us has realized it? There is a difference between theoretical understanding of the science of religion, the science of the soul, and the direct perception of God—actual communion with the Divine Beloved that every human heart (and I know I am speaking of each one of you) is craving.

We are all hungering inwardly for something beyond this world. Even God feels some lack, some longing. He has everything in the universe, with one exception: He is crying for the love of His children—you and me and all of us. And He will never be satisfied, can never be fully content, until He knows that we are out of this terrible mess that we have created for ourselves. When Master first said this to me years ago, it set my whole being aflame, and I determined to devote this lifetime to seeking God alone.

Think of the tremendous problems mankind faces in this world: hatred, prejudice, selfishness; some have plenty and others insufficient for their needs; the struggle between this "ism" and that "ism," each group feeling that its "ism" is better than another's. Why did God create so many different human beings, why did He make so many different mentalities? If we are all children of the one God, what is behind our differences?

Cultivating Stillness and Clear Perception

All of the scriptures of the world say that we are made in God's image. If this is so, why don't we know that we are taintless and immortal, as He is? Why aren't we conscious of ourselves as embodiments of His spirit?

Guruji used to compare the mind to a lake. When the water is still, the moon is reflected clearly therein.

Addressing Self-Realization members during annual Convocation, Los Angeles, August 1989

"How often Guruji had us affirm with him that our lives are to be lived in the joy that is God: 'From Joy I have come. In Joy I live, move, and have my being. And in that sacred Joy I will melt again.' Hold on to this truth, and you will see how that Joy inwardly sustains you no matter what comes into your life."

Daya Mataji speaking to SRF members from around the world during observance of fiftieth anniversary of Self-Realization Fellowship; Los Angeles, 1970

"We are united in divine love, divine brotherhood, divine friendship; and one common goal: seeking God together and serving Him in whatever way we can as we reach out to our greater family of all living beings."

But suppose I toss a handful of pebbles into the lake. You will then see a distorted image of the moon, because the ripples caused by the pebbles have disturbed the smooth surface of the water. In the same manner, man's mind is rippled constantly by pebbles of emotions, moods, habits acquired in this and past lives*—which make it impossible for him even to think clearly, let alone behold clearly the reflection of God that is within himself.

You will say, "Is it impossible, then, to know God?" Again, what do the scriptures say? "Be still, and know that I am God."† "Pray without ceasing."‡ People come to me, here and abroad, and say, "How is it possible for you to sit motionless in meditation for so many hours? What do you do during those periods of stillness?" The yogis of ancient India, who developed the science of religion as no other people on the face of the globe have done, discovered that by certain scientific techniques it is possible to so still the mind that there is not a ripple of restless thought disturbing or distracting it. In that clear lake of consciousness, we behold within us the reflected image of the Divine.

By regular practice of yoga with steady attention, the time will come when you suddenly say to yourself, "Oh! I am not this body, though I use it to communicate with this world; I am not this mind, with its emotions of anger, jealousy, hatred, greed, restlessness. I am that wonderful state of consciousness within. I am made in

* A reference to reincarnation, the doctrine that human beings, compelled by the law of evolution, incarnate repeatedly in progressively higher lives—retarded by wrong actions and desires, and advanced by spiritual endeavors—until Self-realization and God-union are attained.

† Psalms 46:10. ‡ I Thessalonians 5:17.

the divine image of God's bliss and love."

Man Suffers Because He Has Turned Away From God

The goal of life is to know God. And all of the struggles in this world are caused by man's having turned away from God. Now we must turn back to Him. Does this mean we should run away to the Himalayas, or to an ashram or monastery? Not at all. As Master expressed it in a prayer: "Where Thou hast placed me, Thou must come." But it does mean that out of the twenty-four hours each day, which most human beings spend working to feed and clothe the body, reading to improve the mind, or in recreation and sleep, we ought to be able to give at least one hour to God. Can any one of us truly say this is impossible?

Lord Krishna told Arjuna, "Get away from My ocean of suffering."* Unfortunately, all too often, we do not even begin to think about God until we are hit hard by a personal tragedy—something that profoundly upsets us and makes us realize we are not secure in this world, after all. Neither money nor health nor human love is permanent, so what can we hold on to? When we become badly shaken by life's experiences, we look for some way to regain our balance. We begin to search deeper for the real purpose of life. We may start going to church, or studying philosophy or the lives of the saints, for example. Thus begins the quest for God.

If we ask ourselves who truly exemplified ideal balance in this world, the life of Christ, for one, comes to mind. Even when his body was being torn away from him, his consciousness of the joy of God's pres-

* "For these whose consciousness is fixed in Me, I become before long their Redeemer to bring them out of the sea of mortal births" (Bhagavad Gita XII:7).

ence could not be distracted for long. His happiness and security did not depend upon the body, nor on other external, material things. His joy, his security, was in God. He and those other great ones like him are the most balanced beings ever chronicled in the history of mankind.

Why is there so much imbalance in the world today? What is wrong with mankind? Our trouble is that we are striving to find the peace, the joy, the love we seek through the wrong avenues. We have thought that we could get along without the one Everlasting Reality: God. It is He alone who has been with us since the beginning of time, is with us now, and will go with us beyond the portals of this world. Unless and until we return to Him, unless and until we consciously make an effort every day—for at least one hour out of the twenty-four—to find Him, we cannot know lasting happiness.

The Way to Peace

The world is a place of duality, light and shadow, that will never know perfect peace. Each day we wonder what the headlines will be tomorrow, which nations will be next to jump at one another's throats. How can the world know what peace is until man first feels it in his own heart, and then demonstrates it outwardly? Do you suppose that conferences are going to bring permanent peace? No. They help, but they are not the final solution, because peace must come from within. Let it begin in our own hearts. You can know true peace when you take your mind away from this world—so full of discouragement, troubles, and heartache—and anchor it in God.

Some say that those who seek God are merely escapists. Show me who isn't! We are all trying to escape! But wise is that person who has come to the understanding that the only sure haven from sorrow is in God alone, naught else.

The Example of a Great Soul

Living around such a great soul as Paramahansa Yogananda for so many years, I saw countless manifestations of his wonderful spiritual example, which has inspired crowds of souls to want to walk in his footsteps. I love to speak about him because he was such a tremendous inspiration in my life. He had the power to heal. I have witnessed his healing of many, many diseases. And he had the power to read the minds of others. However, he often said, "I never intrude on anyone's mental privacy unless I am invited to by those who have asked for my help and guidance, or if for some reason the Lord tells me to." How many times he read my thoughts and replied to them rather than to my words. In fact, it is not easy to live around a teacher like that, because you could not hide any mood or negative thought from him! He used to say to us, "I don't deal with what you say, but what you think." And, believe me, we knew it!

Yet Guruji was in many ways childlike. I do not mean childish; there is a difference. He had all the simple, trusting, loving qualities that a child shows toward its beloved mother. That is the way he was with God. The Bible says, "Suffer the little children to come unto me, and forbid them not: for of such is the kingdom of God."*

Guruji did not believe that one should wear his love for God on his sleeve. He taught that loving God is

* Mark 10:14.

a deeply personal and sacred relationship between the devotee and his Creator. "Don't talk about your experiences," he would say. "And don't look for miracles and powers. Just develop a simple, childlike attitude toward the Divine Beloved." He taught that phenomenal experiences and miracles often can be distractions on the spiritual path that sidetrack one from the Goal. They come, but they are not the Goal, so do not be lured by them. The whole intent must be toward oneness with God: "Lord, Lord, I want to know You. I want to get away from this ocean of suffering. I know that the more I bring You into my life, and the more I depend upon You, the more I shall find peace in my heart. And when I become a peaceful, loving being, then perhaps it will be possible for me to contribute my share towards a more peaceful world."

An Experience With the Divine Mother

I would like to read to you something I wrote down about one of Master's experiences, which will perhaps give you a deeper insight into his life. (Fortunately, shorthand was one of the subjects in which I excelled at school. It came in handy during the years I was at Guruji's feet. I never went anywhere without my notebook and pencil, so that I could record as many of his pearls of wisdom as possible.)

On one occasion Guruji said this to us:

> While others waste their time, meditate, and you will see that in meditation that Silence will speak to you. "Give my Mother* a soul call. She can't remain

* The scriptures of India teach that God is both personal and impersonal, immanent and transcendent. Seekers in the West have traditionally related to God in His personal aspect as Father; in India, the

> hidden anymore. Come out of the silent sky, come out of the mountain glen, come out of my secret soul, come out of my cave of silence."* Everywhere I see the Divine Spirit manifesting in form as the Mother. Water condensed becomes ice, and so invisible Spirit can be frozen into form by my devotion's frost. If only you could see the beautiful eyes of the Mother that I beheld last night. My heart is filled with joy eternal. The little cup of my heart cannot hold the joy and the love that I beheld in those eyes—looking at me, sometimes smiling. I said to Her, "Oh! and people call You unreal!" and Divine Mother smiled. "It is You who are real and all things else are unreal," I said, and the Divine Mother smiled again. I prayed, "O Mother, be Thou real unto all." And I wrote Her name on the foreheads of a few who were present. Satan will never be able to take over their lives.

Guruji goes on to say:

> Such joy I feel day and night. Day passes into night and I forget time entirely. I don't have to meditate now, because That which I meditated upon has become one with me. Sometimes I breathe, sometimes I don't breathe. Sometimes the heart beats, sometimes it doesn't. I see that I have dropped everything except that one consciousness. Whether this physical engine is running or not, I behold that great light of God. Such is my joy.

How sublime was the realization of that great and divine master from India, Paramahansa Yogananda, the last in the line of Gurus of Self-Realization Fellow-

---

concept of God as the loving, compassionate Mother of the Universe has widespread appeal.

* From *Cosmic Chants,* by Paramahansa Yogananda.

ship.* And if you take to heart the message that will be given to you in this series of classes, and if you deeply and sincerely practice what you are taught, and refuse to give up in your search for God, you will know beyond any doubt, in this life, the truth of his words.

God love you all.

*Mahavatar Babaji, Lahiri Mahasaya, Swami Sri Yukteswar, and Paramahansa Yogananda

Understanding the Soul's Need for God

From a talk given at Bareilly, India

Many questions arise in the minds of those who think about God: What is God? What is the soul? What is Truth? What is religion? What is the *true* religion? What is the right path that leads to God? Why seek God?

First let us consider the question, "What is God?" No one has ever been able fully to describe Him. But those who have tasted the divine nectar of His presence have been able to tell something of what they experience when they commune with Him. One scriptural description of the Infinite is that He is *Sat-Chit-Ananda*—ever-existing, ever-conscious, ever-new Bliss. Ever-existing means that He is eternal; ever-conscious means He is always conscious of His eternal existence; and ever-new Bliss means that He is a joy that never grows stale. Every human being is seeking that kind of experience.

The scriptures also tell us that there are certain manifestations of God that are experienced as one draws close to Him. God is love, bliss, wisdom, peace, light, and the great cosmic sound of *Aum* or Amen.* All

* *Aum:* the universal symbol-word for God. *Aum* of the Vedas became the sacred word *Hum* of the Tibetans; *Amin* of the Moslems; and *Amen* of the Egyptians, Greeks, Romans, Jews, and Chris-

scriptures refer to the devotee's experiencing these aspects when communing with the Divine Beloved.

"Well," we may ask, "if this is what God is, then what is the soul?" The definition Gurudeva Paramahansa Yogananda gave is that the soul is *individualized* ever-existing, ever-conscious, ever-new Bliss. As the tiniest drop of water from the ocean is a minute part of the ocean itself, it contains all the qualities of the ocean, without exception. So, in the same way, this *atman,* the soul, contains all the qualities of the Divine.

Man Has Forgotten His True Nature

Unconsciously man knows he is divine. But consciously he has forgotten his true nature. The five senses were given to man that he might cognize this world, and through his experiences here, grow in understanding. But when he abuses the senses, he becomes engrossed in sensuality and loses knowledge of his infinite nature. Yet that nature continues subtly to manifest itself in pseudo-ways.

For example, every human being seeks power; many crave it. This is natural, because the soul knows it is all-powerful. But since in the ordinary conscious state the soul is not aware of its limitless nature, it strives instead for positions of authority or superiority, or to gain control over other people, or even over nations. The ideal of being all-powerful is not wrong, but too often the method of attaining and using that power is wrong. Those who know God understand and

---

tians. *Aum* is the all-pervading sound emanating from the Holy Ghost (Invisible Cosmic Vibration; God in His aspect of Creator); the "Word" or "Comforter"of the Bible; the voice of creation, testifying to the Divine Presence in every atom. *Aum* may be heard through practice of Self-Realization Fellowship methods of meditation.

rightly use the tremendous power that lies within the soul—the power that can move hearts, that can move nations, that through the centuries has changed lives.

Another way in which man's hidden divine nature expresses itself is through his craving for material wealth. The soul knows that in its oneness with God it is the possessor of all things, and that it has the power to create at will whatever it needs. But because we are not consciously aware of our soul's potential, we begin instead to accumulate material things in an effort to satisfy our buried conviction that everything we need or want is ours by divine birthright.

Man also craves bliss. The soul knows it is blissful, but because the ego is ignorant of that bliss, it succumbs to the temptations of pseudo-joys provided by *maya.** Through the ages, man has used intoxicants such as wine and drugs in an effort to forget this world, because subconsciously he remembers a more blissful one. Isn't it so? That goal is not wrong, either, because man, being made in the image of God, whose nature is bliss, automatically longs for that unalloyed joy. But not knowing how to regain it, he resorts to the pseudo-joy of intoxication. He drinks or takes drugs so that for at least a little while he can forget this world. The tragedy is that when his body becomes saturated with these intoxicants, they destroy his nerves and brain.

Man also seeks love, an unconscious response to the nature of his soul, which itself is love. But because he does not consciously experience that pure, all-satisfying divine love, he goes around like a beggar, pleading for a little affection from human hearts. It is not wrong to crave love, but the means by which most people seek it

* Cosmic delusion.

is ill-conceived. As often as man thinks he has found perfect love in human relationships, he finds instead that death, or unfaithfulness or some other failing, has left him disappointed and disillusioned. As Gurudeva used to say to us, "Behind every rosebush of pleasure there is a rattlesnake of disillusionment." 'Tis true!

There is also a craving in man for unity. Everything in this world is trying to come together. The law of attraction operates in even the most infinitesimal particles of matter. If you look through a microscope, you will see this power at work in many natural phenomena. Man also is always striving for the harmony of oneness. His soul knows that it and all other souls are essentially one with God. But because man identifies himself with this fleshly form, he has forgotten that oneness, so he seeks union with one soul after another in various relationships, trying always to find the lost sense of fulfillment that comes from unity.

So, we see that the goals of man are not wrong, only the manner by which he strives to achieve them. He has forgotten that he is not this body, that he is the all-perfect formless soul. He remembers only this flesh, and so strives unsuccessfully through the limited five senses to regain that which is already his.

Regaining Our Forgotten Divinity

Why should man seek God? Because, as Krishna taught, so long as we are identified with a mortal body, so long will we be subject to suffering. This finite world and everything in it is based upon the law of duality. When the One became many, in that instant He imposed a dual nature upon creation: You cannot know pleasure without knowing pain; you cannot know happiness without knowing sorrow; you cannot know life without knowing death; you cannot know human love without knowing hatred, and so forth. So long as we are tossed about on the waves of duality, we shall suffer—one moment joyous, the next sorrowful; one moment our body is filled with life and vigor, the next it is as dead as a piece of clay. Is the sole purpose of life to be born in these little forms, to grow up, gain a little knowledge with which to deal with this world, marry, beget children, grow old, fall sick, and die? No! The purpose of life—the only purpose—is to know that we are made in the image of God. Knowing this, we realize our true nature, which is ever blissful—ever-existing, ever-conscious, ever-new Bliss.

It is said that before we come to the state of evolution of birth in human form, we have passed eight million incarnations in lesser life-forms. And then as human beings we come on earth again and again, until we have satisfied all the desires that require mortal experiences; and until we have arrived at that state wherein we know our immortal oneness with God.

How, then, can we regain our lost or forgotten divine consciousness? This is what Yoga teaches, and every scripture says the same thing: Sit quietly; go within. That is where God and Self-realization are to be found. Withdraw from this finite world and penetrate deep within the recesses of your soul. There you will realize the ultimate achievement that is the unconscious goal of every human being.

I speak from my own experience, and from what I witnessed during twenty-one years at the feet of our blessed Gurudeva. How often we saw him in ecstasy, as the state of God-communion is known in the Western world—or *samadhi,* as it is known here in India. That state no words can fully describe.

What Is Truth?

Our next question is, "What is Truth?" First of all, let us examine what religion is, and what is the path that leads to God. The true meaning or definition of religion can be only one: That system of behavior and application of truth by which man can remove his threefold suffering—of body, mind, and soul—by the roots, so there is no possibility of recurrence. This is what religion is—or what it is really meant to be.

Unfortunately, religion today has become to many just a system of beliefs and rituals. But these do not satisfy the soul. If they did, millions of people who go regularly to their temples, mosques, or churches would be drunk with the love of God. But this is not the case. External worship is a good and important aspect of religion when the mind is concentrated on Him toward whom we are to direct our love and adoration; but when the ritual or ceremony becomes mechanical, and the Object of worship is forgotten, then such worship has no meaning or value. What has happened is that man has encrusted his worship of God in dogma. That is why he does not know God.

Let us go back to the question, "What is God?" God can manifest as any divine quality or in any form, but He cannot be confined to any particular concept; He is *all* ideas. He is within everything in this universe, and everything is contained within Him. Any thought that man has, the Divine has already thought; otherwise, man could not think it.

Down through the centuries, man has used symbols to remind him of his Creator. The earliest civilizations chose the sun, or fire, or other natural phenomena, to represent Him. These symbols became their gods.

Gradually, as man's understanding increased, religion evolved and clothed the infinite, formless Spirit with human forms and characteristics. Out of this came a whole world of division among religionists—one group saying God is this, another saying God is that, quarreling among themselves. What nonsense! The Lord can assume any aspect, or remain as unmanifested Spirit.

In seeking God, the devotee sometimes finds it much easier if he chooses some divine form as a visible symbol of the Infinite. Because through many, many incarnations man has become used to form, it is simpler for him to think of God in this way. For him who thinks it necessary, form *is* necessary; for him who thinks it unnecessary, it *is* unnecessary. But to have quarrels and divisions over which principle is right is foolishness; for the Divine is formless and with form, impersonal and personal.

I know that my Divine Beloved is essentially without form. But that does not make Him any less real. Love has no form, wisdom has no form, joy has no form; yet we experience them, don't we? They are more real to us than form. Well, that is what God is. In the ultimate sense, He is infinite love, wisdom, joy. Nevertheless, some devotees find it helpful and spiritually captivating to think of Him in one of His divine forms, such as incarnate in Lord Krishna, Jesus Christ, Buddha; or as the Heavenly Father, Mother, Friend, or Beloved.

Experiences of the One God in All Religions

When I entered the ashram as a young girl of seventeen, I had one notion: "Now, my Beloved, I must experience You as You are known in all religions, because I believe in and revere them all." To me, not one is outside the pale of my Beloved's protection and guidance. In my travels around the world, I have worshiped in mosques, temples, churches, and cathedrals. By going within in meditation I experienced in each one the divine bliss of God.

That bliss every person can experience when he rids his mind of prejudices. In the hearts and minds of intelligent human beings there is no room for prejudices. These are hidden fetters that tie the soul and smother it. The Divine is tolerant; the Divine has no prejudices. If we would be like Him, should we not also practice tolerance? If we would know Him, we must!

Tolerance does not conflict with loyalty. For me, it means simply this: I follow my Guru's path, but I revere all others as well. In his invocations to the Divine, Guruji always paid respect to his own line of Gurus. The prayer begins, "Heavenly Father"; and he does not leave it there, because he recognizes that God is all things to all men. He prays: "Heavenly Father, Mother, Friend, Beloved God"—God is all of these. Then he honors by name the Gurus behind his mission. Finally, he invokes the blessings of the saints of all religions—such was his reverence for anyone who lives in the thought of God alone. Truth is one; God is one, though He is called by many names.

So, to come back to the story of my early experiences: I was drunk with longing for God. My mind was aflame with one desire, and I vowed: "I shall not leave this world until I know that my God is my love." Only that was real to me. I was prepared to forsake everything if I could prove that one truth in this life: my God is love, and my God loves me.

The Divine *Lila* of Lord Krishna

My first experience came when Gurudeva gave me a book on the life of the Lord Krishna. For months I was intoxicated by the *lila,* the divine life, of Krishna. My mind was drunk with it, whether I was doing my chores in the ashram, or was in seclusion afterward. I loved to go out alone at night and sit on the ashram grounds and quietly commune with God as Krishna.

Lord Buddha's Path of Right Action

Then, perhaps a year later, Guruji gave me a book on the life of Lord Buddha; and again I was entranced. Krishna was gone, and only Buddha remained. I remember the tears that flowed as I read of the tremendous compassion he felt when he saw the different sufferings endured by mankind. Life was not as he had been taught to believe, surrounded by his protective family within the walled confines of his opulent palace. When he ventured forth to explore the rest of his kingdom, he saw a blind man; he saw a dead man's form; he saw starving beggars; and he said, "Is this how life is? Then I must find its true meaning."

Out of that resolution, by meditating long and very deeply, he came to understand the great wheel of karma—the law that whatever we sow in this world we shall one day reap. Every true philosophy teaches this. You cannot plant an apple seed and get a grapefruit tree. Whatever the seed you sow, you will harvest the fruit of its kind. When you plant the seeds of wrong action, know for certain that in this life, or some future life, those seeds will bear their bitter fruit. When man fully realizes the significance of this law, he will strive—with understanding, not fear—to follow always, to the best of his ability, the path of right action. Such is the truth as expounded by Buddha. So Daya Ma gained that understanding through contemplating the sublime example of his life.

The Divine Compassion of Christ

And then, because I had never understood the doctrine of the Christian world, though I was raised in it, I concentrated my mind upon Jesus Christ. I saw the great compassion and forgiveness he gave to humanity. Though he had converted water to wine, had healed the blind and raised the dead, those miracles could not compare with the miracle of the great example of love he set for the world. The gift from God that man considers the most precious is the flesh. As Christ's body temple was being penetrated and torn apart, in that supreme trial he could say, "Father, forgive them; for they know not what they do."* Then Daya Ma's experience was a true understanding of Christ and the significance of his life.

The All-Embracing Love of the Divine Mother

Later, Gurudeva gave me a book telling of God's appearing to the devotee as the Divine Mother, and then and there my consciousness became lost in Her. In the thought of Divine Mother's loving, tender compassion, every human heart knows there is an opportunity for forgiveness. Just as the mother whose son is a murderer or a thief holds him close to her bosom and says to the world, "You don't understand, but I do; I know why he has done these things," so the Divine Mother looks on each one of us in that way. Her compassion, Her love, Her forgiveness are there for us, if we but seek them. That is why I love to think of God as my Divine Mother. In that thought I find all the comfort, bliss, and love that my soul craves.

So, you see, in the Divine the devotee can experi-

* Luke 23:34.

ence all the various forms of love in their purest and highest state. No love is possible except that which is channeled from the one Cosmic Source. It is God alone who is pouring through human hearts the love of mother for child, of child for parent, of lover for beloved. Though we may taint it with human impurities, all these expressions are God's love.

Gurudeva often said: "In the pages of history how many there are who have vowed eternal love to one another! The path of incarnations is strewn with their skulls. Where is their love today?" But those souls that have been drunk with the love of God, their love lives on. They have changed mankind, because they first transformed themselves by attunement with God's eternal love.

Man Was Born to Know He Is One With God

How tragic it is when man renounces God! I am no renunciant. Those who reject God are the renunciants, because they have forsaken Him who is the Giver of everything in this universe. He is the sustainer of life. So often we say to Him, "My Lord, I have my children to raise, I have my work to do, I have all these things to look after—how can I find time for You?" But suppose He replied to us, "My child, I am so busy with My responsibilities, running all these universes upon universes, I haven't time to think of you." What then? We would cease to exist.

He knows even the tiniest grain of sand, because He is omniscient, because He is omnipresent, because everything in creation is He. Naught exists but Him. Man was born to reclaim his lost divine heritage, to know that he is one with God.

Man is a threefold being: body, mind, and soul. He

has a body, which he wears for a few years, like a coat. When it becomes frayed, he has it mended for as long as he can. Many organs can now be replaced for a certain period of time; but sooner or later, the body has to be cast aside. Man has a mind, but he is not this moody, narrow mind that so often is filled with prejudice, hatred, anger, jealousy, and greed. Man is the soul. How foolish he is to devote nearly all of his life, his attention, his energies, to this flesh. Perhaps a few try to improve the mind by reading good books. But who thinks of his Self—the soul?

Why Wait for Suffering to Prod You to Seek God?

I so love my India because it was in this sacred land that my divine Guru was nurtured, before he went to the West to teach hungry souls like myself—souls who were starving for spiritual nourishment.

Down through the ages God has sent divine messengers who try to rouse humanity out of its dream of delusion. They are voices crying in the wilderness,* "Wake, my child! Wake, my child!" If we do not respond to them, then we must endure the great awakener that cannot be ignored—suffering. Why wait for that? It shakes everyone who sleeps in delusion. At a time of great crisis, even the atheist will automatically cry out, "Oh my God!" Isn't it so? He turns naturally to God because his soul knows there is one Power, and inwardly man is always being directed toward It.

It is often said that suffering is the greatest teacher. It is—provided we take it with right attitude. No one escapes suffering in this world unless and until he has arrived at that state wherein he beholds, not duality,

* "I am the voice of one crying in the wilderness, make straight the way of the Lord" (John 1:23).

but only the One, the one beam of Light pouring through all bulbs of human flesh. Then he transcends delusion; he transcends suffering. But until then, the big and the little earthquakes of sorrow and pain will continue to shake him. Such is the fate of everyone who has not heeded the voices of the divine messengers. It is never too late to seek the Divine Beloved; but what a tragedy to wait until the body is falling apart, and distracts one's attention from thinking deeply of Him. That is why the great ones urge us: "Seek God now."

The Divine Beloved has no favorites. The Mother loves all Her children equally, just as the sunlight falls equally on the diamond and the charcoal lying side by side. The diamond reflects the light, but the charcoal cannot. My Beloved's grace, love, blessings, wisdom, and joy shine equally upon all Her children. The diamond mentalities reflect Her light; the charcoal mentalities have yet to be refined. That is all.

May each one of you make the effort to receive the light of God that graces your life with divine peace, love, and joy.

What Can We Do About the World's Problems?

Compilation from talks at Self-Realization Fellowship International Headquarters

A question I have often received, especially in recent years, is how to deal with the problems of the troubled times in which we are living. People from all parts of the world are concerned about the sad state of affairs affecting our planet.

Throughout history, the human race has gone through so many crises, and these predicaments will continue to come and go. This world revolves in an upward and downward cycle that continually repeats itself.* Right now, the consciousness of society as a whole is progressing upward; after reaching its apex thousands of years hence, it will come down again. Progression, regression; there is constant ebb and flow on this plane of duality.

With these evolutional cycles, civilizations rise and fall. Consider the highly advanced past civilizations, such as those of India and China. From the ancient Sanskrit epics of India,† for example, we see that dur-

* The world cycles, or *yugas,* are discussed in more detail in *The Holy Science* by Swami Sri Yukteswar (published by Self-Realization Fellowship).

† The *Ramayana* and *Mahabharata,* allegorical accounts of great historical kingdoms that existed, respectively, during the reigns of Sri Rama and Sri Krishna.

ing the time of Sri Rama, thousands of years before the Christian era, technology was highly advanced, as evidenced by his marvelous aircraft. And greater still were the mental and spiritual powers of those who lived in that Golden Age. But eventually, civilization began to decline, until in the Dark Ages such advancement became obscured. What caused this? I was thinking about that yesterday after my meditation, in light of what is happening in the world today.

The Nature of the Present Crisis

During the downward part of the cycle, people in general become increasingly ignorant of the spiritual side of their nature, until all that is noble disappears. Then the fall of that civilization is not far behind. This same process can happen to nations in the ascending phase of the cycle as well. If man's moral and spiritual evolution does not keep pace with the upward progress of knowledge and technology, he misuses the power he has acquired, to his own destruction. Indeed, this is the nature of the world crisis we are facing today.

Man's consciousness has evolved enough for him to unlock the mystery and marvelous power of the atom, a power that may one day perform tremendous things that we cannot even dream about now. But what have we done with that knowledge? The primary concentration has been on the development of instruments of destruction. Modern technology has also given us freedom from many of the time-consuming tasks that were once necessary for physical survival. Often, however, the leisure time man has gained is not used to advance his mental and spiritual natures, but to engage in an endless pursuit of material and sensual pleasures. If man thinks only in terms of his own sensuality, ruled by his emotions of hatred, jealousy, lust, and greed, the inevitable result is inharmony between individuals, turmoil within societies, conflicts among nations. Wars have never cured anything; instead, they snowball into greater holocausts—one confrontation breeding another. Only by the evolution of wiser, more loving human beings will the world become a truly better place.

Survival of Civilization Depends on Spiritual Progress

In thinking about world conditions today, I often recall an experience I had in 1963 during a pilgrimage to the cave of Mahavatar Babaji in the Himalayas. I have described this in detail on other occasions.* On the way to the cave, we spent the night in a tiny rest house near Dwarahat. In the middle of the night, I had a superconscious dream in which I beheld a great threatening darkness that was spreading over the earth like a black cloud—trying to engulf the whole world. But before it could succeed, there came a brilliant divine light that resisted the darkness, pushing it back. This was such an overwhelming experience that I cried out, thus waking my companions. Startled, they asked me what was wrong. But I did not want to speak of it, because I understood what this vision signified. I saw that the whole world faces a grave threat from the darkness of delusion with its forces of evil, negation, wrongdoing.

* Mahavatar Babaji is first in the line of Self-Realization Fellowship Gurus. It was he who resurrected the lost ancient spiritual science of Kriya Yoga and ordained Paramahansa Yogananda to disseminate it worldwide. His life and spiritual mission are described in *Autobiography of a Yogi*.

Sri Daya Mata recounts the experience referred to here in her book, *Only Love*, in the chapter "A Blessing From Mahavatar Babaji."

Twenty-five years have passed; and today immorality and the resultant violence are so rampant in society worldwide that it sometimes seems as if we are repeating the days of the fall of the Roman Empire. Especially among large segments of the young people, morality has dropped to practically zero. Everywhere there is so much heartache and suffering. People ask, "Why does God permit this?" But God has nothing to do with it. *We* permit it. He wouldn't punish us; it is we who punish ourselves. We are the creators of the conditions that confront us. They are the sum total of immoral behavior and the decline of ethical standards in all walks of life.

The survival of civilization depends on observance of standards of right behavior. I am not talking about man-made codes that change with changing times, but about timeless universal principles of conduct that promote healthy, happy, peaceful individuals and societies—allowing for diversity in a harmonious unity.

It is sometimes hard for us in our ordinary consciousness to grasp the immensity of the truths behind God's structured universe. But those ultimate verities do exist, and there can be no compromise with the exacting laws by which the Lord upholds the cosmos and its beings. Everything in the universe is connected. As human beings, we are related not only to each other, but to all nature as well, because all life comes from one Source: God. He is perfect harmony; but the wrong thoughts and actions of man have a desultory effect on the manifestation of His harmonious plan in this world. Just as when you try to tune in a radio station, static may prevent you from receiving the program clearly, so man's "static" misbehavior disturbs the harmony of the forces of nature. Wars, natural catastrophes, social turmoil, and the other problems we are facing today are the result.*

Spiritual Change Begins With Morality and Positive Thinking

At the end of that vision I described, the darkness threatening our world was pushed away by the spirit of God through increasing numbers of individuals living according to spiritual principles. Spirituality starts with morality, the rules of right behavior that are basic to every religion—such as truthfulness, self-control, faithfulness to marriage vows, noninjury to others. And we must straighten out not only our behavior, but also our thinking. If we persist in thinking a certain way, those thoughts eventually become actions. So to change ourselves we have to begin with our thoughts.

Try to become a more positive individual. One whose thoughts are always negative—moody, angry, full of jealousy and envy and meanness—is not someone who is progressing spiritually. That person shuts out the light of God and remains in darkness. He spreads gloom and inharmony wherever he goes.

Thought is a force; it has immense power. That is why I believe so deeply in the Worldwide Prayer Circle

* "The sudden cataclysms that occur in nature, creating havoc and mass injury, are not 'acts of God.' Such disasters result from the thoughts and actions of man. Whenever the world's vibratory balance of good and evil is disturbed by an accumulation of harmful vibrations, the result of man's wrong thinking and wrong doing, you will see devastation....When materiality predominates in man's consciousness, there is an emission of subtle negative rays; their cumulative power disturbs the electrical balance of nature, and that is when earthquakes, floods, and other disasters happen. God is not responsible for them! Man's thoughts have to be controlled before nature can be controlled."—Paramahansa Yogananda, in *Man's Eternal Quest*

that Guruji began. I hope you are all involved in it. When people send forth concentrated, positive thoughts of peace, love, goodwill, forgiveness, as in the healing technique used by the Worldwide Prayer Circle, this generates a great power. If the masses were to do this, it would set up a vibration of goodness that would be powerful enough to change the world.*

Change Yourself and You Will Change Thousands

Our role as followers of Paramahansa Yogananda is to do everything we can to put our lives in attunement with God, that by our thoughts, our words, and our exemplary behavior we may reach out and exert some spiritual influence on the rest of the world. One's words have little meaning unless they are manifested in one's life. The words of Christ are as powerful today as they were two thousand years ago because he lived what he taught. Our lives also must quietly but eloquently reflect those principles we believe in. As Guruji often quoted, "Reform yourself and you will have reformed thousands."

You may say, "But there is so much in the world that needs correcting; so much to be done." Yes, the needs are formidable; but the world's troubles will not go away merely by our trying to correct the outer

* Prayers for healing of physical disease, mental inharmony, and spiritual ignorance are offered daily by the Self-Realization Fellowship Prayer Council, composed of renunciants of the SRF Order. Prayers for oneself or one's loved ones may be requested by writing or telephoning Self-Realization Fellowship, Los Angeles. This mission of prayer is supported by the Self-Realization Fellowship Worldwide Prayer Circle, consisting of SRF members and friends around the world, which regularly offers prayers for world peace and the well-being of all mankind. A booklet describing the work of the Worldwide Prayer Circle is available on request.

things. We have to correct the human element that is the real cause of these troubles, and we must begin with ourselves.

You can tell a person a thousand times not to smoke, but if he has made up his mind that he likes cigarettes, nothing you say is going to change his habit. Only when he begins to cough and suffer the negative effects of smoking does it hit home and he realizes, "This is affecting *me;* now it's becoming something *I* have to think about." Similarly, your words alone may have little power to influence an inharmonious person to be more peaceful. But if that person senses a spirit of harmony and well-being flowing from your own peaceful nature, that is something tangible; it will have a beneficial effect on him.

Inner Harmony Comes From Meditation

The peace and harmony so urgently sought by all cannot be had from material things or any outer experience; it is just not possible. Perhaps by watching a beautiful sunset or going to the mountains or seaside you might feel a temporary serenity. But even the most inspiring setting will not give you peace if you are inharmonious in your own being.

The secret of bringing harmony into the outer circumstances of your life is to establish an inner harmony with your soul and with God. Take a little time each day to withdraw from the world, interiorize your mind, and try to feel the presence of God. That is the purpose of meditation. You will find that after you have meditated deeply and harmonized your consciousness with the peace of God within, outer difficulties will not cause you so much stress. You are able to deal with them without losing your composure and overreacting—without "running around like a chicken with its head cut off," as Guruji would say. You have an inner strength that enables you to say, "All right, I will face this obstacle and overcome it."

Two persons may pass through the very same experiences; one may become embittered while the other grows in wisdom and understanding. It all depends upon the individual. When people write to me and say that their burdens are too much, that they are on the verge of giving up, I think, "Oh, if I could just inject some faith into them, so that they would feel, 'Yes, I *can* do it!'" Cultivate positive thinking; and even if you cannot overcome the whole problem at once, start with the first step, and tell yourself, "If I do just this, my situation will be better tomorrow."

Hold On to Inner Peace and Joy in All Circumstances

There is no greater recourse in our difficulties than to take them to God. He may not remove them, for it is in meeting challenges that we grow. But from Him we receive strength to cope and wisdom to act.

I don't know how people can live without having a time to be with God. Yes, we all have many demands on our schedule, duties we must perform as part of our contribution to life. But if we are sincere, each of us can find time daily to give ourselves to God in meditation. I like to arise long before dawn, when everyone else is asleep. The world is so quiet then; you don't even hear the birds singing. It is a wonderful time to converse with God, silently, sweetly, telling Him all the things you would want to tell a dearest friend. We think so many things, but often feel we have no one with whom we can share our thoughts. But we do have. All my life I have had Someone to talk to—and that is God. He gives me so much understanding and comfort—no words can describe. I go to Him with all my joys as well as my problems; and that is what you all should do. Who else will listen as He will? Who else can do for us what He can? He understands us, even when we do not understand ourselves. It is eminently worthwhile to take the time to cultivate that inner relationship with Him.

To reach God, we need the right meditation techniques; these Guruji has given to us. The faithful follower of Self-Realization will set aside a time every day to read and study Guruji's teachings, and to sit quietly at home and meditate. But just sitting still, with the mind flitting like a butterfly in many directions, is not meditation. Meditation is the ability to withdraw your mind from all external objects of distraction and to put that freed attention upon God alone. It takes regular practice to learn to control the restless mind. Running the fingers up and down the scale on a piano is not playing the piano; but such practice is a necessary preliminary. Similarly, disciplined practice of meditation techniques is necessary to learn to truly meditate. We know we are progressing spiritually when each day's meditation is deeper than that of the previous day, and when we can continue to hold on to the inner peace and joy of the meditative state in all circumstances.

Many years ago Master took us to see the inspiring movie, "The Song of Bernadette," about a great Western saint.* I remember particularly her last words. The latter part of her life had been filled with suffering and trials, but as she was leaving her body, she perceived

* St. Bernadette Soubirous, whose sacred experiences at Lourdes, France, in the 1850s have made that site one of the most frequented pilgrimage places in the West.

the Divine Presence and said, with her last strength, "I love You." That to me is what ecstasy is—to live, move, and have our being in this world in the love of God. Every day remember to tell Him, "I love You, Lord." If you do not yet feel that love in your heart, say to Him, "I want to feel that love, Lord. Rouse my heart with Your love."

If God is the focal point of our lives, we are always thinking, "Am I acting in a way that would be pleasing to Him who is my love, Him from whom I have come and for whom I live?" By cultivating that consciousness, we become truly peaceful, happy, understanding human beings.

Perfection Is Not to Be Found in This World

As more of mankind strives for that state, the crises that threaten our world will diminish. But we have to realize that this earth will never be perfect, because this is not our permanent home; it is a school, and its students are in different grades of learning. We have come here to go through all of life's experiences, good and sorrowful, and thereby to learn from them.

God is eternal, and so are we. His universe will go on and on in its ups and downs. It is for us to put ourselves in harmony with His laws of creation. Those who do so continue to evolve upward regardless of their outer circumstances or of the particular world cycle they are born in; and by the refinement of their consciousness, they find freedom in God.

In the ultimate sense, the salvation of each one of us rests totally with ourselves—how we face life; how we behave; whether we conduct our lives with honesty, sincerity, regard for others, and above all, with courage, faith, trust in God. It becomes simple if we concentrate on love for God. We will then want to do good, and to be good, because we find peace and wisdom and joy pouring into our consciousness from that One whence we have come.

How often Guruji had us affirm with him that our lives are to be lived in the joy that is God:

> From Joy I have come. In Joy I live, move, and have my being. And in that sacred Joy I will melt again.

Hold on to this truth, and you will see how that Joy inwardly sustains you no matter what comes into your life. That Joy becomes more real to you than the ever-changing events of this kaleidoscopic world.

The World Is Our Family

From a talk at Gyanamata Ashram (nuns' residence), Self-Realization Fellowship International Headquarters, during gathering to celebrate America's Bicentennial, July 1976

Tonight I am remembering the many Fourths of July we spent with Gurudeva. Our Christmas and Easter observances were in part rather solemn occasions, but the Fourth of July was always a jubilant time. We didn't have much to spend, but we always managed to get a few sparklers and firecrackers, and a little ice cream, and have a gathering on the lawn here at Mt. Washington.* Later, when the Encinitas Hermitage† came into being, Guruji took us to Mission Beach nearby, where we could watch the fireworks display out over the ocean.

It has made me so happy tonight to see how you have all joined in the spirit of celebrating America's two-hundredth birthday. I remember Guruji's saying that he came to America not because he loved other nations less—his consciousness was universal—but because he found here more freedom from prejudice,

* Site of, and by extension a frequently used name for, the Mother Center and International Headquarters of Self-Realization Fellowship on Mt. Washington in Los Angeles.

† Encinitas is a small city about a hundred miles south of Los Angeles, where Paramahansa Yogananda was given a large hermitage overlooking the Pacific Ocean. He spent a good deal of his time there from late 1936 through 1948.

Mrinalini Mata (SRF vice-president), Sri Daya Mata, and Ananda Mata (see p. 263 n.), Janakananda Ashram at SRF Headquarters, 1976

"The secret of bringing harmony into the outer circumstances of your life is to establish an inner harmony with your soul and with God. Take a little time each day to withdraw from the world, interiorize your mind, and try to feel the presence of God."

Following *satsanga* at Ranchi, 1968, Mataji playfully tosses wrapped candies to the assemblage.

Ranchi, 1973

"Anyone who deeply loves God finds it very difficult to be solemn all the time. There is always a divine joy bubbling up from within."

more freedom of worship; and these provided the greatest possibilities for spreading the spirit and ideals that are the very foundation of Self-Realization teachings. Now, this is not to say that America is perfect. But here, perhaps more than in any other part of the globe, there is a greater opportunity to experience and express the four freedoms.*

To be truly patriotic, truly American, exemplifying the ideals on which this great nation was founded, we must learn to cultivate and express love and friendship for all. We begin by loving those whom God has sent to us as our family; and then expanding that love to include our neighbors, our country, and eventually all nations. Applying the Self-Realization Fellowship teachings in our life expands our consciousness, until ultimately we do come to feel and accept the whole world as our family. Then we are expressing the universal love of God.

What Is Freedom?

Today, more than ever, America and all other nations need to work at cultivating that universal love. The world is being torn apart by standards of behavior that do not lead to peace and real freedom. Freedom is not doing as you please, ignoring the rights of others. To be free requires the practice of self-discipline. True freedom, in the ultimate sense, is liberation from the compulsions of bad habits, prejudices, moods, self-interest, self-will, and so forth. When you can exercise free choice in all your actions, guided purely by wisdom, then you are free.

* As outlined by Franklin D. Roosevelt: freedom of speech and expression, freedom to worship God in one's own way, freedom from want, and freedom from fear.

The first time I went to India, it was like stepping into an entirely different world. The spiritual atmosphere overwhelmed my soul with joy, but material conditions were far removed from what we have in this country. I remember being stunned to see so much suffering from poverty and the struggle merely to keep alive. My heart wept, and I vowed that when I returned to America I would stress more than ever the importance of sharing, and of finding freedom and happiness within. We do not need a lot outwardly in order to be content, but we do need soul-freedom. The inner freedom of spirit is not dependent on our environment; but we benefit from an environment that gives us an opportunity to think more deeply about God and to cultivate love for Him.

Master predicted that one day—after great suffering, struggle, and heartache—all nations of the world will unite. That unity will come when individuals within nations begin to find inner freedom. Through the teachings of this path of Self-Realization we have been blessed with the greatest opportunity to find spiritual liberation—freedom for our souls—and through our example, to encourage our family, our nation, and our world to seek their own freedom in God. It has to begin somewhere. Great teachers come and speak fervently about the importance of unity of humankind. Crowds cheer and wave flags and agree that universal brotherhood is necessary. The ideal lives in minds and hearts for a while, then dies away again. Why? Because each one is waiting for someone else to start practicing the requisite spiritual principles. But that practice must begin with himself.

Soul freedom is "where it's at," as they say nowadays! And that freedom comes from surrendering yourself to God's will for you each day.

Right Activity Begins With Right Attitude

To serve God is the ideal of the karma yogi. What does Karma Yoga mean? First of all, it means to develop the right attitude, by which you can eventually put into practice right activity. Right activity is action performed not for self, but for God. The perfected karma yogi offers all his actions and the fruits thereof to God alone.

To start with, we must realize that the world owes us absolutely nothing. I find such freedom in that thought. Too often, people feel that the world owes them something, even if they have not worked to merit it. On the spiritual path, one must adopt the attitude: "The world owes me nothing, but I owe the world much." From this truth, let your thoughts continue: "I owe God much: I owe Him my life; I owe Him everything I am. So long as I breathe, there is no time when I am not drawing in His life. So long as I think, there is no time I am not borrowing from His intelligence. I depend utterly upon Him." When you reason in these terms, you begin to realize that your life and everything you have has come from God. Then you want to give of yourself to Him in return.

After we have this straight in our consciousness, we should think: "How can I serve Him?" Many feel that God has sent them into this world with a special mission. This is a false notion, because the only calling He has given to us is to find Him. Thus, the devotee says: "Lord, use me in whatever way You will. If You choose to use me here, if You decide to use me there, I am happy; it is all the same to me. My sights are fixed on You. You alone are my Goal."

It is not enough to do our work mechanically or grudgingly, all the while holding back inwardly. Right behavior, or right activity, is not just an external practice. We must guard against inner resentment: "This is my discipline; and, much as I dislike it, I guess I've got to do it." If we do not surrender within—letting go of our resistance and allowing the Lord to use us exactly as He wills—we will not gain the spiritual freedom we are seeking.

Whatever crosses our path at any given moment, in that circumstance God wants us to display the best possible attitude, with cheerfulness. St. Francis de Sales said: "A saint that is sad is a sad saint!" Anyone who deeply loves God finds it very difficult to be solemn all the time. There is always a divine joy bubbling up from within.

It is so nice to laugh—above all to be able to laugh at ourselves. We should overcome that sensitivity which induces hurt feelings. If our feelings are easily wounded, it simply means we are catering to our ego. We do not have the right attitude if we cannot bear to have anyone criticize or say anything unkind about us. Let others say what they will. If our minds are on God, and if we are striving to do our best, does it really matter what people think of us? Whenever negation has been directed my way, I have made it a practice to pray: "Lord, what do *You* think of me? If I am wrong, correct me, discipline me. Change me." We should always look for what He is trying to teach us in every situation.

Loving Service to All God's Children

It is only by looking to God, loving Him, and then serving Him in all who cross our path, that we begin to know that universality in which real freedom lies. Cultivate this consciousness:

"Lord, I am in this world because You sent me here. I am here for one purpose: to love You and to love Your children, whoever they are, wherever they are, be they Americans, Africans, Asians, Europeans; Buddhists, Christians, Hindus, Jews, Muslims." Whatever our faith or nationality, we are all kin, with one common Father.

Think of others in these terms: They are my own. They are a part of my God. In each one my God is manifest. Let me serve them to the best of my ability.

These principles we should practice as a part of our daily life. Be thoughtful of one another, empathize with one another, do for one another. And while doing so, respect one another as images of God.

If America, or any other nation, is ultimately to become a land of true freedom—that which is founded on freedom from spiritual ignorance and delusion, the birthright of every soul-citizen—it must begin with the nurturing of the divine qualities inherent in each individual. That is the ideal freedom to be extolled and emulated. It is the surest foundation upon which to build any nation, for it fosters the fullest potential of the human heart and spirit.

America is still an infant in years when compared to many nations of the world. But when you go elsewhere you realize how much she has achieved, and how blessed one is to live in this great country. I am staunchly patriotic in that sense; I appreciate all this country has given to me. Yet when I travel abroad, I find that all countries are my own, because all humanity is my family. There are no boundaries in the consciousness of God, and there should be no boundaries of nationality, race, or creed in the consciousness of His children.

Happy birthday to America, and God bless her!

The Hope for Peace in a Changing World

From a talk at Yogoda Satsanga Society of India Branch Math, Ranchi, Bihar, India

In every country I visit, I see in people the same deep yearning: "How can I get peace?" Gurudeva Paramahansa Yogananda taught us that peace will never come from external means. We may rest assured that as often as we pin our hopes on external conditions, any peace that we find in them will be short-lived.

Paraphrasing Lord Krishna's words to Arjuna in the Bhagavad Gita, Gurudeva used to say, "If you want to find peace, become anchored in That which is changeless." Nothing in this world is stable; nothing is without change, except God. In Krishna's words, spoken thousands of years ago, "Become thou settled in the Self."* He was showing the way for all mankind, for we can never know true peace without becoming "settled" or "anchored" in God.

That was one of the first truths I was taught by Guruji after I entered the ashram: Become anchored in God, the only changeless Principle in this world of change. How to do this? By meditation, and by keeping our minds always fixed at the *Kutastha* or Christ-consciousness center, between the eyebrows. Here, and in the heart, is where we commune with the Divine.

* Bhagavad Gita II:45.

The ordinary person's mind is constantly wavering with restless thoughts, and fluttering among all kinds of worries about his work, his family, his social standing, his material success. As a result, he is a bundle of nerves. Even if one renounces the world to live in an ashram, it does not mean that suddenly all his problems are wiped away. He has just as many troubles as every other human being; but in the ashram he learns that no matter what comes into his life, there is hope, there is security, there is a solution, there is One to whom he can always turn, confident of getting help—and that One is God. This is a lesson everyone should learn.

Our trouble is that we are reluctant to depend on God, because we are not certain that what He will give us will be what we want. We think, "If I give my life to Him, He might not look after me, He might not give me security, He might not fulfill my desires." That is man's failing. And it is also false reasoning, because if we put our minds on God and practice a little self-surrender every day, we will see that He is looking after us, without fail.

India: Spiritual Leader of Humanity

Of all the nations of the world, India is the most blessed spiritually. Guruji used to say, "As the West has concentrated upon material and scientific efficiency, so for centuries India has concentrated upon spiritual efficiency." India is a land of great spiritual giants. No other nation has produced as many saints. They have been born of your holy traditions, which are your sacred heritage.

I have visited many of the countries of this world. When devotees know that I come to India, the one thing they all ask about is your spiritual leaders. So many dream of coming here to seek God: such is the inspiration India gives to the rest of the world. She must never lose that.

India is certainly going to progress materially. There is no question about it. After all, India is only twenty years old, you might say; it has been only twenty years since she gained independence.* You have made rapid strides in those years, and you are going to make many more. But I plead with you, especially the young people of this holy land, that in seeking material improvement, you do not cast aside that which is your greatest treasure: your spiritual heritage. This is something for which the whole world looks to India.

You are the only nation that is so steeped in the ideals of *darshan* and *satsanga*.† Though you might take these traditions for granted, because they are so familiar to you, they stem from a deep spiritual nature that is inborn in the Indian. Use it rightly, and encourage this natural inclination. It is important for souls to come together for meditation and *satsanga*—friendship, fellowship with the divine *Sat*, with God. If you will remember this, you will make India the greatest nation of this age. But if you cast aside these spiritual qualities and become drunk with materialism, you will miss the most important opportunity the nation has

* This talk was given in 1968.

† *Darshan*, the blessing received by seeing or being in the presence of a holy person or place. *Satsanga*, divine fellowship with other truth-seeking, God-seeking, souls. Deeply ingrained in the Indian is the understanding and appreciation of the value of spiritual company and of holy personages and shrines. These are his source of strength and inspiration for meeting the travails and challenges of daily life.

ever had to lead the world. I say this to you from the depths of my soul, because I love this land so much.

This is the way I have talked in universities around the country. The young are confident that they can conquer the world. Their interest is focused on fulfilling their dreams and aspirations. They tend to imitate; and because youth is a time of the awakening of desires and ambitions, they usually pick up the worst habits or traits of their peers in other nations, because the appeal to the senses is strong. This is such a tragedy. So while striving always to improve your lot materially, do not throw aside the thought of God.

This is what the materialists of the West have done. They think, "So long as I have whatever else I want, I don't need God." He has no place in the lives of so many. This is wrong; and America today is an example of the troubles that come from such an attitude. I have seen thousands of young people in a sad state of bewilderment, unrest, unhappiness, confusion, for the very reason that God has been cast aside. And now you will find more and more of them turning to India. You have read in your newspapers about the many who are following Indian teachers. They have come full circle and found that materialism does not give satisfaction. They are trying to find peace and a reason for living, and they find these in India's spiritual teachings.

I was blessed that at a very early age—seventeen—I met Gurudeva. He transformed my life. To him I shall be eternally grateful. I cannot say or do enough to express adequately or repay my debt to him for the wonderful way in which he has affected my life. He went from India to the West, and appreciated the material accomplishments there, but he did not throw aside his divine heritage; he never forgot God or the spiritual ideals on which he had been nurtured. He took them with him and transplanted them in the West. And that is why today, in every land, you will find thousands of followers of Gurudeva Paramahansa Yogananda.

"To Thine Own Self Be True"

So how shall we find an inner peace we can cling to in this troubled world? Very simply: while striving always to improve our lot, we should keep God in our hearts. While looking after the body—feeding, clothing, housing it—we should not forget to devote at least a little time, even if only ten or fifteen minutes every day, to thinking of God, to meditating upon Him. How foolish we are if we forget Him!

I tell you frankly, I do not know how it is possible to live without being anchored in God. No wonder there is so much unnecessary misery. I have seen the suffering of mankind, how it becomes an unbearable burden to many. I could not endure life without God. How different life is when it is anchored in Him. It is so easy to know Him. The way is meditation. Man makes it complicated, because he does not really want to make the effort. Instead, he tries to justify his mental laziness.

"To thine own self be true, and it must follow, as the night the day, thou canst not then be false to any man."* It is as simple as that. In everything you do, always first ask yourself, "Am I being honest and sincere with myself?" Never seek excuses for your weaknesses. That basic principle is bound up in the first two steps of Patanjali's Eightfold Path of Yoga:† *yama* and *niyama*,

* Shakespeare: *Hamlet*, Act I, Scene 3.

† Patanjali was the foremost ancient exponent of Yoga. He outlined eight steps by which man attains union with God: These are (1) *yama*, moral conduct; (2) *niyama*, religious observances; (3) *asana*, right pos-

the proscriptions and prescriptions of right behavior. You can sum them up in just one phrase: be true to yourself. That means, be true every moment—not to the ego, the pseudo-soul—but to the *atman*, your true Self, or soul. This means to strive earnestly to be honest, sincere, kind, and loving; and to avoid hatred, dishonesty, and anything else that disturbs the soul, that creates nervousness and unrest within, and does not give peace.

"To thine own self be true," and a little bit of meditation every day: then one finds freedom; then one finds peace of mind. Otherwise these remain elusive.

The Greatest Lovers in the World

Every human heart, without exception, is hankering to love and be loved. Plants, animals, and above all, man—being made in the image of the Divine—respond to love. The way to receive love is to give love. Yet how few in this world know how to love sincerely, deeply. By meditation, as we learn to love God more and to feel His love, it becomes possible for us to love, even without asking anything in return.

The greatest lovers this world has ever known are those who have loved God. Down through the ages they remain an inspiration to all mankind. To produce true lovers of God, true knowers of God, is the purpose of India's teaching; this is what her scriptures have proclaimed to mankind. Long before the era of Christianity, Buddhism, or other religions, India showed the

---

ture to still bodily restlessness; (4) *pranayama*, control of *prana*, subtle life currents; (5) *pratyahara*, interiorization; (6) *dharana*, concentration; (7) *dhyana*, meditation; and (8) *samadhi*, the ecstasy of oneness with God.

way. This is why I love her so much. And her teaching is what the world needs today.

As I have said, you in India have that spiritual background. It is very simple for you to know God if you make the effort; but you have to make that effort. Practice meditation every day; and even if it is only for a few minutes, be deeply immersed in God. Then His response comes.

Many seekers have said to me, "But I *have* been praying." The Christian may say, "I have said my prayers every day for twenty-three years"; the Muslim, "I have been faithful in performing *namaj* for twenty-three years"; and the Hindu, "I have been practicing *japa* or doing my *puja*."* But still each one complains, "I don't feel I've made any progress. My mind is so restless. I'm so nervous. Why is this?"

It is because these practices have become mechanical. You cannot win the love of anyone by half-heartedness or mechanically spoken words of love. Love must come from the heart. That is what is so often lacking in spiritual practices. We must cease being parrots, merely repeating God's name without feeling or understanding. Master taught us that the heart and mind should be so fixed on the Divine Beloved that the first utterance of His name stirs deep feeling within. This comes by daily meditation; the moment you take the name of God, your whole heart is there: "My God, my God, my Love."

I have such a wish to plant deep within your souls the seed of yearning for God—to rouse that yearning in you not for just a few weeks or a few months, but

* *Namaj:* The chief prayer of the Muslims, repeated five times daily. *Japa:* Repetition of a concentrated thought of God. *Puja:* Ceremonial worship.

until it finds spiritual fruition. Do not wait for life to go by and then suddenly say, "Oh, I have missed Him." Now is the time to seek God.

Guruji used to say, "Each one of you, before you go to sleep tonight, sit in meditation and deeply call to God." Like a child, talk to Him. If you do this every night, your life will become anchored in Him. You will become like a strong tree, which bends in the wind, but never breaks. A brittle tree cracks and falls in just a little gust of wind. The devotee of God learns to bend with life's experiences, without breaking. His roots are anchored deep in the Divine.

God-Communion: The Thread Uniting All Religions

From a talk at Janakananda Ashram (monks' residence) at Self-Realization Fellowship International Headquarters

Religious prejudice should not exist in the hearts of those who follow in the footsteps of Paramahansa Yogananda, but loyalty must. Respect all religions, but be loyal to your own. Having recognized that the universal Truth is expressed in different ways and in varying degrees in all religions, find the path that suits you, and do not waver from it. Honor all, but be true to your own way. That was Gurudeva's ideal; and it should be the ideal of all who follow him.

With this understanding of loyalty, I have always believed it possible to experience the Divine Presence in any church or temple dedicated to God, because the various paths all lead to Him. When I travel for Guruji's society, my one "hobby" is to visit various temples and churches, which are dedicated to the One I love—God—to commune with Him, and to behold and respect Him in all His devotees there who have dedicated their lives to Him according to their chosen way. I hope that we of Self-Realization will always hold to the ideal of broad-mindedness. Narrow-mindedness is against the principles of God. When an individual becomes narrow, it is impossible for the light of God to shine through him. All great lovers of God have opened wide their arms to all religions and religionists. But they followed only one: their own path. Love all, but do not be fickle. Be steadfastly loyal to one. That attitude must be there if we would know God.

Experience of God Removes the Barriers Between Religions

The spirit of God is indeed omnipresent. I was blessed with a tremendous experience of His divine presence while meditating before a huge statue of the Lord Buddha in a shrine at Nara, in Japan. I remember also a unique and rather humorous experience in the great Shwedagon Temple in Burma. In many Hindu and Buddhist temples you find not only a large central altar of worship, but also a number of small shrines—just as in Catholic churches you will find niches dedicated to different saints. I had been meditating long and deeply, immersed in divine love, in a corner of one of these shrines in the Shwedagon Temple. A Buddhist priest was nearby, and some other people were present. As I rose to leave, the priest, radiating kindness and goodwill, spontaneously offered me a cigar! Perhaps it was all he had on hand at the moment. I politely declined, but I deeply felt and appreciated his gesture of friendship and recognition of a fellow devotee.

In the Tarakeswar Temple, during my first visit to India, I was healed of an illness by the presence of the Divine. It was an immediate healing; not a gradual improvement over several days. I had forgotten that this temple is famous for healings—like the shrine at Lourdes in France. But while reading Guruji's autobiography after my return to the ashram that evening, I was reminded of the healing that a member of his family had invoked in that same temple.*

* See *Autobiography of a Yogi,* chapter 13.

In Puri, I was privileged to be one of the first Westerners ever to set foot inside the sacred Jagannath Temple. Ordinarily, only Hindus are permitted to enter, just as in the West only a practicing Mormon may enter the sacred Mormon temples where their religious rites are performed. The purpose of this is that only the truly devout be present, not the merely curious. We sometimes forget that we have accepted certain rites of behavior in our Western religions, and then do not want to grant others the same privilege, and respect their customs. Just a month before our visit to Jagannath, a European had tried to enter that temple, and a serious disturbance resulted because the people felt so deeply about the intrusion. But, through the intercession of the late Shankaracharya of the Gowardhan Math in Puri,* my companions and I were permitted to enter. And in that temple I had an overwhelming experience of the presence of God.

Later, when we visited the sacred places associated with Christ in the Holy Land, and when we traveled through Europe and saw the shrines in Italy dedicated to St. Francis, I was again blessed with wonderfully inspiring experiences.

I mention these things only to show you the universality of God, and that by personal experience of Him we break down the barriers of misunderstanding and prejudice that have been built up in religion.

Yoga: Direct Perception of God

The different religions teach different doctrines, and dogmatize their followers in those ideas, and this is all right. But I often remember Master's saying to me,

* Sri Jagadguru Shankaracharya Bharati Krishna Tirtha, ecclesiastical head of most of Hindu India. See photo following page 198.

"We must be very broad, but we must dogmatize"—and that was the only context in which he ever used the word in relation to his work—"we must dogmatize our members in the practice of Kriya Yoga." I thought to myself, "Ah, how wonderful!" For I understood his meaning: "I am interested in holding the devotees of Self-Realization by only one tie—their own direct perception of God, as experienced by the practice of Kriya." We don't say that Kriya Yoga is the *only* technique of realization, but our Guru found it to be the best method by which the devotee can attain direct experience of God within.

That is the real purpose of every religion: to help reacquaint man with his Maker. It is not sufficient just to adopt a certain set of religious ideas or principles. This is good, but we have to go deeper. The church, regardless of what religion it embraces, has one primary mission to fulfill: to help the devotee to attain direct communion with God. I believe, as Master said, that the time will come when all churches will more and more emphasize meditation, which gives actual experience of God. That alone will save mankind, and indeed the world. And because Self-Realization teaches that direct communion, I also believe, as Master said many times, that this is the religion of the new age.

Communion with God is the touchstone that proves His one presence hidden behind all true religions. When God is actually experienced, the superficial differences of dogma lose their meaning. Devotees of any religious path, by going within in meditation, find the same God. God-communion is therefore the key to tolerance and understanding among followers of various faiths.

Above all, God-communion is a vital personal necessity to every one of us, His children, because in the ultimate sense our happiness and well-being depend on it. In the Self-Realization teachings, Gurudeva teaches us how to attain that experience of God, through meditation and devotion. Let me review, just briefly, some of the points that help the devotee reach the Goal of meditation.

Keys to Deeper Meditation

First of all, when it is time for meditation, let the world recede. Forget everything else. Whatever problems you have, leave them at the door as you enter the chapel or your place of meditation. Do this consciously. Mentally shrug them off. Feel that you have actually taken hold of them and thrown them out of your consciousness. Train yourself to thus immediately empty your mind not only of all burdens of worldly responsibilities, but also all love of bodily comfort, all attachment to self-will. It is vital that you so discipline yourself that simply by using your will power you can throw out of your mind every mundane preoccupation and say truly, "Nothing exists for me now but God."

If you knew at this moment that your death was imminent, what would you do? I know, because I have faced that crisis. You would be thinking just one thought: "I'm going to lose my life!" And you would feel such an urgent need for God that you would instantly realize that nothing else is important. Take with you into meditation that consciousness of the urgency of finding God, and the realization that at any moment death could come—as it will, one day, to each of us.

When you meditate, cling to the thought that God is the only reality. He is the only Eternal Existence. Everything else in this universe is unreal, an evanescent part of the great mayic veil that clouds Reality.

The next point is to develop the patience to sustain meditation. Be content with taking small steps first; do not become impatient or tense when you meditate. There has to be an attitude of unconditional surrender: "Lord, I am on fire for You. I am plunging toward You. But do what You will. Come when You wish. I shall go on seeking You no matter what." Pray in this way, and you will be amazed at how the divine consciousness, that divine intelligence, that divine love of God responds to your soul's call. But not if you are impatient.

When devotees have difficulty going deep in meditation, usually the reason is that they are anxious for a quick response. Do not look for results in meditation, because that attitude creates anxiety within you. Then you become restless and tense because you are not getting some hoped-for response from God. Instead, forget results, forget time, and persistently pour out your heart to the Lord. Call to Him, cry to Him, weep for Him. If you do not feel that longing, mentally take His name, or pray, "Reveal Thyself, reveal Thyself." Go deeper and deeper, plunging your attention within. He will come when He wishes. This you must understand. You cannot force God; you can only surrender to Him. Then He will respond.

If you meditate in a hurry, or with a sense of anxiety, the very Object you seek will elude you. For example, suppose you are rushing to keep an appointment. You are nervous and tense, and you drop something that rolls under the couch. Frantically you look for it, worriedly thinking, "I've *got* to find it; I have to leave—they're waiting for me." You may look and look and still not find the object. We have all had this experience. Eventually you get hold of yourself and relax, stop hurrying, and just concentrate—and there it is! Then you say with amazement, "I looked in that place a dozen times and didn't see it!" So it is with meditation. When anxiety, tension, and restless impatience cloud your consciousness, you will be unable to behold God's presence within. There has to be a calm, quiet waiting. Rabindranath Tagore expressed it beautifully in these words:

> Have you not heard His silent steps?
> He comes, comes, ever comes.

"Silent steps"—the devotee has to abide in the inner stillness, with an attitude of devotional, worshipful waiting. Then he begins to perceive that Joy, that Love, that Divine Presence welling up within himself: "He comes, comes, ever comes."

The Purpose of Life's Tests

The things we do all day long are nothing but acts in this great drama of God's. They are not important, except to the degree that we can learn through them, so as to go on unfolding spiritually. That is all life is. Tests are part of the drama of life. Never, never be dismayed. How easy it is to be in love with God when everything is gloriously going our way. The test is whether we can hold steadfastly to the joy of divine consciousness when everything about us tries to shake us loose. That is why Guruji said, "Learn to stand unshaken midst the crash of breaking worlds."

When things become difficult, that is the time to rush to God's feet, to cry to Him within, to demand as His child that He help you; and to invoke Him to enter the temple of your consciousness. It is often when the devotee is enduring the greatest trials that he most strongly and sweetly feels the loving, understanding, comforting presence of God. And these are the times when the devotee makes great spiritual strides, when he allows these difficulties to drive him to God. Never forget that; never be afraid of any trial. Face it with courage, faith, and devotion. That is the way to cope with hard times.

So if you are crucified by trials, if through ignorance you are misunderstood, if you are faced with some superhuman task, if you are overwhelmed by temptation, remember that these do not come to destroy you. They come only to shake you out of delusion. That is why the devotee should always pray for right attitude, that he might at all times keep his attention on God as the goal of his life. In this way, life's tests neither make us bitter, nor plunge us into despair, nor give us desire to retaliate. The heart and mind turn constantly to the One: "My Beloved, my Beloved, my Beloved. You are the only One who understands me. Reveal Thyself to me."

Understanding and Empathy for All

What right have we to expect the world to understand us? We do not understand the world. What right have we to expect any individual to understand us, when we cannot truly say we understand anyone else? And we never will until we understand ourselves—not this body or this mind, but the consciousness within. Having understood ourselves as the soul, we are then able to master and guide the body and control its senses and moods, emotions, and mental restlessness. From that state, one understands and feels empathy for all.

As we reawaken and strive to express the divinity that is locked within us, we will behold the divinity in others. Analyze it in this way: When we are extremely happy, when we feel love in our heart, we can take all the jibes or sharp words of others in our stride. We are not sensitive, not hurt by them. When we are happy within our true Self, we *understand* why others behave as they do, and we are prepared to show that understanding, and our compassion. But when we are cross, sensitive, or hurt, we carry a real "chip on our shoulder," just waiting to be knocked off by someone who says a wrong word. By getting right within ourselves, we behave rightly toward the rest of the world. The way to do this is to get back to God.

Practice humility and surrender; these are absolutely essential. The struggle to surrender the ego-self is the purpose behind religious vows. Simplicity, or poverty, teaches surrender of desire for material possessions; chastity, surrender of bodily attachments; obedience and loyalty, surrender of egotistic self-will. The householder devotee as well as the renunciant can follow these vows in principle by performing all actions with detachment. Eventually, the practice of these principles frees the soul: we are released from the mental and material attachments that have enslaved us to the body and kept us from God.

Gurudeva's teachings take us to the very essence of Truth—God. We do not have to wade through a lot of dogma and theory. He has given to us the sum and substance of the Eternal Religion: the way to direct communion with God.

Harmonizing Spirituality With Outer Achievements

From a talk to monastics at Self-Realization Fellowship International Headquarters

Gurudeva [Paramahansa Yogananda] used to say to us that we must make each day's meditation deeper than that of the previous day. If you make a sincere effort to meditate more deeply, to call on Divine Mother with all the anguish, all the yearning, all the hunger of your soul, you will know for certain you are progressing on the spiritual path.

Life is fleeting; it is like a bubble that one day bursts as it is carried along the cascading stream. Though the tiny bubble bursts, it is not lost; it only changes its form. Similarly, our life is not lost, though one day it leaves the bubble of this particular fleshly form. When meditating, it is good to contemplate the insecurity of this mortal form, that we may realize the illusory nature of our earthly experiences. The only Reality is God; everything else is part of His cosmic dream. Meditate upon that Reality, realize the need to relate to that Reality, that you may know you are not a mortal being, but an immortal part of the Divine Beloved.

[A period of meditation follows; then Daya Mataji resumes speaking.]

I've entered a deep state of stillness or peace. As Guruji used to tell us, peace is the first proof of God's presence. When we were with Master, he taught us to work toward this state of inner stillness by practicing, with ever-increasing attention, Self-Realization meditation techniques. And he often used this illustration: After one milks a cow, filling the pail to the brim, if he then carries it carelessly, spilling all the contents on the way to the house, there was no point in collecting the milk, because it has all been wasted. The same is true about meditation: After achieving stillness within, it is important to very carefully, watchfully carry that pail of peace with us throughout the entire day, drinking deeply from it, so that we can benefit from what we achieved in meditation.

God put us here on earth in the midst of endless trials, heartaches, and burdens; with very few joys, and with pleasures that are so short-lasting. This is a world of delusion He has created. But He also gave us a means of escape, a way to remember that we are individualized reflections of His Being. That means of escape lies in the stillness which all of us have within us, but which very few know anything about.

Every scripture has taught man the importance of meditation or prayer or communion, but only a few seekers have taken the time or made the effort to experience it. Master used to say to us that this divine path of Self-Realization can take the devotee as far as he wants to go. The key word there is *want,* which has the same meaning as *yearning*. To the degree that you yearn for God, to that degree He responds to you. The important point is to nurture that yearning constantly. When each one of you entered the spiritual path, you felt a yearning—a longing to know God, a longing for joy, a longing for divine love. It is up to you to keep feeding that ardent desire, to not let it die out, to not let it evaporate.

Drawing From the Good in Every Culture

Guruji taught that to some degree every individual and every nation is unbalanced. God is both active energy and transcendental stillness; man, having been made in His image, should also express both constructive activity and the inactive state of absorption in Spirit. The problem is to balance the two. From the different temperaments of the various nationalities we should draw the best qualities, and by a balanced blend create a common brotherhood amongst all of His children in all nations.

When we look to the good in every nation, we become freed from the limitations of nationality and realize that we are universal children of God. This can be accomplished only individually. We are here to strive for that balance in our own lives, and our common problem is how to achieve it.

Guruji's mission was worldwide. India nurtured him, but he belonged to the world. When Master came to the West, his guru, Swami Sri Yukteswarji, told him: "Babaji is sending you to the West; all doors are open for you now. Take the best of the West and hold on to only the best of India." Sri Yukteswarji meant that the ideal is to rise above all circumscriptions of nationality and adhere to those virtuous qualities of God which He has instilled in all of His children throughout the world. Only that which is of God is real.

When we die, we will not know whether we were Hindus or Americans. We will only know we are souls, eternal reflections of God. This is the truth that God is determined to try to bring into this world. He is doing His best! And we who live in the Guru's ashrams here and in India uphold this principle: We are not Americans, we are not Indians—we are God's children. Guruji's message is spreading to every continent to awaken that love, that realization of one nationality: God.

Master came to the West to help Westerners understand the importance of balancing their activity with inner stillness, and his message to India and the Orient is to help them understand the importance of balancing spirituality with greater material accomplishments. We all must learn to blend in our lives activity (constructive service) and inactivity (inner stillness and communion with God). This balance comes by having periods of daily meditation wherein we milk the peace in the temple of silence, wherein we milk the awareness of God in that temple of meditation. And foolish is the devotee who then wastes that milk as he carries on his duties throughout the day.

Maintaining Awareness of God During Work

Master taught us to live more within; to dwell more in the thought of God; to practice the presence of God all the time. There is no time when we ought not to be silently conversing with God; there is no excuse for not doing so. No environment, no activity can keep us from God. If we do not feel Him with us, we have nothing and no one to blame but ourselves. When we blame activity for our forgetfulness of God, we are not facing the truth. The fault lies in our making excuses.

Throughout the day we have countless opportunities to take our minds within, even if it is for only an instant, and talk to God. It is the greatest joy then to be involved in His activity.

There is a science in India called *Karma Yoga,* based upon the path of right action, of doing everything in life out of love for God. When a mother loves her child, or the child loves the parent, or a husband loves the wife, there is a tremendous joy in doing for that loved one. How dare we not find that same joy when we are serving or doing for our Divine Beloved, our Divine Mother, our divine Guru? That is the attitude that is missing, my dears. That attitude must be cultivated, so that when we are in the midst of activity—as I find in my own life, and as many of you find who are devoutly loving God—picking up a straw in the kitchen is as great a joy as the moments spent in meditation.*

This is what God wants us to achieve, that we perform all our activities with the thought of Him, so that there is no difference between the hours spent toiling with our hands and the hours spent toiling with our minds, you might say, in meditation. They become one.

I remember Guruji standing in the hallway upstairs, giving me so many instructions as to what he wanted done. And he concluded by saying, "And don't forget to meditate." I said, "Master, how on earth can I do it? How can I keep my mind with God?" I expected some profound, miraculous flow of wisdom from his lips. But all he said to me was "Yes, I understand. I said the same thing to my Master and he said to me the same thing I say to you: You have to keep on trying; you have to keep on yearning, keep on wanting."

As Guruji had once said, "When I first came to America, I was busy night and day with so much activity. One day in my meditation I prayed, 'Lord, You keep me so busy carrying Your mission here that I haven't had time to meditate, but I am always hankering to meditate.'"

* An allusion to the life of Brother Lawrence, a seventeenth-century Christian mystic and lay brother of the Carmelite monastery in Paris, and author of the spiritual classic *The Practice of the Presence of God.* See also page 289.

God responded: "When you are not meditating, isn't it true that in your thoughts you are missing Me and thinking about meditating? When you meditated you thought of Me, and when you didn't meditate you missed Me; therefore the thought of Me was always predominant."

Master said that a great peace, a great sense of relief, fell over his consciousness, and he replied to God, "'Tis true, that though I have not been able to meditate as much, that hankering is within me, and so my mind has been with You just the same."

The Way to Inner Balance

"Now," said Master to us, "don't use this as an excuse not to meditate." See the fault in human nature? It constantly makes excuses for us, constantly rationalizes our behavior. That is the delusion. But we were taught by Master to critically analyze ourselves—not to cast us into dejection, but that we might begin truly to know ourselves. If you practice self-analysis, you will become more honest about yourself. You will not make excuses before God and Guru for the flaws that lie within you by placing the blame on some external circumstance or some other individual.

"Know thyself" means just that. Begin to see yourself as others see you, and as God and Guru see you, not as you would like to think you are.

If you look at your life, you will see countless moments that could have been spent thinking of God, practicing His presence, even in the midst of your duties or recreation.

It takes self-discipline to cultivate peace and happiness; and to know God. Self-discipline is what is missing in the life of the average person. It is absolutely essential for the devotee. It helps him to overcome the little "I," so that the ego-emptied vessel of his life may be totally filled with the waters of God's wisdom, love, truth, bliss.

Set aside a day once a week for concentrated practice of the presence of God, when you can be filled with His consciousness and remain in that inward stillness which comes from long hours of meditation. Just as Master told us to allocate one day a week for a longer period of meditation, I ask all of you to do so. By that practice you will gain greater strength, and begin to be more aware of that blessed joyous Presence within. You will find renewed energy and enthusiasm with which to carry on all the duties God has placed upon your shoulders.

This is the way to balance, my dears; I speak from many, many years of experience. None of you carries greater responsibilities than I, but I carry them while practicing the presence of God. You can do the same.

What Is Missing in the World Is Communion With God

The world tries to pull you downward toward slavery to the senses. When we allow the world to claim our consciousness, we may get a little temporary pleasure from sensory experiences, but we also get everything else that is a part of worldly consciousness—sensitivity, jealousy, anger, negation. You can't pull the tail of the cat without getting the whole cat. And so it is with worldliness: it draws the mind down to all those things that embroil us in discontent and unhappiness. Meditation reverses the searchlight of the senses and places the concentrated light of attention upon God, uplifting us with sublime love, peace, and joy. It takes us out of the consciousness of the flesh into an expansion of consciousness. We begin to see that we are not these little fleshly, self-centered, ungenerous human beings, but the divine children of God, offspring of the Divine Mother, bearing Her likeness within us. Let us never mar that image by smallness of mind, meanness, hatred, jealousy, ugly gossip.

It is because all of you are striving so sincerely that we have such a spiritual harmony in our ashrams, which is felt by all who come here. The divine vibrations of our blessed Guru, and of his ideals, permeate his ashrams; and you contribute to that by your efforts in meditation, your efforts to expand yourself beyond "me, me, me" so that you include others in your thoughts of service, helpfulness, love, and goodwill.

The world needs such souls, and is uplifted by them. Guruji often said to us that no matter what the world is doing, no matter what it is passing through, you keep your mind fixed in God. If you want to know God, the mind must be with Him at all times. Keep on working toward it, and you will see that it will come. You must nourish that wanting, that yearning, with meditation. Nourish it by practicing the presence of God. Nourish it by constantly telling God, "I love You, I love You." Even at those times when the heart feels dry, keep trying to feel love for Him. It must become a way of life; not for just a few minutes or hours a day, and not for just a few years, but through all the moments of the rest of your days. Then you will find at the end of the trail that the Divine Beloved is there waiting for you.

Each day along the way can be a day of joy, cheerfulness, courage, strength, love, when you unceasingly commune with God in the language of your heart. Remember this always, for it is the way to Self-realization.

Karma Yoga: Balancing Activity and Meditation

From a talk at Self-Realization Fellowship International Headquarters

Balance in life comes by practicing the principles of Karma Yoga. There is no way to find peace of mind while carrying on your duties except by performing them as a karma yogi, leaving the fruits of actions in God's hands.

Gurudeva Paramahansa Yogananda used to say, "Always think that what you are doing, you are doing for God." Now, "thinking" means you have to really believe that what you are doing is for God. Every act must be dedicated to Him. I am grateful that through Guruji's training this consciousness remains with me now. This does not mean it is easy all the time, but I truly feel that in all my actions I am striving to please God. That is the right attitude to have.

God Is Looking After You

When problems arise, most people blame them on somebody else. The disgruntled worker feels: "He's out to get me; that's why he's giving me these hard tasks." Or, "He resents me, so he's giving me extra work." Do not look at life that way. It is much healthier to face our problems as having come to us bearing

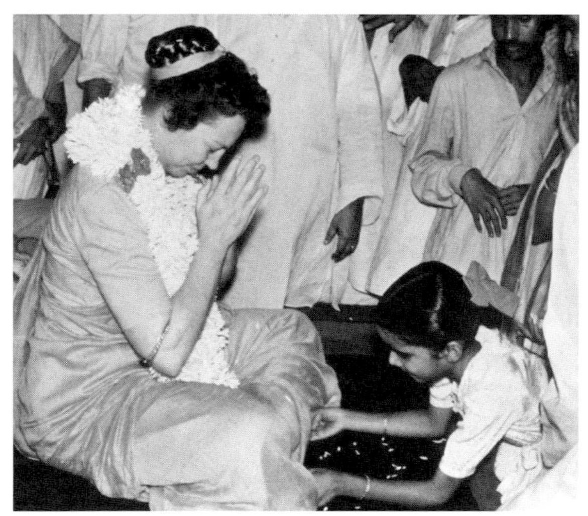

Calcutta, July 1961. Mataji greets little girl with ancient Indian gesture, *pranam,* which signifies "my soul bows to your soul."

Reception by YSS members, Delhi, November 1972

"Whatever our faith or nationality, we are all kin, with one common Father. Think of others in these terms: They are my own. They are a part of my God. In each one my God is manifest. Let me serve them to the best of my ability."

Paramahansa Yogananda seated between two disciples who would later become his spiritual successors: Rajarsi Janakananda and Sri Daya Mata; SRF Encinitas Hermitage, 1939

Mataji speaking at SRF Lake Shrine, July 1965

In meditation in front of portrait of Paramahansa Yogananda at SRF International Headquarters, March 7, 1980, during observance of Mataji's twenty-fifth anniversary as SRF/YSS president

"Transcendent peace is within you, not flowing from some heavenly sphere in space. There is an opening up of the heart, an opening up of the mind, which comes by meditating deeply, until one reaches the inner source of peace."

(Left) Reception on return to SRF International Headquarters, 1964, after extended trip with Ananda Mata and Uma Mata to serve Paramahansa Yogananda's work in India. *(Right)* Leading devotional chanting during *satsanga* at Self-Realization Center in Mexico City, February 1972.

some inherent benefit—a learning experience, if nothing more. How are we to behave? What are we supposed to do in this situation? What should be our attitude in these circumstances?

If you really believe there is a Divine Power in this world, then believe that this Power has control over your life. No matter what happens to me, I am firmly convinced that no one can do anything to me, no condition can come into my life, that God has not first permitted, because He is in charge of my life.

There has to be faith that God is in control. I look at it this way: God brought me into this world, and nobody but God is going to take me out of it. He has been looking after me every moment since He first created me.

Once that thought is set in your mind, it becomes much easier to believe that at every moment, whether you are "eating, working, dreaming, sleeping, serving, meditating, chanting, or divinely loving,"* God is the One with whom you have to do. That is the thought the devotee should place first in his consciousness. In other words, begin to cultivate a more direct relationship between yourself and God.

"Always think that what you are doing, you are doing for God." I have practiced that; and I am sure I will have to be given more opportunities to prove this in my life, because no one can say, till this life is done, that he has risen above all tests. But the way to succeed is to accept that God has something to do with whatever comes to you. No matter what it is, even if it seems impossible, face it. It is important not to try to run away from any test or trial, because through that experience God is giving you an opportunity to grow in spiritual stature.

* Daya Mata is quoting from the poem "God! God! God!" in *Songs of the Soul* by Paramahansa Yogananda. *(Publisher's Note)*

Union With God Through Selfless Activity

In the last years of Master's life he said to me, "Now you have to become a karma yogi." I was terribly upset; that concept had never appealed to me at all! Karma Yoga was the last path I would have sought.* But because Master said it and I trusted him completely, I accepted it. And I set out to learn as much about it as I could.

In Guruji's words: "The path of Karma Yoga is the path of uniting the soul with God through selfless activity." Now, doesn't that tell us something about how we should balance our lives?

"When you are doing things for yourself," said Master, "your consciousness is united with your limited ego. But when you act for God, you are identified with Him. Perfection may be attained through Karma Yoga only if one dedicates all the fruits of his actions to God." Do the best you can and be not overly concerned with results. Leave the fruits in God's hands. If you are doing your best, your actions are bound to produce good fruit.

What does it mean to perform all one's actions without looking for or desiring their fruits? I give you this illustration: An ambitious man plants a flower seed and tends it lovingly. After long months of care, just as the plant begins to blossom, insects destroy it. Such a man becomes angry or discouraged, and may stop his gardening. The divine man, on the other hand, will tend his plant even more lovingly and with greater care than the possessive man. But if insects destroy it, he

* As readers of her book, *Only Love,* will have understood, Daya Mataji's lifelong desire was to know God as love, the primary realization of the *Bhakti Yogi.* Under her Guru's guidance, she realized that God can be known through each of the yogic disciplines: love, service (right activity), discrimination, and meditation. *(Publisher's Note)*

says, "Lord, I grew it for You. I will plant another." He does not become upset. His attitude is that he will try again and again and again. Why? Because he is not doing the work for self, and he finds joy in doing it for God. So it does not matter how many plants die. He goes on with his replanting and caring.

"It is important," said Master, "to remember this point: Why should anyone think he has a right to the things of this world? He does not even know why he came on earth, how he got here, or when he is going to leave." Nor do we know whither we will go when we leave here. We are utterly dependent upon God. So why wait until the end of life to realize this? Begin to think of Him and seek Him now.

Suppose I tell you all to go out tomorrow and sweep the grounds. Half of you would be bored with the idea of just sweeping, sweeping, sweeping. But when Master had us perform this chore, he taught us to think of the Power that is allowing us to move. If That were taken away, we would not be able to use our hands or feet, or even to think. Since it is God upon whom we are wholly dependent, Master taught us to do all tasks in this consciousness: "My hands and feet, my thoughts and speech, were made to work for Thee." He instilled that spirit in us. Try to feel it when you are working. Don't talk idly, but practice the presence of God while performing duties. It is a marvelous experience.

Master said, "Give everything to God. Give Him even the responsibility for your actions." Now, this does not mean that you can do something stupid and then say, "Well, the Lord is responsible!" That is a misinterpretation of Master's counsel. God gave us common sense and He wants us to use it, so that when we perform an action it is based upon reason and discrimination.

"He wants you to make Him responsible, for He is the true Doer of everything. You have attempted to rob Him of both the fruits of your actions and the responsibility for performing them." That is why, when I asked Master how to carry on the vast array of duties he was leaving with me, he said two things—and not a day goes by but I remember them and try to realize more fully what they mean.

The first was: "Lord, Thou art the Doer, not I." When you live that way, you feel less the burdens you are carrying—this organization, as an example. You realize you are just doing your part in the Lord's work.

And the other one was: "Lord, Thy will be done, not mine." I am always saying to Him, "What I may want is not important. What do *You* want? And if ever I start to follow my own will, Lord, don't allow it. Disappoint me. I want only to do Your will." Do not be so attached to your own ideas and desires that you try to twist God's arm, so to speak, to make Him tell you to do what *you* want to do. There is spiritual danger in that.

Guruji continues: "You say, 'I, I, I,' morning, noon, and night, but who are you? Don't you know that only God exists? You are but His expression." That is beautiful to me. Only God exists and every one of us is only His expression. Let us always be honest, sincere, truthful, humble expressions. Let us be sweet, fragrant, understanding, willing, devoted, dedicated, intelligent, serviceful expressions of God. That covers everything—but it is a big order, isn't it?

Freeing Yourself From the Sense of Being Burdened

"Adopt a neutral attitude toward life," Master continues. "Instead of creating more desires and becoming entangled in this cosmic dream, just say, 'Lord, You put me in this body. It is You who are dreaming my existence. All that I own and all that I am belongs to You.'" That is another beautiful thought. When things get too rough, just think, "Well, Lord, You gave me this responsibility. I will do my best, but You must guide me. And while I am acting, Lord, don't let me forget You. Let me just cling to You." The more difficulties we have, the more we should cling to God. Don't permit troubles to separate you from God, as so many people do. Hold fast to Him. Let go of everything else and cling to Him.

Guruji goes on to say, "How wonderful it is to live that way. How wonderful to think, 'Lord, I am living just for You. And I am working just for You.'" With that consciousness, the burden of your responsibilities is lightened; you do not feel that the whole world is resting on your shoulders. You know it is on His shoulders, and you are just doing your best to help Him.

If the Lord wished, He could replace all of us with persons far better, far more qualified. I often think of this: He has the power, if He decides that any of us are not doing very well, to replace us with others much more efficient, much more talented. But He has given us this blessed opportunity to grow by carrying responsibilities and performing duties for Him. It is we who should be grateful. We should thank Him for letting us work with Him.

Once when I was feeling the pressure of so much work to do, Master said to me: "Don't ever give Divine Mother the impression that you are doing Her a favor." That hit me very forcefully; it sank in very deeply and I never forgot it. Sometimes our problem is the attitude, "I'm working so hard for You, I'm just too busy for words!" Every day I say, "Lord, thank You. It doesn't matter what my pains or problems are. I thank You."

I don't want to be caught up in delusion. I am trying to get out of it. I wish to be free. When you get a little glimpse of divine joy, divine freedom, it makes you eager for more. This does not mean you want to leave the world, but to be free from the delusion that limits you to this tiny fleshly cage and to narrow, small thoughts. I like to think big, to think vast thoughts. Master said, "If you just once got a taste of divine freedom, your heart and mind would race to the Infinite, wanting to have that joy and bliss all the time." This is so true.

The more you meditate and become anchored in the consciousness of God, the less importance you will give to externals. Problems will always be here. Dealing with them is like trying to straighten out a pig's tail, as they say in India; it always curls back again. You resolve one problem and another rears its ugly head; sort that one out, and you are faced with yet another. That is part of life, and you cannot escape it. We have to learn to do as Master did. He used to say, "When I don't like this world, I go into the other world." How often I think of that. When you get weary of this world—and we all do now and then—just take your mind away from it. You need not walk away from your duties, but mentally you can divorce yourself from them for a little while, recharge yourself, and then get back into them again.

It does not matter what our problems are; we can overcome them and learn from each experience. So let us never be dismayed or discouraged. Yes, I admit there are times when you may want to "throw in the towel." But always pick yourself up and say, "It doesn't matter. When the Lord decides that I should have a breathing spell, He will give it to me."

"Everything I do," said Guruji, "I do only for God. If you follow that principle, karma can never touch you. In that way you become a true karma yogi."

We might all prefer a simple remedy for balancing our lives, such as: "Take two teaspoons of this and one tablespoon of that, and all will be better." But that is not the way life works. Each person has to find in his own consciousness the way that gives him perfect balance between work and meditation.

The Importance of Meditation

Devotees who bypass meditation will gradually lose the desire for God. That is why I tell you all again and again, you cannot find God without meditation. And you cannot find happiness on the spiritual path without meditation. Service alone will not suffice.

Make up your mind to set aside a specific time for meditation. You will then find it much easier to maintain a balance in your life. If you meditate and carry over into all of your activities the peace born of your meditation, eventually you will come to the state wherein your entire day is one long stream of God-communion. Whether you are in meditation or working, there is an unbroken flow of divine awareness. But that does not come unless, as well as serving, you meditate deeply, without being absentminded or falling asleep.

If any of you have the problem of sleeping in meditation, do not let that tendency continue; because once it takes hold and becomes a habit, you might as well say, "Good-bye, God!" That habit can become so deeply ingrained in your consciousness that it will be very difficult to overcome. Correct this weakness at the outset by making up your mind to do so. Will power and determination are what are necessary.

It helps to exercise before you meditate, to fill your lungs with fresh air and thereby vitalize your whole system with oxygen. And when you meditate, go deep. If you cannot, it means that your attention is not yet concentrated enough, not really riveted on your practice of the meditation techniques. If you find yourself nodding, pull yourself up and bring your mind back to the practice of the ancient technique of concentration taught by Guruji.

Nowadays, when I practice that technique, almost immediately my mind and breath become calm. I cannot tell you how much I value it. When you have many responsibilities, just taking the mind within and resting briefly in that inner peace helps to give the balance you need. This technique is marvelous for that, very soothing and calming. It helps you to maintain your equilibrium, and keeps you from getting uptight. And as you go on practicing, those moments of utter stillness become longer. If the whole world practiced this technique, there would be fewer problems.

In the beginning, it is difficult on your own to establish the habit of regular meditation. But you cannot get anywhere spiritually if you are spasmodic in your efforts, and in your practice of the techniques. That is why Guruji used to say it is important for devotees to come together in groups for meditation. Many of you are not yet meditating deeply because your will is not sufficiently strong—you cannot sit still long enough to get results. It takes time to cultivate the right habits of meditation, because you may never have done anything like it before in this life. Group meditation strengthens each individual present. Christ said, "Where two or three are gathered together in my name, there am I in the midst of them."* Paramahansaji's guru, Swami Sri Yukteswarji, stressing the same principle, said to him, "Surround yourself with your spiritual bodyguards." You don't know how much you help one another when you meditate with other devotees. The vibration that is created supports and encourages each one.

Work With Joy and Creative Enthusiasm

Practice the presence of God. I remember going many times into Master's rooms, excited or distressed about something, and he would say, "Why don't you just keep your mind here?" pointing to the *Kutastha,* or Christ center. How often I heard him say that; it is something he taught us to practice all the time, so that we would develop the habit of letting our consciousness rest there during the little gaps of time when our attention is free. Because of this training, I find that now my mind is always concentrated there. That point between the eyebrows is the center of concentration and will, and of creative thought.

Guruji said, "When you begin work, *think of God.*" Now, that does not mean just a light, off-the-top-of-the-head thought of Him. Sit for a few moments, concentrate, and pray, "Lord, let me be with You this day. Let me see how much I can carry You in my thoughts and into my work." Then plunge into your activities with joy and enthusiasm, because you are doing them for God. At noon, take a little time again to think deeply of God, and then go back to your work.

Sometimes our thoughts of God are too shallow; we are saying halfheartedly, "O Lord, I am thinking of You. Bless me. But I've got to go now!" Rather, pray

* Matthew 18:20.

with deep feeling: "I love You, God. I want only You. I have all these duties, but You know they have no meaning for me, except that I am striving to do Your will. I don't want anything but You. I just want to please You. If You ask me to scrub floors, I'll do it gladly. I am here to do whatever You ask of me. That is my joy." It is possible to develop this consciousness and to find joy in it. It does not make you dull-minded. In fact, you become extremely creative, because it fills your thoughts with the energy and wisdom of God. It is the most creative state of consciousness. Try it.

"Learn to Live a More Interior Life"

Master used to say to us frequently, "Learn to live a more interior life." Cultivate interiorization of the mind so that you live more in the thought of God; and so that when you have finished your activities of the day, your thoughts turn automatically to Him. The more you interiorize your consciousness, the more you will find it opens up a whole new world, one that is far more interesting than this external one in which we live. As Guruji would say, "That is where God and the angels reside."

But you will not know that world unless and until you meditate more deeply. We are living on the surface of life, unless and until we draw closer to God. Only then do we really know what life is, and what we are. Master said, "Let each day's meditation be deeper than that of the previous day." Ask yourself, "Am I doing that?" "Deeper" means that when you meditate your mind becomes much more concentrated, much more on fire to experience the divine state of God-union. That is the natural state of your soul, your true being.

The Spiritually Healthy Attitude Towards Work

From a talk at Self-Realization Fellowship Ashram Center, Encinitas, California

Looking back over my life in the ashrams of my guru, Paramahansa Yogananda, I see that it has been one of intense activity since the day I entered Mt. Washington many years ago. And I can truthfully say that hard work has been a tremendous benefactor in helping to strengthen me and uplift my consciousness in God. Of course, meditation was also essential; but my attitude has always been the one Master instilled in us: Meditation does not consist only of sitting quietly with the thoughts turned inwardly on God. We should learn to so conduct ourselves, to so train the mind to dedicate all activities to God, that our whole life will be lived in the awareness of His presence. In that consciousness, dutiful action becomes a form of meditation.

I have heard many people say, "I meditate for hours every day," or "I have done hundreds of Kriyas,"* but when I look into their eyes I see not one whit of spiritual growth. To them spirituality meant only spending time in the sanctuary of silence and seclusion. As long as they did their Kriyas, they were not concerned with

* Reference to the practice of Kriya Yoga, an ancient technique of God-realization given to the modern world by the line of Gurus of Self-Realization Fellowship.

how they conducted themselves after meditation. That was not the guidance we received from Master. If practiced correctly, Kriya enables us to achieve the physical and mental stillness necessary to commune with the Divine in meditation. Then we are to make the effort to hold on to that communion in the midst of activity, drawing on it to guide and inspire our behavior and actions. Seeking God is not just the practice of meditation techniques; it is a way of life.

Hard Work: A Valuable Spiritual Discipline

Work is a valuable spiritual discipline. It purifies our consciousness, because in order to perform our duties correctly we must develop right attitude. Beginners on the path sometimes think they do not have to be too concerned about doing their job well, because seekers after God are not supposed to be attached to material things. Frankly, this is an excuse for physical and mental laziness. How many times through the years Master said to us disciples (I can still hear his voice): "If you do something, do it right!" He was so strict about this that very often he would insist that we redo a task if he felt that we had done it carelessly.

This doesn't mean Master was attached to the fruits, or results, of endeavor. Rather, he was teaching us to strive for the highest in whatever we do, because that is how we bring out our innate soul perfection. Look at the law and order that is manifested by God in His gigantic universe. Everything runs with precision. He is the archetype of efficiency; and we, being made in His image, ought to strive to express the same in our little corner of activities.

Never be afraid of hard work. People who dislike work are always dodging it; and I can tell you without a doubt that they do not succeed on the spiritual path. Over the years I have seen again and again the negative effects of this wrong attitude in devotees: "I will give *this* much, but no more" or "I will do only this because I don't like to do that." It is not easy to know God; it cannot be accomplished merely by wishful thinking. To gain the greatest Treasure requires that we dedicate the whole of our lives to Him—whether in an ashram or in family life. As Jesus said, "Whosoever will save his life shall lose it, but whosoever shall lose his life for my sake and the gospel's, the same shall save it."* He who thinks only of his own comfort, fearing that if he overextends himself in service he will "go to pieces," does not find God. But he who holds back nothing of himself, who wholeheartedly gives his life in service to God and his fellow beings, finds his true life, the life divine.

Dealing With the Pressures of "Impossible" Workloads

I speak from experience. I have had to pass through what seemed at the time to be great difficulties during my years in the ashram, as have all the disciples who received Guruji's training. Master was divine love and kindness personified, but he could also be firm where our spiritual discipline was concerned. Sometimes we would feel discouraged, that we would never be able to measure up to his expectations and lofty standards. My discipline centered primarily around the duties he assigned to me. He gave me so much to do that at times I felt I would die if I tried to get it all done. Under that kind of pressure, there is the tendency to think, "Well, let me die, then, if that's what he wants!" (Human nature loves to indulge in self-pity, and to draw attention

* Mark 8:35.

to itself by putting on a show of "martyrdom.") But by accepting what he asked of me, I learned a wonderful lesson: When the pressures of your workload become so great that you honestly do not see how you can deal with them, the best thing to do is to say sincerely, "Lord, it makes absolutely no difference to me what You place in my path. I accept whatever You ask of me. I will weed out from my consciousness all thought of holding back for the sake of my little self. If I fail, that is in Your hands; but I will do my best." When you thus inwardly surrender, and truly do your best, God responds. How many times I have seen Him make possible the impossible.

The Guru's Training

To each of us on the spiritual path come the particular experiences that will help us to learn unconditional surrender to God. I will share with you an example from my own life with Guruji. In the latter period of Gurudeva's life, he began to prepare us for that time when he would leave his body. He and many of us disciples had been living most of the time at the Hermitage in Encinitas since he returned from India in 1936; but one day in 1948, he said to me: "I want you to go back to Mt. Washington and take charge of the administration of the society."

This was very painful to me. First of all, I wanted to remain where Master was; and secondly, I had always resisted the idea of being a leader. I had only one desire in this life: to be a *bhakti yogi.* For me, only devotion had meaning—only love for my God, to remain forever at the feet of my Beloved, adoringly worshiping. My ideal was to be always in the background, loving God and humbly serving my Guru. Now that life I cherished was being swept away. I didn't voice my feelings to Master. Deep within I knew I had to accept the lesson we all have to learn on the spiritual path: Worry not about the external changes that are an inevitable part of life in this world of duality. Be of even mind, inwardly anchored in that which alone is changeless—God.

So I packed up and went to Mt. Washington to take up my new duties. Master was full of glowing ideas about organizing the work to better disseminate the Kriya Yoga message of the Gurus; and I, too, was brimming with enthusiasm. But there was a surprise in store for me. Shortly after I began this task, Guruji moved to his little ashram in the desert, and took with him most of the key disciples on whom I had been counting. He left me with only a handful of people, most of whom were wholly untrained.

My first reaction was, "This is impossible!" Then I resigned myself to the fact that Master knew best. Much of what time was left to him he would spend at the desert. He required help with the writings he was working on, and he also wanted those disciples to be with him so they could receive his guidance. This I could understand. I had had many years in his blessed presence; now it was the turn of others. So I adjusted myself to the situation.

But then another blow fell. Master came in from the desert for a short time, and called me to him. "I think we ought to have a Convocation* next year," he said. "I want you to organize it." I was shocked. "This time he's gone too far!" I thought.

* A gathering of Self-Realization Fellowship members from all over the world, consisting of a series of classes, meditations, and other spiritual programs.

"Master," I said, "I cannot do it; it is physically impossible." I could see so many reasons why he should not ask me to assume this responsibility: I knew nothing about organizing Convocations; there were no personnel to do the work—he had taken them all to the desert; and, besides, I was completely burdened down by the enormous demands of supervising the offices—correspondence, centers, financial, ashram matters.

Master returned to the desert that night, and I could see he was very unhappy with my attitude. I went to my room in tears, for I could never bear to displease him. But this time I was determined not to give in, because I felt my reasons were fully justifiable. I tried to meditate, I tried to sleep, but I couldn't; my mind was too upset. So I began to analyze my attitude.

The trouble with most people is that they can't stand to look at the truth about themselves. They keep busy with outer things because they do not want to be alone with themselves, even for a few minutes. Sometimes this refusal to face oneself goes to such an extreme that it leads to mental illness. Master taught us the art of healthy introspection, and I hope all of you are practicing it. Learn to examine your thoughts and behavior when things go wrong. The cause will be found more readily in your own makeup than in outer conditions.

So as I introspected that night in my room, and objectively analyzed why I was so distressed, I had to admit the truth of the matter: I was not *unable* to take on this task Master had asked of me; but I was *unwilling* to do so. That was really what was wrong with me. To my mind, the reasons why I could not organize the Convocation had seemed justified; but now I realized that I was just rationalizing my own unwillingness to assume such a great responsibility.

The moment I recognized the true motive behind my resisting his request, my consciousness changed. "You have given your life to God unconditionally," I told myself. "You cannot say to your Guru, 'I will accept this discipline from you, but not that one.' If you have such an attitude, then how can you think your devotion is unconditional?"

I resolved that I would do what he had asked, and instantly a great peace came over my soul. Before I fell asleep, I determined that in the morning I would get in touch with Master at the desert and promise him to do my best in organizing the Convocation he wanted.

Master was always attuned to our state of consciousness. Even though he was 150 miles away, he was aware of the struggle I was going through. The first thing the next morning, he telephoned from the desert. I quickly said to him, "Master, please forgive me for my unwillingness. My attitude was wrong. I don't know how to organize a Convocation, and I confess that I already feel overburdened, but I promise you this: I will do my best."

I can never forget how sweetly he replied: "That is all I ask of you."

Willingness: Key to Spiritual Growth

Well, we had the Convocation, and it was a success—and furthermore, my world did not come to an end! From that experience I learned what great strength and blessings come from willingness. Unwillingness is a formidable stumbling block on the spiritual path; so often our failure to progress is caused by this one obstacle. Examine yourself and you will find it to be so. When the devotee stops rationalizing his own desires and approaches God with a pure heart and a sincere determination to accept whatever the Lord wills, it is then that he begins to grow spiritually. His life becomes so simple and uncomplicated. I don't know of any saint who found God whose life did not reflect this attitude of willing surrender.

I thought of this when I saw the film "The Ten Commandments," especially during the scene that shows the tremendous hardships Moses had to undergo in the desert. The narrator explains that when Moses was driven out into the wilderness, God severely tested him, and molded and shaped him into the instrument He needed to do His work. Only then was Moses ready to carry out the will of the Divine. That episode inspired me so much, because I knew from my own experience that this is exactly what the soul goes through in learning surrender to God. How grateful I am for those years of discipline and hard work Guruji gave me, because I see that hand-in-hand with my meditations these have molded my being as nothing else on earth could have done.

What Is Right Activity?

So we should never think that spiritual unfoldment takes place only during our periods of meditation. We have to make time for meditation, yes. But both meditation and right action are necessary, as the Bhagavad Gita teaches. What is right action, if not work? It certainly does not mean we should play hopscotch all day! Right activity, a basic tenet in all religions, means willing, constructive service. Whether you are carrying on your duties and pursuits in the world or in an ashram, if you are performing them as perfectly as possible as offerings to God—and if you are taking every opportunity to serve others by giving love, kindness, and encouragement, and material assistance where appropriate—then you are fulfilling the principle of right activity.

It is not enough to spend our lives merely thinking noble thoughts. God has put us in a physical form because service is an essential part of our spiritual evolution. When we no longer need that kind of activity, we will no longer be required to reincarnate on this material plane.

Cultivate the attitude of willingness, and leave the results in God's hands. Many times, concerned devotees have said to me, "You've got to slow down for the sake of your health; you are trying to carry too much." But I know that for all these years it is God who has been looking after this body. I have lived with that faith. As long as He wishes this body to be well, He will look after it. I do my part, but ultimately it is His responsibility. My joy, my privilege, is to serve in whatever way He asks.

This attitude gives such mental and spiritual freedom; I can't describe it to you. Certainly there will be times when the body gives trouble. While giving it its just due, we should carry on, uncomplaining, doing the best we can. It may not be on a par with what we could do if the body were feeling better, but that we do our best at each given moment is all God asks of us.

God Will Never Send Us a Cross We Cannot Bear

So never be afraid of hardships. Know for certain that God does not permit any human being to be tested with a trial or burden heavier than that individual can bear. The crosses we are given, we are capable of carrying; their purpose is not to punish, but to strengthen.

When we give up and refuse to try, we are actually refusing God's grace.

The way to overcome the weaknesses of our mortal nature is to face our obstacles squarely; otherwise we will remain forever timid and worried and crying over the difficulties life puts in our path. The muscles in our arms become strong only if we exercise them. Similarly, we have to confront life's troublesome situations with the "spiritual muscles" of right attitude, courage, faith in God, and willingness to do His will. Then every hardship that comes will serve to strengthen us. Devoted meditation and cheerful, dutiful action—thereby we shall reclaim and manifest our omnipotent divine soul-nature.

Free Yourself From Tension

From a talk at Self-Realization Fellowship International Headquarters

Many in the world today are filled with tension and insecurity. This is because man has not learned the teaching of Christ: "All they that take the sword shall perish with the sword."* When to attain its ends, self-centeredness resorts to the sword of aggressive behavior, destruction is the inevitable result of that conflict. In other words, so long as we think—as we have for centuries—that the way to success, happiness, and freedom is through indulging our lower nature and fighting anyone who gets in our way, so long we will never know peace of mind. Negative feelings and attitudes—selfishness, hatred, greed, prejudice, worldliness—create tension within the individual; and, on a universal scale, result in war. Here are a few practical ideas that can benefit all of us, on how to avoid tensions.

Practical Methods to Reduce Tension

"Keep the mind calm through practice of meditation." When we become tense, we are excitable. Our thinking is too fast. We lose the natural harmonious relationship between mind and body. We know that all our physical responses originate in the mind, so to overcome tension

* Matthew 26:52.

we must first bring the mind under control. When we learn to calm the mind, we can calm the body. That is one reason why there is such a great interest in meditation throughout the world today. The value of the Hong-Sau technique* of our Gurudeva Paramahansa Yogananda is its remarkable effectiveness in calming the mind. I encourage all of you to practice it regularly; I never miss it. Whenever I have a few spare moments in my room, or when waiting for people, I practice this technique. By doing so, one arrives at a wonderful state of inner peace.

"Think one thought at a time." When too many thoughts crowd in on us, pressure begins to build up inside. Get into the habit of thinking calmly—one thought at a time.

"Don't interrupt others while they are talking. Let them complete their sentences." We have a tendency to interrupt others when we feel under pressure. Learn to let others finish what they have to say before you respond. On the other hand, we must take this a step further and say, "Let the person who is talking not go on endlessly." The individual who talks too much is insecure; he feels he must constantly explain his ideas and actions to others. This is not necessary. Learn to be a listener rather than a talker.

"Read books that require deep concentration." Do not read trash. Take just one or two paragraphs from a good book, such as one of Guruji's, and read slowly. When you have finished, ask yourself if you have understood. If not, reread the passage until you feel you have completely grasped its meaning. Then go on to the next thought.

* An ancient yoga technique of concentration and meditation taught by Paramahansa Yogananda in the *Self-Realization Fellowship Lessons.*

The Importance of Proper Eating Habits and Exercise

"Learn to eat slowly." Gulping down food is an expression of nervous tension. Scientists say that we should chew our food more, even liquid foods. Additionally, Guruji discouraged talking at the table, because it distracts you from concentrating on what you are eating; and this in turn inhibits the proper functioning of the life force that is responsible for digesting and assimilating the food. So learn to eat more slowly, and in silence. Another advantage is that the more slowly and thoughtfully you eat, the less food you require. When you eat quickly and absentmindedly, you gulp it down and cannot wait to get more into your mouth. And that, if it goes to an extreme, becomes compulsive eating—all the result of tension.

"Exercise regularly." Master was an avid advocate of this. Every night at Encinitas, no matter how late it was, Guruji took us out on the veranda, and we did our Energization Exercises* with him. Sometimes it was bitter cold outside, but that did not mean a thing to him. So that habit was formed; and now, even if it is eleven at night before I am free, I never miss doing those exercises. And in addition he encouraged us to walk or run regularly. Don't forget to combine it with the deep breathing Guruji teaches. This is especially important for those who lead a somewhat sedentary life, and therefore do not get sufficient oxygen into their lungs.

Guruji used to have us go out every afternoon and play on the tennis court. Because we had so many duties, we were reluctant to do it. We were going in one direction and did not want to be pulled in another. But

* A special series of exercises, originated by Paramahansa Yogananda and taught in the *Self-Realization Fellowship Lessons,* that recharge the body with all-pervasive *prana,* or cosmic energy.

such was his discipline that when the time came for recreation, we had to go, even if it meant coming back later to finish our work.

What Paramahansaji Did for Recreation

Someone has asked: "Tell us what Master did for recreation. What sports did he play?" Guruji encouraged recreation. He believed there was a time for everything: for meditation, for work, for recreation; and often quoted that saying, "All work and no play makes Jack a dull boy."

Master recommended simple and wholesome forms of recreation and exercise. People in the West, particularly, have gotten away from enjoying the simple things of life, and are always looking for new thrills. One who does this will never be satisfied; he will always end up being bored or jaded by excess.

Keep life simple. Learn to appreciate and enjoy unsophisticated pleasures. I am happy to see so many people today getting back to that ideal. Some individuals are so full of tension and restlessness, it is impossible for them to look at the beauties of nature—a tree, or a sunset—and appreciate them.

Guruji sometimes took us on little outings. I remember one time, when we were all in the desert with him, he suddenly said, "Come on, we're going on a picnic." No fancy preparations or foods; we took a loaf of bread, a little butter and cheese—no cookies or soft drinks. Guruji had a small plastic lunch box that was always packed for him to take in the car, with a few raisins, nuts, apples, sliced carrots, and so on, which he would share with all of us—so sweet! That was all. We were ready for our picnic. Sometimes we might stop later and be treated to an ice-cream bar.

On another occasion we drove up toward the mountains. I was much looking forward to this outing in nature, but there were crowds everywhere, and we couldn't find any place to have our picnic. We kept on driving, driving, until—toward sunset—we found ourselves back down the mountain, in the city of Banning. Finally we pulled up in front of the Department of Water and Power—there was some grass in front—and had our picnic in the car there! Now, many people would have been bored with that; but we had such fun! Simplicity was part of Guruji's nature, and he taught us to enjoy simple ways. He showed us that it is not what we do that makes us happy, but the attitude with which we do it.

When I came to Mt. Washington in 1931, I was the youngest devotee living here. Every afternoon, when we had finished our office duties, Guruji used to call me—I think more for my sake than for his—and say, "Come, let's play." We had an old badminton set, but no net. We used to string up a rope across the hall on the third floor and hit the shuttlecock back and forth. Master was very good at it. You could never win against him. He had a way of seeming to be playing very casually and then with a playful smile, suddenly, a big swat, and before you could get to it, the shuttlecock had flown past you!

Later on, other young devotees came. Our brother Dick* was a very good tennis player, and he and Master used to play on the tennis court here. Sometimes we younger disciples would join in. Guruji was also very good at tennis; he was quick on his feet.

* C. Richard Wright, Daya Mata's older brother, known through *Autobiography of a Yogi* as one of the devotees who accompanied Paramahansaji to India in 1935.

Someone made a small Ping-Pong table—it was not standard size—and we also played table tennis.

Swimming, of course, Guruji loved. When at Encinitas, he would go down to the beach with the monks and swim, even in winter, no matter how cold it was. We always marveled at that, because everyone else would be freezing; but Guruji paid no attention to whether the water was cold or not. He would plunge in and stay as long as he enjoyed it — and sometimes that seemed a long time to those who were with him!

Another sport, which reminded him of his childhood in India, was kite flying. He enjoyed this out in the desert, and at Encinitas. At Lake Hodges, near Encinitas, he had a little rowboat, only large enough for three people. He loved to just sit quietly while one of us rowed him around the lake. I enjoyed rowing; we used to do it in Utah, on a lake in Salt Lake City, before I came into the ashram. I think perhaps Guruji included me on those outings because I had told him that. On one occasion, we were on the water for hours, meditating. At sunset, the wind came up and the ripples began to get stronger and stronger; and I became a little concerned. By the time Guruji said, "Now let us get back to shore," I had a tremendous battle, because the current kept pushing us out, and I had to pull with all my might to get the boat back to shore. We finally got in, but that was the last time he took me rowing!

Guruji did not approve of playing cards, or games of that nature. But like a little child, he was fascinated by mechanical toys, and the human ingenuity behind them. As a result, at Christmas he was often given some new toy that would move about or gesture or speak in some amusing way. This he enjoyed very much.

He loved animals, and at one time we kept a goat

here. I remember Guruji sitting here leading a service, back in 1931 or 1932. The door to the stairs outside was open for fresh air. On that day, wandering up the stairs so casually, came the goat! It rambled down the aisle, and this was Master's only comment: "Well! He's come to hear us today."

Another of Guruji's main forms of relaxation was looking at the stars. On clear nights, when the stars were shining, he liked to go out and sit quietly and gaze at them. He also had a telescope he used at times. He loved to relate everything he did to God. My reason for telling you this is because it is good to choose forms of recreation that are associated with nature—an expression of God. God has a physical form—this world. In whatever we do or create on earth, let it be to express appreciation of and to decorate this form, His nature, with all that is beautiful, all that is good, all that is wholesome.

Keep the Mind on God—In Seclusion and in Activity

The next guideline to help reduce stress in our lives is one I like very much: *"Relax. Don't get bogged down in little things."* Make that one of your mottoes. When we are under tension, minor annoyances become exaggerated in our minds. Ask yourself, "Why am I getting so upset about it? Why don't I relax?" Then just let go. You have to do it—for your own sake.

"Set aside time for seclusion, when you can be alone with God and have time to think." We all have some opportunity for that if we use our time wisely. You may feel you need two or three days, but that is not necessary. Every evening, or on the weekend, or one day a week, or for half a day a week—whatever your responsibilities permit—set aside time to be alone. Take

a vow of silence for that time and do not speak; just inwardly be with God. Make whatever adjustments are necessary in your schedule. For even a short period every day, and a longer period once a week if possible, maintain silence and keep your mind with God. You will be amazed at the strength it gives you within.

"Keep your mind fixed, all the time, on the polestar of God's presence." Whenever we came to Guruji with troubles, he would just say, "Keep your mind here," pointing to the Christ-consciousness center. Some devotees might have thought, "Well, he's not giving anything to help me." He was, but because it was so simple, not everyone understood. Keep the mind on God; for He is the ultimate answer to all problems.

Be Receptive to the Guru's Guidance

And the last suggestion: *"Try always, to the best of your ability, to walk in the footsteps of the Guru."* This is simple if you have a well-developed conscience. Any time emotions begin to build up and you want to lash out, all you have to do is think, "Gurudeva is watching me." He used to say to us, "Don't think that when this body is gone I will be away from you. I will be silently watching you." I know that to be so. We may be able to conceal things from everyone else, but not from our Guru. So be honest before him. When we have done something wrong, let us turn to him and say, "Master, I know I have done wrong; help me." He does not expect one hundred percent perfection, but what he does expect—and has a right to expect, if we accept him as our guru—is honesty, sincerity, and truthfulness. He demanded these from all of us who were around him. He used to say, "No matter what you have done, don't try to conceal it from me." In the relationship between guru and disciple, there must be complete openness of heart and mind; otherwise you limit his help. We enjoyed that relationship with Guruji. As a result, I admit, we received more scoldings than if we had been less candid with him. But we came for correction, we came to change ourselves; and his guidance was the best thing in the world for us.

Whenever you find yourself getting uptight, remind yourself, "Relax, relax. I came for God." Remember that some day others will be doing the work we are doing now. None of us is indispensable. This is not a justification for neglecting your responsibilities, but simply a reminder that you should let go and let the mind rest in God—and then, in a more detached frame of mind, take up your duties again.

I have had some of my most wonderful experiences with the Divine Mother when there has been a lot coming at me, and I suddenly reminded myself that I would not be here forever, and inwardly let go and said, "It's not my responsibility. I'll do my best as long as I am here, but You are my Love." Every time the mind goes within, I feel such a sweet response from the Divine. When you say, "I love You, my Lord," and feel immediately the divine joy springing up within your soul, that comes from daily effort to practice the presence of God. The search for Him is so simple, but sometimes we make it difficult because we put everything else first and God last.

To sum up, to free yourself from tension:

- Keep the mind calm through practice of meditation.
- Think one thought at a time.

- Don't interrupt others while they are talking. Let them complete their sentences.
- Read books that require deep concentration.
- Learn to eat slowly, and preferably in silence.
- Exercise regularly.
- Relax. Don't get bogged down in little things.
- Set aside time for seclusion, when you can be alone with God and have time to think.
- Keep your mind fixed, at all times, on the polestar of God's presence.
- Try always, to the best of your ability, to walk in the footsteps of the Guru.

A Heart Aflame

From a talk at Self-Realization Fellowship International Headquarters

In the *Self-Realization Lessons,* Gurudeva Paramahansa Yogananda has said: "The purpose of the practice of the SRF Technique of Concentration is to gain conscious passivity." Let me explain what conscious passivity is, and why there is no contradiction between that state and the ardent longing necessary to know God, such as expressed in Guruji's chant, "My heart's aflame, my soul's afire, just for You, You, You, just You."

Passivity is a state of peace. *Conscious* passivity is a deeper state, a great calmness in meditation, of which you, the soul, are fully conscious. Passivity should not be interpreted to mean unconsciousness. There is nothing in the teachings of any scripture—and certainly not in yoga—that tells the devotee to strive for a passive state in which he is not conscious. One never loses consciousness in meditation. That is not the purpose or the result of any yoga meditation technique. In deep meditation, one's consciousness expands and is keenly perceptive.

Now you may comprehend this intellectually, but the only way you will really understand is through your own experience in meditation. But how are you to arrive at that state of conscious passivity in meditation? Let me put it to you this way: When you meditate, it must be with a relaxed mind. Do not hold a sense of "When is it going to be over?" Do not put a limit on your meditation; that you will meditate five or ten minutes. When you come together to meditate in the temple, avoid restless anticipation: "When is the leader going to start praying? When is he going to close the meditation?" When you are meditating in your room alone, throw out such restless thoughts as "I don't feel like meditating, but I have to." These are all indicative of mental tension.

But when you put all your concentration and enthusiasm into your meditation, when you feel the divine ardor of "My heart's aflame, my soul's afire," you enter the state of conscious passivity. The thoughts are still, but you are fully conscious, enfolded in a marvelous peace—and a feeling of tremendous love and joy. This experience is not something superimposed on your consciousness from any external source—though peace and love and joy are all around us. These qualities are also within you, in the soul. Meditation gradually pulls away the various leaves of thought, of consciousness, of sensation, which have heretofore hidden your awareness of these soul-treasures.

It isn't that peace suddenly descends upon you, but rather that you suddenly glimpse your real nature. It is the most thrilling experience! Transcendent peace is within you, not flowing from some heavenly sphere in space. There is an opening up of the heart, an opening up of the mind, which comes by meditating deeply, until one reaches the inner source of peace. To achieve this, apply what Guruji has taught us: the techniques of concentration and meditation, and the practice of the presence of God, or what we call mental chanting.

The Measure of Meditation's Depth

The devotee comes to that state, during and at the close of meditation, wherein his thoughts are expressed

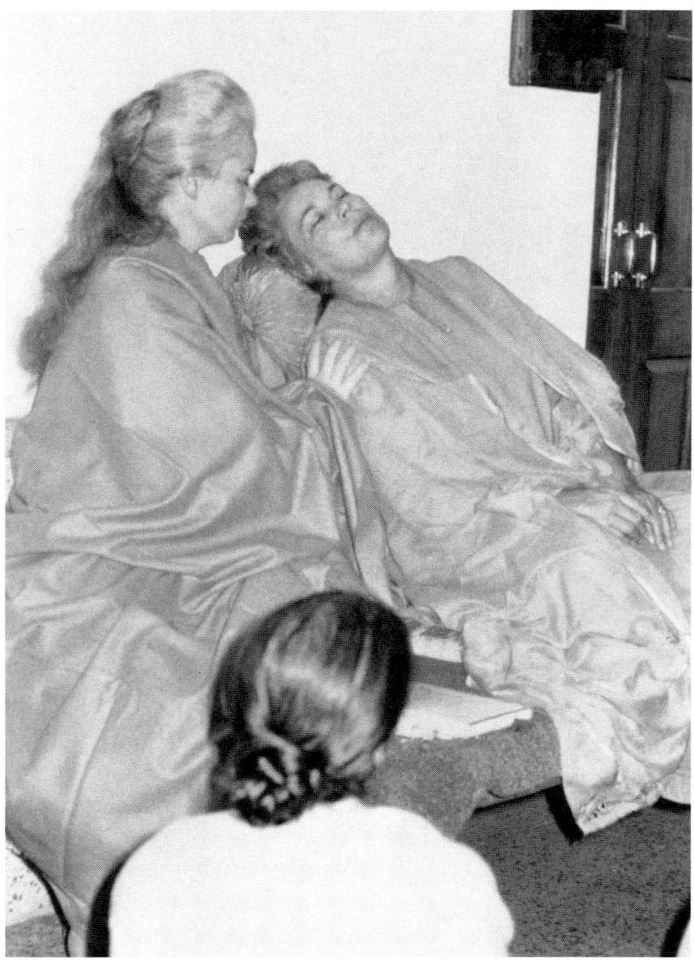

In a deep state of *samadhi,* wherein the consciousness has withdrawn from awareness of the body in an inner ecstatic experience of God-realization; Ranchi, 1967

"No human experience can match the perfect love and bliss that inundate the consciousness when we truly surrender to God. It is the most sublime fulfillment the soul can ever know."

After Christmas *satsanga*, Pasadena Civic Auditorium, 1978

"The best way to change people is by the example of our own behavior; not thinking we are better, not showing off our spiritual endeavors, but expressing the kindness, thoughtfulness, love, understanding, that begin to develop within us as a part of Self-realization. That is what touches people."

in a very simple way: "Lord, I only know that I love You." When he mentally converses with the Divine Beloved and feels that love in his heart, then he knows indeed he is holding steadfast to the hand of God. This has always been the test by which I have been able to judge my own meditations and their depth. There is just this sincere expression from the heart, the mind, and the soul: "I have nothing to ask, Lord. I have nothing to demand. I have nothing to say but 'I love You.' And I want naught but to enjoy this love, to treasure it, to clasp it close to my soul, and to drink of it always. There is nothing in the world—no power of the mind, no craving of the senses—that draws my thought away from this avowal of my love for You."

The greatest temptation, the greatest ignorance, is to permit anything to stand in the way of achieving that goal. We will not reach it by forsaking our duties, which have, in fact, been given to us by God and by our karma. That attainment comes by accepting with strength, with courage, with faith, whatever we must face each day, while keeping our minds fixed on the polestar of God's presence. This is what life is all about. Its only purpose is to prompt us to overcome this terrible delusion of separation from God, our Creator, and by the simple act of love, of devotion, of silent conversation, regain our lost divine heritage as the children of God.

God has given us freedom of thought and privacy in the sanctum of our minds. No one can intrude upon that freedom and privacy. Therein, He has given to each of us the unbounded opportunity to express love for Him and to commune with Him. No one need know of our silent worship within—a sweet and sacred exchange of love and joy between the soul and the

Lord who has sustained it through millions of incarnations, and who will sustain it through eternity.

A Simple Avowal of Love for God

To me it seems a disgrace and a tragedy that we human beings have turned away from, and actually evade, the very One who alone sustains us. If we follow worldly ways, we will know temporary pleasures, but we will never know eternal happiness or peace of mind—that wonderful sense of well-being, joy, divine love and understanding, which we seek in all of our activities and in all of our relationships—until we begin to know God and the part we have in Him.

It is so simple, this search for God by loving Him. It is the one ingredient that millions of religionists lack. They substitute other ingredients in their search for God. They would much rather enjoy deep philosophical discourses about Him, or engage in debates about Him and His various aspects and manifestations, or become interested and engrossed in His powers. But who ever thinks of a simple avowal of love for Him?

It is easy to know God in the way Master taught us, and as he showed us in his life every day. We are so busy giving our love to everything God created—to the world and worldly ways, to the flesh which one day decays, to our ego: "I hurt, I hate, I, I, I"—but who gives love to God? To love Him is what Master taught us. Get into the habit of telling God that you love Him. How many do this every day, even once a day? How many do it many, many times a day? This is what is called practicing the presence of God. No saint of any religion ever found God without this practice.

We always say, "I love this. I love that." How easily we use the word "love" and cheapen it. So much of the time it is confused with sensuality. In the ultimate sense, love and sensuality have no bearing upon one another. Love is the greatest power, the greatest force, in the world. Without this divine ecstasy flowing from the One Source into every heart, we could not love anything or anyone. We receive this love freely from God, though we do not acknowledge it as coming from Him. And when it comes to giving love, we give it very unwisely: we give it to the world and shut Him out. That, my dears, is why mankind suffers. And we will go on suffering until we begin to open our hearts to include Him.

Connect All Your Experiences With the Divine

How much sweeter life becomes, how much more beautiful, when in the use of the senses I relate them back to God. I can look at souls and say, "My friends, I love them." I can look at the birds and the trees and say, "I love them." But I know, "It is You I love, my Lord. You have given me eyes with which to see beauty in everything and everyone You have created. You have given me ears to hear goodness. You have given me a voice, not to speak vulgarity, but to use to shed some light in this world—to say something encouraging to others as I pass down this short, short hall of life.

"You have also given me a mind, my Lord, with which to reason and discriminate; and so I dare to ask You any question. I never feel shy or embarrassed or blasphemous, because You are my Beloved. You know the simplicity of my soul. You understand my longings for understanding and wisdom. I come to You totally naked, my Beloved. You see me with my good qualities, and with all of the darkness I have not yet been able to throw off. You don't punish me because of the flaws that have gathered around the purity of my soul;

You help me. I do not try to hide my imperfections from You, my Lord. I come to You in humility, in devotion, in simplicity, in trust like a child, asking You to help me. And I will go on asking until You respond. I will never give up."

Think of all that God has endowed us with that sets us apart from the tree or the animal. Is it not an insult of ingratitude when we do not use rightly this Self which is made in His image? While I am busily engaged in pondering the worldwide problems of this society (Self-Realization Fellowship/Yogoda Satsanga Society), while I am standing out-of-doors doing my exercises, or while walking on the grounds among the trees and flowers—no matter what I am doing—it is the simplest thing in the world to recollect my thoughts for a moment and say inwardly, "I love You, God. I don't know anything else but that I love You. And I ask You always to give me enough strength, enough understanding, enough courage, enough compassion to serve my fellowmen, to love them as I would be loved, to love them as I feel Your love flowing over my consciousness."

The habit of inwardly talking to God and loving Him should be cultivated not only by those who live in monasteries, but also by those who live in the world. It can be done. It just takes a little bit of effort. All the habits you have developed up to now are actions you performed regularly, either physically or mentally, until they became second nature to you. But you had to start sometime to create those habits. Now is the time to initiate those kinds of actions and thoughts that develop the habit of silently conversing with God. It does not require long magnificent prayers, just a silent call from the heart, a simple sweet expression: "My God, my Love, to whom else could I turn to receive the love I feel in my heart whenever I turn to You? No one could satisfy me as You do. Indeed, my Lord, You fulfill Your promise to those who heed Your command, 'Forsake all else and follow Me.'"

Tell God That You Love Him

Simply tell God in your own words—quietly, unheard by any other—that you love Him. Tell Him when you are sitting in silent meditation. Tell Him when you are on the busy street or at your desks: "I love You, God. I love You, my Lord." Let this be your last thought at night before you go to sleep. Try it tonight. It is so beautiful, the greatest joy. As you are falling asleep, as your soul begins to enter the state of restfulness, let your mind softly, sweetly, quietly chant, "My Lord, my Lord, my Love, my Love, my God." Feel what you are saying to Him.

When you awaken in the morning, let the first thought be, "Good morning, Lord. Another day. Let it be one in which I make greater effort toward that perfection which is my real nature. Let me give understanding. Let me be more calm. Let me say something kind in response to unkind words that may be said to me. Let me today try to manifest You in my life." When you feel sad and when you feel happy; when your body is not well and when it is strong with vigor; when things go wrong and when things go right, during all these times let there be a silent, steady flow of one thought: "My God, I love You." And say it from the heart.

When you use the word "God," never take His name in vain. Though swearing is considered smart and sophisticated, it isn't right. The fact that the whole world does it does not make it right. Whenever you take the name of God, let it be with deep thought, devotion, and feeling. I have often told you about Gurudeva's ecstasy in God (in 1948) when he repeatedly uttered only one word. He didn't say "God, God," because even in that there is a sense of distance from God. By the word he used—how it touched my soul!—I could see that he was in the very presence of the Divine. He repeatedly uttered only, "You, You, You." What a thrill went through us with that one word! He was standing in God's presence, speaking directly to the One before whom he stood, the Divine Beloved of all mankind.

Keep your mind similarly on that high devotional plane. Guruji taught us to live simultaneously in two realms. Sometimes we would be completely absorbed in Divine Joy in Guruji's presence; and then suddenly he would bring us down to the level of dealing with mundane matters. He was teaching us that while our minds are fixed in God, and our souls resting in Him, we must be able to deal effectively with everyday concerns. That is the highest state of consciousness: the mind in the clouds, but the feet firmly planted on the ground, down to earth. It is what God intends for us, because that is also His nature. He is the Father, Creator of the universe. And He is very practical. Were this not so, He might have created us, but no water for our thirst, nor food to feed us. He would not have established cosmic laws that set the orderly course of the planets, and the patterns of the stars. They all would have collided long ago. The earth would have come to naught. So God's feet, we might say, are firmly planted on the ground. Yet He is always intoxicated with His divine bliss, with His divine love. We are made in His image and this is the consciousness He expects us also to manifest.

Deepening Your Love for God

Compilation from talks given at Self-Realization Fellowship International Headquarters

The search for God begins with yearning. We must yearn for truth, for some relationship with God. So the first quality one needs to develop is a deep, sincere longing for God, for His love.

In the beginning, you may not yet feel love for Him, but you can cultivate the desire to know Him by reflecting on how much you need Him. It has often been said that suffering is the greatest teacher. To a degree it is true that people turn to God when they have been disappointed by human beings or by the things the world has to offer. I think I was born with that—not disillusionment with people, because I love them—but the knowledge that neither the world nor any human being could give me what I wanted.

Every one of us is looking for perfection; not one of us craves anything less than perfect love, perfect relationships with others. As a young child I had the idea that such perfection was not to be found in the world. I realized I had no right to expect it of other people, because I myself am imperfect. How dare I demand from others something I myself am incapable of giving? Out of this kind of reasoning grew the desire: "Let me then begin my search for God." Only He can fully satisfy our longing, our need, for perfect love and understanding. No ordinary human being can. Having understood that

God alone can fulfill our deepest needs, our desire for Him begins to unfold.

One of the first thoughts that impressed me from the scriptures was this: "Seek ye first the kingdom of God, and His righteousness, and all these things shall be added unto you."* I kept revolving that truth in my mind. We draw many beautiful thoughts from the scriptures, and become inspired for a moment; then we forget them, without really applying them in our lives. But the scriptures are a textbook of principles that, if we live them, produce proven results as surely as do the laws of mathematics.

I decided to apply that one quotation in my life. I wanted to know whether it was true, or whether it was just a glorious statement from some exalted human being who did not really have to face the "nitty-gritty" of daily life. I kept to that one point: seek God first; then, the scripture tells me, everything else will fall into its rightful place, everything else will be added unto me. Whenever there was any kind of temptation or distraction, I held to that: seek *Him.* I proved to my own satisfaction that the truths taught and lived by the Great Ones can transform our own lives, too; for they had to face the same struggles, heartaches, and disappointments that all mankind faces.

Once a person grasps this, he will look for a way to approach God. The practice I have followed, as have many other disciples of Guruji, is simply, first of all, yearning for God; and then cultivating a personal relationship with Him through devotion.

To have an intimate relationship with God, you have to get to know Him. If you were asked to love

* Matthew 6:33.

someone you didn't know, you would find it very difficult to do so—even if told of that individual's wonderful qualities. But if you were to meet that person and spend some time with him, you would begin to know him, then to like him, and then to love him. That is the course to follow in developing love for God.

The question is, *how* to get to know Him? That is where meditation comes in. All scriptures encourage the individual who is seeking God, who wants to know Him, to sit quietly to commune with Him. In Self-Realization Fellowship we practice meditation techniques as well as chanting and prayer to achieve this. Some method is essential. You cannot know Him by reading a book about divine joy or love. Though spiritual writings do inspire fervor and faith, they do not give the end result. Nor does merely listening to a lecture about God. You must sit quietly in deep meditation, if even for just a few moments each day, taking the mind away from all else and focusing it on God alone. Thereby you gradually come to know Him; and knowing Him, you cannot help but love Him.

The Purpose and Value of Group Meditation

Devotion is strengthened by association with others who are also deeply seeking God. That was the ideal on which Guruji started meditation groups and centers all over the world. He used to say, "I am not interested in building huge edifices of stone wherein God is absent. We should have many small temples filled with a true spirit of devotion for God and of united seeking of God." Groups of devotees should come together to commune with God, each the spiritual friend of the other, and each interested in serving the group as a whole.

I remember once, years ago, Guruji went to the eastern part of the United States to give classes and Kriya Yoga initiation. During that period we had a service leader here who was very dry, uninteresting, boring. No inspiration came to me, so I decided not to go to the chapel anymore. As I thought I did much better in my room, I would stay there and meditate.

When Guruji came back, he called me to him, and said, "I understand you are not going to meditation?"

I said, "But, Master, I am meditating." We love to rationalize, don't we? We always have seemingly logical excuses.

"But you're not going to the *chapel* anymore?"

I replied, "No, I meditate better in my room; I can go much deeper. Down there, the teacher is very boring."

He said, "You go just the same. Go, not to be inspired by the teacher, but to seek deeply within yourself. Don't be dependent on anyone else; you are there for one reason, to commune with God." I never forgot that. It was a great and wonderful lesson that has remained with me.

When you gather with others for meditation, forget everybody else. Go there just to commune with God. There is no question about it, when our own will is weak, joining a group with like interest helps to strengthen us. If you are in your own home, and there are problems to be solved, or you have had a hard day, you may say, "I won't meditate tonight. I'll just rest. Today has been really hectic." You put off meditating, and then you put it off again, because every day there is some seemingly legitimate reason. I see someone nodding his head in agreement, so you are understanding me!

When anything tries to deter you, say, "No, I must

join the group for meditation." But go for the right reason, because you want to make the spiritual effort to change yourself. You are not there to impress or reform anyone else. In that meditative environment there is an exchange: others in the group give you strength, and you give them strength.

Cultivating a Personal Relationship With God

Do not think that you must forsake the world and enter an ashram in order to seek God. No matter how active you are, you can find time to cultivate a loving, personal relationship with Him. With my responsibilities, looking after the affairs of Guruji's society not only in this country but in India and other parts of the world, I am as busy as the busiest of you. But God comes first. I allow nothing to interfere with that. What is necessary is yearning for God, and the will power to make time for Him in daily meditation.

Meditation must never become for you just a routine, humdrum activity. In my travels I have gone to temples, mosques, and churches, and around the world I have seen devotees saying their prayers with distracted minds. I remember visiting the holy places in Jerusalem where Jesus Christ walked and communed with God, and seeing that the priest conducting the service was praying mechanically, more interested in his audience than in Him to whom he was praying. My inner feeling was: "No, no, no! You are here to commune with Christ!" Similarly, in temples in India, I saw other priests perform their *pujas,* busily looking at the other people all the while they were talking to God. The One to whom their prayers were addressed was not listening, because those devotees were not thinking of Him! The deep flaw in modern religion is that the One around whom it should revolve is totally forgotten in the preoccupation with what is going on externally. What Guruji taught is that when we sit for meditation, it is God with whom we have to do. Talk for even five minutes with God, letting no other distraction enter in, and you will find that your relationship with Him gradually becomes more real.

One way to develop one-pointed devotion is to chant mentally over and over again the name of God or some short thought or prayer addressed to Him. This is what India calls *Japa Yoga,* and the West knows it as a form of "practicing the Presence."

It is also helpful to express longing for God in a song addressed to Him—such as one of Guruji's *Cosmic Chants.* There are many beautiful love songs that can be addressed to God, even if they were not written for Him. One that Guruji liked was "Indian Love Call." How thrilling it is to offer such sentiments and longing, not to a human lover, but to God.

Also, read the lives of great souls, such as the life of Guruji, who was always immersed in the love of God.

A great help in awakening devotion is to think of someone you love very much, someone whose love has been an inspiration to you. Guruji thought of the love he had for his mother, which was beautiful, noble, and pure; he revered her. As you recall the love you feel for that person—your mother, for example—turn your mind and feeling to Divine Mother. "Oh, Divine Mother, I know it is You who came to me in the form of my mother." It can be a parent, husband, wife, child, or friend. Think of the sweet quality of that individual, and when love wells up in your heart, immediately put your mind on God. Think in those moments: "This person could not love me unless You had instilled love in him." It is from God that all love comes. When you think this way, gradually you begin to cultivate love for the Love behind those you love.

During the day, whenever anyone does something to help you, always see God's hand in the bestowal of that gift. When anyone says anything kind about you, hear the voice of God behind those words. When something good or beautiful graces your life, feel that it comes from God. Relate everything in your life back to God. Think in those terms, and you will suddenly find one day, "Oh, it is He alone with whom I have to do." God is the common denominator in the lives of all human beings. He the prime mover behind all of our activities, our greatest well-wisher and benefactor. Can there be any greater incentive to love Him and to receive His love in return?

Chanting as a Form of Meditation

From a talk at Self-Realization Fellowship International Headquarters

Let me say a few words to you about the purpose of devotional chanting, as taught by Paramahansa Yogananda. In *Cosmic Chants** he tells us:

> Sound or vibration is the most powerful force in the universe. Music is a divine art, to be used not only for pleasure but as a path to God-realization. Vibrations resulting from devotional singing lead to attunement with the Cosmic Vibration or the Word. "In the beginning was the Word, and the Word was with God, and the Word was God."†...Words that are saturated with sincerity, conviction, faith, and intuition are like highly explosive vibration bombs that have power to remove the rocks of difficulties and to create the change desired....One who sings these spiritualized songs, *Cosmic Chants,* with true devotion will find God-communion and ecstatic joy, and through them the healing of body, mind, and soul.

To learn the chants, take one at a time. In the begin-

* A book of devotional songs by Paramahansa Yogananda; published by Self-Realization Fellowship.

† John 1:1.

ning, of course, you will have to concentrate upon the notes and the correct rendering of them on the harmonium.* But when you have learned the chant well, your attention should be on the words you are singing. With increasing depth of concentration, repeat the chant over and over and over again, until your consciousness becomes wholly absorbed in the meaning behind the words. By this practice, you will arrive at that state wherein you are one with the chant. No distracting thoughts will penetrate your consciousness; nothing else will exist for you but the concept of God you are invoking.

For instance, consider the chant we have just sung, "Blue Lotus Feet:"†

> Engrossed is the bee of my mind on the blue lotus feet of my Divine Mother. Divine Mother, my Divine Mother! Divine Mother, my Divine Mother!

The repetition of the name "Divine Mother" begins to draw Her loving presence. The key is to continue chanting until you feel that blissful awareness. Then you know you have drunk the nectar from the flower of that chant. Such chanting becomes a form of meditation.

We were often blessed to sit around Gurudeva while he composed a new chant, or rendered a traditional Indian chant into English. Then we would join in with him as he sang that song over and over again, sometimes far into the night, until we went even beyond the words and the music and were glorying in devotion to God and the wonderful feeling of His nearness. This experience is the goal of chanting.

I cannot stress too much the importance of a devo-

* A hand-pumped reed organ, much used in India, which is particularly suited for accompaniment of *bhajans,* devotional chanting.

† A chant to God in the aspect of Divine Mother, from *Cosmic Chants.*

tional spirit in chanting. When we chanted with Master, he would often remind us, "Sing with all your heart. Forget that I am playing the harmonium; forget me. Just become absorbed in the thought behind the words. Think of the One to whom you are singing." Sometimes, as he sang to Divine Mother, my consciousness would become absolutely intoxicated with love for Her. The very thought of Her seemed like an ocean within me, swelling with Her infinite, loving presence.

When one goes deeper and ever deeper into the realm of a single spiritual thought or realization, everything else fades into the background. I remember one occasion in Encinitas while we were meditating with Gurudeva and Rajarsi.* The blessed Master was singing to Divine Mother, pouring out his heart to Her. His love for the Mother, and his joy, lifted us into a rapturous state. My mind became so engrossed in longing for Divine Mother and Her love that I entered a very deep ecstatic state. The Master stopped chanting; he touched me on the forehead, and then turned to Rajarsi and said so sweetly: "See, she has stolen my ecstasy."†

What a blessed experience! To touch that inner divine joy, we have to forget everything else when we chant or meditate. God's presence is felt only when we divorce ourselves completely from all other mental preoccupations. So whenever you take the name of Divine

* Rajarsi Janakananda, beloved and highly advanced disciple of Paramahansa Yogananda, was the Guru's first spiritual successor as president of Self-Realization Fellowship. He held that position until his death in 1955, at which time it passed to Sri Daya Mata.

† In moments of attunement with a divine personage, the devotee can draw from the spiritual vibration of the holy one. This principle was expressed by Jesus when, in the midst of a crowd, a woman devoutly touched the hem of his robe: "Somebody hath touched me," he said, "for I perceive that virtue is gone out of me" (Luke 8:46).

Mother, do not let it be just words to you. Lose yourself completely in the thought of Her. By your concentration and devotion, make Her a living reality in your consciousness. She is real to those who think Her real; but far away—only a name or a vague mental concept—to those whose call to Her is mechanical.

In one of the chants* is this thought: "Will that day come to me, Ma, when saying, 'Mother dear,' my eyes will flow tears?" I shall never forget the thrill that went through my being when first I heard Master sing that chant. That same thrill returns whenever I dwell on those words. So should it be with all of you. Every day you should repeat to yourself that thought, and feel the divine longing of those words welling up from within your soul.

It is said in the Hindu scriptures that just taking the name of God can give one salvation. When I first read this, I did not understand how it could be possible. But I learned that it *is* possible, when behind that mental prayer is all the hunger and longing of your soul: "My Lord, I love only You, I want only You, I crave only You. Do with my life as You will." When you have complete dependence on God—by which I mean deep devotion, faith, and surrender—then He does indeed respond.

So, dear ones, meditate regularly and sincerely. Sing to the Divine One with all the love of your soul those chants that have been spiritualized by Gurudeva. And pray for devotion: pray that your heart, mind, and soul be afire with such divine hunger, divine fervor, that your life becomes one great longing for God. Then will your feet be truly, firmly, set on the spiritual path.

* "Will That Day Come to Me, Mother?" in *Cosmic Chants.*

Learning to Like Yourself

From a talk at Self-Realization Fellowship International Headquarters

Introspection, self-analysis, is essential to self-improvement. The first *sloka* of the Bhagavad Gita says: "Gathered together, eager for battle, my children [my good and my evil traits]—what did they?"* In other words, let me review my thoughts and actions of this day: Are they leading me toward my goal? How did I behave? Was I mean? Did I lie? Did I cheat? Was I selfish or covetous? Was I unkind? That is how we should introspect.

Introspection is a very healthy practice as long as you do not employ it to dwell on your weaknesses until you are plunged into depression, or into such feelings of guilt that you begin to hate yourself. That is a misuse and abuse of self-analysis. To concentrate on your defects defeats your purpose, because the more you identify yourself with them, the stronger they become. You are not your flaws; you are the ever perfect soul. The aim of introspection is to help you dispassionately recognize the character flaws that obscure your innate divinity so that you can overcome them. If you have a weakness or do something wrong, you do not have to go around telling everyone about it. But *do* something

* Daya Mata is here using Paramahansa Yogananda's interpretation that the warriors in the Bhagavad Gita represent the warring good and evil tendencies in each human being. *(Publisher's Note)*

about it. Look at yourself honestly; and try to correct whatever you see that is unattractive. That is the right way to introspect.

Do not worry about what you feel are sins committed in the past. They are not part of you now. That is something Gurudeva Paramahansa Yogananda very much stressed to us. Correct yourself, and then whatever you did that was wrong does not belong to you anymore. Forget it. Christ told many that God had forgiven them, but he also advised: "Sin no more"—do not do it again. Hold to the thought that your past is forgiven, and learn to like yourself more. This liking of self has nothing to do with ego; it means accepting yourself as God accepts you.

There is nothing any one of us has done that is not forgiven by God when we truly turn away from that wrong behavior. It makes no difference what it is. And there is nothing you have ever done that all of us here have not also done in some life. Not only that, there is nothing you have ever done that was not already thought of by God, or you could not have done it in the first place. We must never be afraid to let Him see us as we are. He already knows every flaw, and every mistake we have made throughout many, many lives. But He has not forsaken us. He loves us unconditionally, and that will never change.

Some have the notion that they are unworthy, and they brood on this thought. Their minds are not on meditating deeply or loving God. All they think of is their unworthiness. That is a terrible pitfall. We are all worthy, because we are God's children. We have the right, the privilege, and the opportunity to seek God. Do it! Don't entertain the thought, "I am unfit." That notion is harmful because you then waste so much time wallowing in self-pity. It is also an unconscious excuse for not making greater effort to seek God more earnestly: "I am so unworthy; He couldn't really want me very much, because I'm not a good person." Those are weak arguments. Unconsciously, one is saying: "And besides that, I don't really feel that deep a desire for God; so it's convenient to blame my flaws in order to justify my lack of effort."

Whatever be my imperfections, I only know that love for God is what I am trying to perfect in this life. By concentrating on trying to think positive thoughts and to perform positive actions every day of my life, to the best of my ability, I have no time to think of my flaws or to dwell on whether or not I am fit to seek God. I am seeking Him!

Learn to accept and like yourself for what you are striving to become. Take each day as it comes. Someone has said, "Each day is like a fresh sheet of writing paper." You have the marvelous opportunity every day to write your life anew. Let it be beautiful, creative, constructive thoughts that contribute to your own spiritual well-being and that of others.

The more you put your mind on God and the less you dwell on yourself and your flaws, the more you will be in tune with God and Guru. Negative thoughts about yourself cultivate and encourage spiritual weakness, so don't entertain them; dismiss them from your mind. Your past does not belong to you. Only the present and the future are yours. Write fresh thoughts and new wholesome actions on the pages of your life that are left. That is the important thing to remember.

Surrender: Relying on the Unlimited Power of God

From a talk at Self-Realization Fellowship International Headquarters

At one time or another every one of us reaches a point at which our problems seem so overwhelming that we feel we cannot cope with them. We say to ourselves, "I've reached the end of my rope—physically, mentally, and emotionally. I've tried everything I can think of. What on earth can I do now?" Many people seek the help of a medical doctor or a psychiatrist; this is sound common sense. But there comes a time when the doctors can do nothing for us. What then?

I very much believe in the power of surrender to God, of placing our lives totally in His hands. He can bring us through every crisis, regardless of the dire pronouncements of any human being. I have been through many illnesses and have never let go of that Divine Power, because I know It sustains me. Time and again He has given me proof of this.

To draw on God's unlimited power, we need to develop more trust and faith in Him. Gurudeva once said to me, "Inwardly hold always to the thought: 'Lord, let Thy will be done, not mine.'" Too often, people are afraid to surrender to God because they do not really trust Him. They are not sure if what He will give to them will be what they want. So even if they say, "Thy will be done," they do not mean it sincerely. That is where they make their mistake.

So long as we think we can run our lives by ourselves, we do not make contact with God. The delusion that the little ego is sufficient has to be abandoned before we can receive from the Divine. How many become lost because of the notion, "I can do it by myself." No, we can't! We cannot even breathe, we cannot even lift one little finger by ourselves. Every moment we are totally dependent on the Divine; every instant He sustains us.

The more we rely on Him, and the less on material remedies, the better off we will be. Through the years I have seen the effectiveness of this faith in God demonstrated in the lives of many of the disciples of Gurudeva Paramahansa Yogananda. This is not to say that we should disregard the advice of doctors or the value of the treatments they offer. But while cooperating with professional assistance, we should realize that God's power in the mind is the true source of healing; the outer methods merely stimulate the mind to release some of that divine energy.

The mind as an instrument for tapping the power of God is limitless; I want to emphasize this to you all, as Guruji did to those of us around him. The body, this magnificent physical form man wears, is a product of his own consciousness. Each of us is unique because we have used our minds differently. All the ills of mankind stem from wrong use of the mind; scientists today are beginning to understand this more and more. As we cultivate the right thoughts and attitudes, and practice the techniques of Self-realization that Master has taught, we become increasingly able to express that perfect Divine Consciousness whose reflection is hidden within us as the Self, the soul.

Removing the Obstructions That Separate Us From God

Years ago Guruji told us (and psychologists nowadays would certainly agree) that chronic worry, fear, nervous tension, and the other negative emotions—guilt, hate, jealousy, bitterness—close off the channels through which wisdom and healing flow from the deeper levels of consciousness. People become so tense and anxiety-ridden in struggling with their problems that they get emotionally "hung up." So when we have tried everything possible to solve our problem and nothing seems to do any good, the wisest course is simply this: *Relax.* Stop trying to deal with it through the limited human resources of the rational mind, which has brought you to your present state of frustration and tension. Surrender the problem to the Divine with one hundred percent faith and trust. In other words, "Let go and let God."

Is that not what the scriptures of every religion have taught? Endeavor to surrender fully to God your heart, your mind, your life. This will begin to remove the mental blocks that give you the consciousness of separation from Him. Accordingly, you will find His power flowing into you in a greater way. Creative thinkers, inventors, people who perform extraordinary feats of strength in moments of emergency, saints who commune with God—all successful human beings—have learned in varying degrees to tap that divine reservoir within, the sole source of creative inspiration and power.

Psychiatrists would say that these qualities reside

in the "unconscious" mind.* They may not use the word God, because science looks at everything in terms of natural laws. But you cannot separate God from His laws. Regardless of what terminology is used, everyone who looks deeply enough will discover the similarity between the scientific principles governing the universe—including man's body and mind—and those truths spoken of by God-knowing seers throughout the ages. Any science that denies the existence of these spiritual truths has not yet fully understood that which it is studying. There is, in fact, no conflict between the spiritual teacher who says, "Have faith in God," and the psychiatrist who says, "Draw on the inner resources of the unconscious mind." It is by contacting the deeper levels of the mind that we begin to perceive God.†

The tendency in our time, especially in the West, has been to try to divorce the universe and its beings from God. Nowadays, however, we see that many people are trying to get out of the ruts of materialistic thinking; they are seeking again the deeper metaphysical experiences of the mystics of old. Unfortunately, they often erroneously assume that by getting out of the misleading old ruts they are not going to fall into any new ones. But they do. For instance, some have tried to explore the inner realms through drugs, which only confuse the mind and distort the understanding of what is real and what is unreal. Some people become

* Paramahansa Yogananda referred to the subconscious and superconscious minds rather than the "unconscious." He said: "There is no actual *unconsciousness;* consciousness may sleep or rest, but it can never be unconscious. In sleep the consciousness is resting, i.e., not active. The soul is never unconscious."

† "The kingdom of God is within you" (Luke 17:21).

fascinated by hypnosis, trance channeling, or other methods of passively attaining altered states of consciousness. All of these have dangerous pitfalls; all of them lead their practitioners to get into a whole new set of mental ruts. The only way to keep from getting "hung up" in this world is to become anchored in God. Then you are not hung up; you are soundly anchored!

The mind is a wonderful world whose powers should be investigated, but through the proper methods. The real spiritual seeker follows the right way—meditation taught by one who knows God—and he never loses touch with reality or common sense or the eternal laws of truth.

Relaxation and Meditation: Keys to Tapping Inner Resources of Strength

Whether one defines it as "tapping the power of the unconscious mind" or as "making contact with God," meditation is the highest way of finding the strength to overcome life's obstacles. Everyone should arrange his schedule in order to have time daily to free the mind from worries, responsibilities, and outer disturbances, so that he can give himself up to the thought of God in meditation.

One of the first necessities in meditation is learning how to relax the body and mind. Now, I am not going to suggest that you lie down in order to become relaxed for the practice of meditation, because the first thing you know you'll fall asleep, thinking, "Well, Daya Mata told me to lie down and take a nap!" It is human nature to stretch the truths we are taught so they suit our inclinations. Master told us that when he was first teaching in this country, he encouraged his students not to eat bacon. Some of them reasoned, "He told us not to eat bacon, but he didn't say we couldn't have ham." So Master then told them not to eat bacon or ham; but they rationalized to themselves, "Well, he didn't tell us not to eat pork chops!" This is the way the ego works. We should always ask ourselves, "Am I being hypocritical?" We may be so prejudiced by what *we* want to do that we seek "loopholes" in the Guru's instructions. To follow the spirit of his teachings, not just his literal words, is to develop wisdom and common sense.

So remember, relaxation does not mean going to sleep! Instead of lying down to meditate, sit up straight—spine erect—in a chair or cross-legged on a cushion. Close your eyes to reduce distractions; gently lift your gaze to the Christ center;* tense and relax your body a few times while inhaling and exhaling deeply; and then let go, mentally and physically. Maintain the erect posture, but consciously relax all undue tension in the muscles. Make yourself as limp as a wet noodle hanging on the rigid rod of the spine.

Do not think about your problem; otherwise you will remain stuck on the conscious level. Practice Kriya and the other techniques, and deeply surrender heart, mind, and life to the Divine. When we relax and calm the mind by meditation, we begin to draw on the higher levels of consciousness, the eternal vault in which resides everything we have learned in this life and in our countless previous incarnations. When we tap the

* Paramahansa Yogananda explained that the position of one's eyes has a definite correlation to one's state of consciousness: lowered or downcast eyes correspond with subconsciousness (and tend to produce that state); eyes focused straight ahead are indicative of the conscious, active state of outer consciousness; and eyes uplifted help to elevate the mind to superconsciousness.

superconsciousness—the intuitive, all-knowing insight of the soul*—wisdom begins to percolate up into the awareness, and we find a solution to our difficulty or guidance in the right direction.

Some people expect that God will appear out of the clouds and say, "My child, first do this, and then do that, and you will solve your dilemma." This is ridiculous; He will not come to us in that way, and we should not want Him to. Faith does not mean forsaking our reason and common sense and will power. It means using all of these God-given abilities in attunement with His will. As Master said: "Lord, I will reason, I will will, I will act; but guide Thou my reason, will, and activity to the right thing that I should do."

God wants us to use these divine powers that lie within each of us. That is how we grow. When I look back over my own life and remember my early years on the spiritual path, I am grateful for every hard struggle that I have had to go through. These have brought out of me strength and determination and a total surrender to God and His will that I might not have developed in any other way.

Often, when we get sick or experience some crisis in our lives, we feel helpless and want to give up. But don't you know that facing and overcoming problems is what life is all about? That is why we are here—not

*According to Professor Jules-Bois of the Sorbonne the superconsciousness "is the exact opposite of the subconscious mind as conceived of by Freud; [it] comprises the faculties that make man really man and not just a super-animal." The French savant explained that the awakening of the higher consciousness is "not to be confused with Couéism or hypnotism. The existence of a superconscious mind has long been recognized philosophically, being in reality the Over-Soul spoken of by Emerson; but only recently has it been recognized scientifically."

to whine or despair, but to accept what comes to us and use it as a means to bring us into a closer relationship with God. When adversity strikes, do not think it is because God has forsaken you. Nonsense! If in those moments of trial you turn to Him in childlike trust, you will find Him with you, perhaps even more tangibly than He ever was during the good times in life.

The Power of Positive Attitude and Affirmation

No matter what happens, constantly look to the bright side: "Never mind, soon things will be better." By God's grace that is something I always have: hope. I never allow myself to become depressed. But I had to work at developing this, and all of you should do the same. Some people have a tendency to look always to the dark side of a situation. Invariably, their reaction to suggestions or conditions is one of negation or fear or pessimism. Scan your conduct every day, and if you catch yourself thinking or behaving in this way, remind yourself that this is the wrong attitude; it destroys peace, happiness, and constructive will. Yes, there is evil in this world; in the realm of duality there cannot be light without dark, joy without sorrow, health without sickness, life without death. But to dwell constantly on the negative side is an insult to the soul and to God. Never give in to discouragement!

Create an atmosphere of positive thinking around yourself. It has been said that to the mind, attitudes are more important than facts; and this is very true. If we consciously look for the best in every situation, that positive spirit and enthusiasm acts as a wonderful stimulant to the mind and feelings, and to the body. Right attitude is a tremendous help in removing the mental and emotional obstructions that cut us off from the divine resources within us.

Guruji gave us a perfect example of positive thinking. He went through untold struggles in building this work of Self-Realization Fellowship and Yogoda Satsanga Society in India, but we never saw him dejected or complaining. And he would not permit us to be discouraged, either. He taught us to pray, "Divine Mother, teach me to stand unshaken midst the crash of breaking worlds." In other words, "No matter what happens in my life, I will never admit defeat, because You are with me. It is You who have given me life, and it is You who sustain me."

Develop this kind of adamant will power. In the midst of all crises, affirm with deep conviction, "Lord, I *can* succeed, for You are in me." Then set your will on trying to find a solution. You will see that in mysterious ways the Divine Power is helping you. While making your best effort, keep your mind in attunement with the inner Source of strength and guidance by affirming, "Lord, Thy will be done, not mine." That is the secret.

Affirmation, as Master taught us, is an excellent way of tapping the power of the mind.* When you are troubled or fearful, for example, affirm with each breath, "Thou art in me; I am in Thee." You will feel the assurance of His presence. In India this science of continuous repetition of a spiritual thought is known as Japa Yoga; in the West it is called practicing the presence of God. Affirmations repeated over and over with concentration and will power sink into the subconscious and superconscious minds, which respond by creating the very conditions we are affirming. That is

* See *Scientific Healing Affirmations,* by Paramahansa Yogananda, published by Self-Realization Fellowship.

how we change. We do not have to remain as we are; we needn't become "psychological furniture," as Guruji used to say. Furniture never changes. If it were in its original form, a living tree, it would go on growing and producing; but when it is molded into a chair or a table it stops improving. It just gets older and deteriorates and falls apart.

To grow spiritually we must be trying constantly to change ourselves. Spirituality is not something that can be grafted onto us from without—a "halo" we can fashion and put on our heads. It comes from a continual, day-by-day, patient endeavor and a relaxed sense of surrender to the Divine. It isn't that suddenly the light of God descends on us and makes us instant saints. No; it is a daily effort to change ourselves and to surrender heart, mind, and soul to God, in meditation and in activity.

Sublime Fulfillment Comes Through Surrender

We might as well accept the fact that we belong to God and stop running away from Him. There is no way anyone can escape Him. Master often quoted the poem, "The Hound of Heaven":* "I fled Him, down the nights and down the days; I fled Him, down the arches of the years; I fled Him, down the labyrinthine ways of my own mind...." But in the end that Divine Hound caught up with the fleeing soul and held it fast, saying, "Thou dravest Love from thee, who dravest Me." Until we let Him catch us, we will never know real love or security or fulfillment.

I have found that my deepest spiritual awakenings come when I surrender; and you too will find it so. As

* By Francis Thompson.

long as we are looking for some thrilling experience in meditation, some tangible "miracle" or phenomenal demonstration, God will not respond. Inwardly turn to Him and say, "Lord, I surrender my heart to You. I care not what You do with me. Whether You come to me or not, I only know that I love You." That is divine love. No human experience can match the perfect love and bliss that inundate the consciousness when we truly surrender to God. It is the most sublime fulfillment the soul can ever know.

God has no favorites in this world; He loves each of us as much as He loves the greatest saints. They receive more only because they give more and are thereby more receptive.

Never be afraid of God, no matter what mistakes you have made in the past. Many people get hung up in strong cords of guilt and fear and doubt, and seek professional help to talk out these complexes. If we have enough faith, we can just as easily cultivate that communication with God. He is the real Father-Confessor to whom we should take our problems. He knows us as we truly are; it is impossible to hide one thing from Him. Yet He loves us unconditionally as His children. When you feel the burden of negative emotional hang-ups, take them to God with deep faith: "Father, naughty or good, I am Thy child. Help me to have greater understanding of my true Self, and strength to manifest the innate perfection of my soul."

That sense of trust and surrender brings such a sweet relationship with God; no words can describe it. I can only tell you that it gives meaning to everything else in life. What joy comes when you awake each morning and look within and can say, "Divine Mother, what do I want this day? Only to do Your will. Guide me!" When you go about your duties in that consciousness, you feel strength and love pouring into your life from that inner Source. Your only desire is: "Lord, let my heart be a channel for Your love, not to draw people to myself, but to You whom I adore; because I see how much people everywhere need Your love."

That is the way all of us are meant to live in this world. Wherever God has placed you, do the best you can to manifest a positive spirit, an inner strength of mind, a sense of faith and trust and surrender at His feet. It is so simple to know God; just let go and let Him enter your life. This is the whole purpose of the spiritual path. Accept each experience that comes to you as coming from Him, and try to learn from it. Otherwise you will go on making the same blunders, the same mistakes, day after day, year after year, right up to the end of life—never realizing what a wealth of divine fulfillment lies within you.

Do not remain the same old "psychological antique"; use God's power within you to change your life. Therein lies complete freedom from all limitations of body, mind, and this world of delusion. Therein lies the supreme victory for all of us.

Death: Mystery Portal to a Better Land

From a talk at Self-Realization Fellowship International Headquarters

Someone has asked: "What view does Self-Realization Fellowship take on the 'right to die'?"

Gurudeva Paramahansa Yogananda taught us that it is not the role of Self-Realization Fellowship to debate these complex social issues, because a categorical answer cannot be given to this type of question—it very much depends on the particular circumstances. In the ultimate sense, God is the only one who has the right to take our lives. He brought us into this world, and He alone has the right to remove us. On the other hand, I am certain Master felt that it is not right to prolong life artificially if there is no hope of survival and the body is being sustained only by means of equipment. So this is something that must be determined in each individual case by those who have the legal responsibility to make that decision. Our duty is to give people an understanding of moral and spiritual principles, and show them how to go within and find in their personal relationship with God the answers to every question. That is the way to know what is right or wrong in any situation.

It is tragic when people suffer, and this is what raises

questions about the "right to die": "Why should a person for whom there is little or no chance of recovery have to suffer so long and terribly, when death would end their agony?" But we do not know the great lessons a soul may be learning during the period of a lingering illness; this is what is not always understood. Our faith in the compassion and justice of God must remain steadfast, especially during those times when life appears so unjust. We should pray for the individual who is afflicted, and help that person find strength and courage.

Now, I am not arguing in favor of suffering. But I accept the ways of the Lord; there is nothing else to do! And I am convinced beyond any doubt that what He does is right. His love and compassion are unconditional. But with our limited human understanding we sometimes do not comprehend His ways—especially when faced with suffering and death.*

Death Is Not to Be Feared

Guruji frequently said to us: "Why fear death? As long as you are alive you are not dead; and when you are dead it is all over—so why fear it?" That reasoning used to impress me very deeply.

"Death," Master said, "is the mystery portal through which every soul enters into a better land." Everyone goes through this experience—and has throughout aeons gone through it countless times, incarnation after incarnation. It is not something to be feared. In this life we are carrying a very wearying bundle of flesh; but eventually the angel of death comes and tells us to drop

* "For My thoughts are not your thoughts, neither are your ways My ways, saith the Lord. For as the heavens are higher than the earth, so are My ways higher than your ways, and My thoughts than your thoughts" (Isaiah 55:8–9).

that burdensome bundle and return to our infinite home, where we are free from the encumbrance of suffering and disease and troubles.

Having had that experience myself, I can tell you that it is a wonderful state of consciousness. One doesn't like to speak of divine blessings such as this; they are too personal. But I will tell you about this one because it has to do with Master.

Throughout his life, Guruji had often entered *samadhi* [conscious union with God in meditation], but in 1948 he began spending long periods of time in that state. He gradually withdrew from the administration of his worldwide society, trying his best to coax a reluctant Daya Mata into assuming more of that responsibility. One evening at the Encinitas Hermitage (where Master and some of us disciples were living at the time) he called me to him and said, "I want you to go back to Mt. Washington and take charge of the ashram and the work."

After having spent so many years at Guruji's side, the thought of seeing him less often was quite painful. However, I knew that the training he had given through those years was not just for my personal benefit, but so I would be able to carry these responsibilities. I summoned my courage and replied, "All right, Master, I will do my best." I don't think I had even one day to prepare to move!

Returning to Mt. Washington did give me more time to meditate after my daily duties were completed. (When serving Guruji personally, we were usually active nonstop from morning until late at night; often he dictated on his manuscripts and correspondence until the wee hours.) Now my evenings were devoted to long and deep communion with God.

About this time, Guruji went to his little ashram in the desert, taking several of the disciples with him. I remained at Mt. Washington. It was a Friday, and the previous evening I had had a wonderful six-hour meditation. My consciousness had been enraptured with love for Divine Mother, and the bliss of Her response was intoxicating. All day Friday I was filled with the thought of Her; my heart was singing with such joy. (I pray with all my heart that each of you will work to attain that state. It comes easily when you get in the habit of inwardly practicing the presence of God.)

Around nine or ten o'clock in the evening, after I had finished my duties in the ashram, I went to my room and gave myself wholly into that inner joy. Suddenly a tremendous pain stabbed me in the side. "Good heavens!" I thought. "What is this?" I had never before felt such throbbing, searing pain. Thinking it would pass if I rested for a moment, I lay down on my bed. But as I did so, I drifted into a semiconscious state, feeling some physical pain but still aware of the blissful presence of Divine Mother. I remained in that condition all night long.

When I did not come to breakfast the next morning, one of the other nuns stopped by my room to find out if I was all right, and saw that I was not well. She quickly called a doctor. When he at last arrived and examined me, he said that I must be rushed to the hospital for an emergency operation. But I replied, "No, I will not go unless Master gives his consent." I had faith that if my actions had Master's blessing, everything would turn out all right. Over the years I had experienced his protection too many times to doubt.

Now, Guruji was 150 miles away, and there was no telephone at his secluded desert ashram. It wasn't until

Sunday morning that word finally reached him, by our phoning a taxi company and asking a driver to take a message out to the retreat. Master was walking around the grounds; and when he heard that Faye (as I was known then) was stricken ill and that the doctor said I should be taken to the hospital at once, he stopped and reflected for a moment. Then quietly, with deep thoughtfulness, he turned to the monk who was with him and said, "You know, this is her time to die." He sent this message back to Mt. Washington: "Tell Faye to go to the hospital. My blessings are with her."

An Experience of the World Beyond Death

I was rushed to the hospital by ambulance and was immediately wheeled into the operating room. Throughout all of this I was still in an inner blissful state, the state of joy that had been with me since my long meditation Thursday evening. Though I was given a general anesthetic, I remained acutely aware of the doctors and everything that was going on in the operating room. There was also the intuitive feeling that they had not correctly diagnosed the ailment. As the surgeon made his incision, I felt a sensation, but not pain, in my right side. I knew he had made a mistake, but I couldn't speak to tell him so. Then I heard one doctor exclaim to the other, "Oh, oh!" He had discovered that his incision was in the wrong area, that he was operating for the wrong condition.

Suddenly I had a wonderful experience. The entire room became filled with a soothing golden light; and the beautiful spiritual eye,* which I had seen many times in my life through the years, became visible in

* The single eye of intuition and omnipresent perception at the Christ center *(ajna chakra)* between the eyebrows; the entryway into the ulti-

my forehead, growing and growing until it seemed to fill all space. I heard the great sound of *Aum* engulfing me, pouring over my being. What joy I felt as my soul melted into the love of Divine Mother!

Now, I must tell you that when you are facing the other world, it is true, as they say, that your entire life passes before you very quickly. The consciousness of time vanishes. In reality, there is no such thing as time; it is a relative term. As Master has explained, in the consciousness of God there is no past, present, and future; everything is taking place at once. If, for example, there were partitions within this large room, you would be able to see only one section of the room at a time. However, if you could see the room from above, your perception would not be limited by those divisions; the whole room would be perceived as one. Likewise, in divine consciousness everything is seen as part of the Eternal Now.

In this state I was beholding my whole life from childhood on up as happening in the present moment. Then something very beautiful happened. A Voice, emerging out of the *Aum* sound, gently said to me, "This is death. Are you ready for it?"

In that great light of the spiritual eye, I saw into the world that was ahead of me; it was filled with such joy, such communion with the Divine. In comparison, this physical world seemed so gross—burdened by darkness and filled with the heaviness of matter. Usually we do not think of it in this way because we are used to this plane of being; but if you had to choose, for example, between diamonds and rocks, it is obvious what

---

mate states of divine consciousness. The deeply meditating devotee beholds the spiritual eye as a ring of golden light encircling a sphere of opalescent blue, and at the center, a pentagonal white star.

your choice would be. This was my consciousness as I replied to the Voice: "Yes, Divine Mother! One does not come this far into the other world and then want to go back. Why would I hold on to such grossness, when this divine bliss lies ahead of me?"

Then the Voice said so sweetly, "But if I ask you to stay for Me?" Oh! I can't tell you what those words did to me. Such a thrill of joy! "You would ask *me* to stay for You? Yes, Divine Mother. Let me serve You!" Then the Voice said—so soothingly; I can't convey to you what a soothing sensation bathed my whole consciousness—"All right, My child. Now sleep." I lost consciousness and the operation proceeded.

A day or two afterward, the doctor said to me, "Well, young lady, we didn't think you would make it. You gave us quite a scare!" Then he said, "When you are feeling stronger, I would like to talk with you." Two days later he told me: "We thought you had appendicitis, and we made the incision with that in mind. But then we discovered that was not your problem at all." I won't go into the details, but it was much, much more serious than appendicitis.

He continued, "Tell me something about your life. What is your religion?" I told him, and then he said, "I must tell you that you made a deep impression on all of us who were present. Throughout the operation you kept repeating over and over again, with such feeling, 'My God, my God; dear God, dear God.' We were overwhelmed—deeply stirred by it."* I never told him

* In 1983, Sri Daya Mata related: "The doctor later met Guruji, and Guruji had a profound impact on him. About a year ago, I happened to meet him in a public building in Pasadena. He told me then, 'I have never forgotten you, nor your teacher. That experience made an impression on me that has lasted through all these years.'" *(Publisher's Note)*

what took place in my consciousness; I just inwardly smiled. When you have a deep spiritual experience, it is best not to talk about it, otherwise you lose something of it. I'm telling you in this case only because I feel that Master wants me to do so.

Through the years since 1948 I have mentally relived this incident many times. The recollection of it is as fresh as the day it occurred, renewing my soul with great joy, and filling my mind with peace in the thought that I am here for Divine Mother alone, striving only to do Her will.

It was not until much later that I told anyone about this experience. One evening, about three or four days before his *mahasamadhi,* Guruji asked me to go for a drive with him. (Sometimes he would go out in the car for a little respite from the many demands on his attention.) He was giving me certain instructions about the work, conveying his wishes for its future. During this drive, I told him what had happened to me in the hospital. He listened, then asked me to repeat it. After a while he said, "That was your time to go. Many times Satan has tried to take your life. But know this: The Lord has given you great position and spiritual freedom. None can balk you. Keep that spirit to the end of life and you will be saved."

Guruji's words assured and encouraged me, for he knew my deep inner conflict against accepting any leadership in his work. I came not for that, but to find God; and position had no meaning for me. Authority and titles do not give one God-realization, and my mind was bent on that achievement alone.

Find Joy in Accepting God's Will

Now, my reason for telling this story is so you will

know that we need never fear death. This does not mean we should invite it! The point I am making—and it was the most valuable lesson I learned from this experience—is that we should find joy in surrendering to the will of God. This world is in such a mess today because people do not try to attune themselves with God's will. We should make more of an effort to practice the ideal of surrender, inwardly praying, "Thy will be done, O Lord, not mine." And try to *feel* what you are telling Him; there must be deep sincerity.

Those who crave individual power make a grave mistake; for one gains so much more by striving to become attuned with the Divine—through devotion, meditation, and the constant thought, "Lord, Thou art the Doer, not I." This is the way we ought to live our lives. Tell Him, "My Lord, You are everything. And because I am part of You, I am a part of everything—but only insofar as I am aware of You. Of myself I am nothing." There is great joy in this thought. To me, the very foundation of the spiritual life is humility. Without humility the cup of one's consciousness is so filled with "I, I, I" that there is no room for "Thou, Thou, Thou."

To find God takes self-discipline; it takes effort. But every human being has the strength to succeed. The only failure is in the mind. As Guruji said again and again, each one of us can know God in this life, if we make the effort. And we will know Him to the degree that we strive to be in tune with His will for us.

Life on this plane comes to an end for every human being, and each of us must ask himself, "What have I gained? What did I get out of life? Have I frittered away my time in idle things? 'O My saint, wake, yet wake! You did not meditate, you did not concentrate; you passed your time in idle words.'"* We should so live our lives that at the time of death we will neither know fear nor harbor any regret; but will pass joyously into the higher realms of Spirit.

* From the chant, "Wake, Yet Wake, O My Saint," in Paramahansa Yogananda's *Cosmic Chants.*

Solving Your Problems With Guidance From Within

Compilation from talks given at Self-Realization Fellowship International Headquarters

Gurudeva Paramahansa Yogananda often quoted this saying: "The Lord helps him who helps himself." When having to make a decision, we would like nothing better than for some divine force to just tell us what to do. It would be so easy; we would not have to make any effort if at any given moment we knew we were receiving God's direct guidance. But it is not meant to be so simple, and the reason is this: We are a part of God, but we don't know it—and we will never know it if all we do is put the burden on Him and say, "You tell me what to do," as though we were dumb puppets and He the Puppeteer. No, He expects us to use the mind He has given to us, *while* asking His guidance.

Jesus prayed the ultimate prayer: "Lord, let Thy will be done." Now, many people interpret this to mean that they are not supposed to do any willing or thinking at all, but just sit and meditate, and wait for God to do something through them. This is wrong. We are made in His image. He gave man intelligence such as He gave to no other creature, and He expects us to use it. This is why Guruji taught us to pray: "Lord, I will reason, I will will, I will act; but guide Thou my reason, will, and activity to the right thing that I should do."

We practice this religiously in the ashram. In our meetings about the work, we meditate for a few minutes and then offer that prayer. Only then do we enter into discussion and make decisions.

So do not sit back and expect God to initiate the necessary actions. Applying the principles of reason, will, and action, pursue what seems to be the best course. Work conscientiously using your will and intelligence, and at the same time pray throughout: "Lord, guide me; let me follow Thy will. Only Thy will be done." By doing this, you keep your mind receptive to His guidance. You may then find that you will suddenly see clearly, "No, I must go in this direction now." God shows you the way. But remember, when asking God to guide you, your mind must never be closed; let it be always open and receptive. This is how God helps him who helps himself. It works, but the initiative and effort have to come from us.

You do not have to live in an ashram in order to serve God and follow His will. Each one of us is at this moment where God and our past actions have placed us. If you are not satisfied with your present condition, meditate and ask God's guidance. But while doing so, apply your God-given reason. Analyze the options you have in connection with your life and your future.

Listen to the Divine Voice Within

The Divine Voice within us will help us to solve all our problems. The voice of the conscience is a God-given instrument of divine guidance in every human being. But in many, it is not heard because over a period of one or countless lives they have refused to pay any attention to it. Consequently, that voice becomes silent, or very, very faint. But as an individual begins to put right behavior into action in his life, the inner whispers grow stronger again.

Beyond the semi-intuitive conscience is pure intuition, the soul's direct perception of truth—the infallible Divine Voice. All of us are endowed with intuition. We have the five physical senses, and also a sixth sense—all-knowing intuition. We relate to this world through the five physical senses: we touch, hear, smell, taste, and see. In most people, the sixth sense, intuitive feeling, remains undeveloped from lack of use. Blindfold the eyes from childhood, and years later when that blindfold is removed, everything will appear flat. Or immobilize the arm, and it will not develop properly for lack of use. Similarly, through lack of use, intuition no longer functions in many.

But there is a way to develop intuition. The sixth sense is not able to function until we quiet the body and the mind. So the first step in developing intuition is meditation, entering a state of inner calmness. The more deeply you meditate, and then put your mind on some problem, the more your intuitive power will express itself in resolving that problem. That power develops gradually, not all at once; just as a muscle or limb is strengthened gradually by exercise—it doesn't happen overnight.

To be intuitive, one must learn, as Guruji said, to be "calmly active and actively calm; a prince of peace sitting on the throne of poise, directing the kingdom of activity." When an individual is excited, restless, or emotionally overwrought, he cannot feel or express intuition, but becomes confused in thinking and makes wrong decisions. This is why it is important for all mankind—not only those who are seeking God, but everyone—to learn to be quiet by practicing meditation. Guruji's techniques of concentration and meditation are therefore invaluable.

As you live more in a state of calmness, you begin to perceive yourself less as a physical being. You become aware of an inner stillness coming from the soul, the real you. That stillness is the foundation of the intuitive sense.

Intuition can be developed by those persons who are deeply contemplative, those who have reached by meditation that state of absolute calmness of heart and mind. One must be neither overcome by emotion nor bound by intellect. Intuition is a blend of thinking (the thought process) and the heart (the feeling process). Many people have intuitive experience through reason—a sort of guidance of their thoughts. In my own case, very often intuition expresses itself through feeling. When I have certain feelings about things or persons, those impressions are like subtle vibrations around my heart, and then I know, from years of experience, that these intimations are correct.

When you have developed intuition to some degree, you will find that as you make decisions, something within you says: "This is the right way to go." That is intuition guiding you. Do not expect this to happen all at once. There will be some mistakes in the beginning as other factors within you impede the flow of intuition. But as you go on practicing meditation, and living more in the state of interior calmness bestowed by this practice, you will find increasing improvement in the development of your intuitive power.

Very often now, when something comes before my mind, I see not just the present matter, but projecting ahead, I see the end result. That is intuition. And if you act on it, you will find that everything runs smoothly—well, not always. Even though you have made the right decision, there will be some rough times. They are part of the growing process, learning how to deal with conditions that are normal in life. But your intuition tells you that even though there are problems, you have taken the right course of action.

Learn to distinguish when inner "guidance" is an authentic intuitive message, or only imagination or emotionalism (which in some people are very strong, and are sometimes misinterpreted as intuition). You can recognize intuition if whatever guidance you feel from your experience produces the correspondingly right result. If the effects are contrary, you know it was nothing but imagination. Intuition will always bring forth the correct positive response for the good of one's own life or that of someone else. Only time and experience will enable you to tell always whether a strong inclination is imagination or a natural, intuitive feeling.

In summary: Learn to enter the state of deep calmness that comes during the practice of concentration and meditation techniques; become a more peaceful being throughout all the day's activities; and use your God-given intelligence to make the best decisions of which you are capable, while at the same time continuing to ask divine guidance and remaining open to it as you proceed.

Developing an Understanding Heart

From a talk at Self-Realization Fellowship International Headquarters

The individual who is sincere about spiritual growth strives to keep his mind always clear and unruffled, so that in every circumstance he may express the divine quality of understanding. Gurudeva Paramahansa Yogananda gave a beautiful definition of this attribute: "Understanding is your inner vision, the intuitive faculty by which you can clearly perceive the truth—about yourself and others, and all situations that arise in your path—and correctly adjust your attitudes and actions accordingly."

Guruji used to say to us, "Understand what I *mean* when I say something to you. When you try too hard, you don't get my thought. Your rationalized thoughts get in the way. Remain calm so that you are in tune with what I am telling you; then you will understand." He was teaching us to listen with the ears of intuitive understanding.

"With all thy getting, get understanding," the Bible tells us.* How many of us really take that to heart and try to practice it? Usually, whenever we encounter anyone or anything that is different from what we are used to, our prejudices are immediately aroused and

* Proverbs 4:7.

we raise mental blocks. We do not make an effort to understand; we cling blindly to our own opinions, no matter how shortsighted they may be. That is one of the great flaws in all cultures, and why there is so much misunderstanding and conflict in the world. In school we are taught intellectual subjects, but who is taught the art of understanding others? Each culture thinks its ways are the best, and we do not learn to see beyond the horizon of our own idiosyncrasies and customary manner of doing things.

Master had a unique way of expressing this: "In this world we are all a little bit crazy, but we don't know it. People don't see their own 'craziness' because they mix with those who are similarly crazy. It is only when people who are differently crazy come together and try to understand each other that they have a chance to find out about their own craziness."

Do you see his point? Always keep your mind open. When someone says something that is foreign to your own particular personality or way of thinking, do not be closed-minded or permit your prejudices to influence your understanding. Listen calmly, willingly, and respectfully. In this way you may learn something valuable from others whose views and background are different from your own.

Emotions and Moods Are the Enemies of Understanding

Emotions and moods are vicious enemies of understanding. They blur our perception so we cannot see circumstances correctly. Many people go through life so enslaved by their uncontrolled mental reactions that the moment anything conflicts with the way they are thinking or feeling, they get irritated or upset, obliterating any chance for understanding.

Master was very, very intolerant of moods; he insisted that we strive to conquer them. He explained that moods are the manifestation of bad habits we have brought over from past incarnations. That is why they are so automatic, why our temper flares up or we get moody for seemingly no outward reason—perhaps over some trivial incident that occurs or some little thing that is said to us. These habits of wrong thinking and behavior have become so deeply ingrained over lifetimes that the instant they encounter resistance, irrational emotion takes possession of the mind.

So long as we allow ourselves to be victimized by these negative states of consciousness, it is impossible to develop understanding—and it is impossible to know God. Do not cater to your moods. Do not slavishly carry them with you. Resist them! Get rid of them at once, because they will block your progress—not only on the spiritual path, but in all of life.

This does not mean suppression of our feelings. Suppression is unhealthful—physically, mentally, and spiritually. The individual who holds his emotions inside of himself is like a pot of boiling water that is tightly covered. As the water boils, it builds up more and more pressure, until eventually the lid is violently blown off. Likewise, by trying to stifle our emotions we may be able to maintain the temporary illusion of calmness, but sooner or later those feelings will vent themselves. Meanwhile, their boiling within disrupts not only our peace and well-being, but also our understanding. Master taught us to control our emotions, not to suppress them.*

* A student once asked Paramahansa Yogananda: "Aren't your teachings about controlling the emotions dangerous? Many psy-

The way to accomplish this is to pause before you react, and do some serious thinking. The next time you are tempted to strike back or speak harshly to somebody who has antagonized you, stop for a minute and ask yourself, "Is it worth it? Who am I going to upset? Myself, first of all. Let me calmly listen to what the other person has to say, and fairly analyze it, before I close down that gate of nonunderstanding. Why shouldn't I give due respect to that person's opinion? My views are not always infallible! Maybe there is something I can learn from him."

Learn the Divine Lesson in All That Happens to You

As our understanding develops, we see that there is a divine reason for all that happens to us. Nothing in this world occurs by accident. Everything that takes place is governed by universal law, and that law operates with perfect justice. No matter what particular ordeals you have to face, always try to understand the spiritual lesson inherent in those experiences. Never feel that outer circumstances are the cause of your difficulties, or that others are trying to do you in. Those who constantly blame their troubles on their spouse, their boss, their childhood upbringing—anyone and anything but their own thinking and behavior—develop deep emotional problems.

Realize that it is God alone with whom we have to

---

chologists claim that suppression leads to mental maladjustments and even to physical illness."

The Master replied: "Suppression is harmful—holding the thought that you want something but doing nothing constructive to get it. Self-control is beneficial—patiently replacing wrong thoughts by right ones, changing reprehensible actions to helpful ones."—*Sayings of Paramahansa Yogananda.*

do. It is He with whom we are dealing at every moment —no one else—in our speech, in our actions, and above all in our thoughts. When that truth becomes well settled in our consciousness, it is much easier for us to react properly when some unpleasant incident occurs. We do not waste time defending ourselves; we realize how much more profitable it is to inwardly cultivate our relationship with God, for then He will defend us, if necessary. He is looking after us; beyond doubt I have found this to be so.

The Divine is always there. It is not that He suddenly comes from some point out in space and draws near to us. He is always with us, but we don't know it because our minds are not with Him. We allow moods, emotional upheavals, oversensitive feelings, anger, and the misunderstanding that comes from these, to so ruffle and cloud our perception that we remain unaware of His presence.

Train yourself not to "fly off the handle." The moment you lose control, your contact with the Divine vanishes. Sometimes it is very hard to regain that inner tranquility so that you can again pick up the threads of communion with the Divine.

Mean words and sarcasm have no place in the spiritual life. Displays of bad temper have no place in the behavior of one who is seeking God. But neither are we expected to become "doormats." Rather, we learn to speak with the voice of reason and understanding. Firmness, yes! I am not suggesting we become like milk toast. What I am saying is that we should learn to think before we speak.

The difference between temper and firmness is this: When we lose our temper, we are out of control. When we are satisfied that we are speaking truth, then we can be so firm that the whole world will not be able to change our position, but we never lose our calmness, self-control, or respect for others.

As we grow in understanding, we come to the point where, in all circumstances, our interest is: "What is truth?" Wondrous wisdom and thrilling realizations of God pour over the soul when we live in that consciousness! The development of such clear understanding begins when we put aside moods, prejudices, likes and dislikes, which distort our view of reality. Show me a man of God, and I will show you a man of great understanding.

Inner Calmness Helps Us to Make the Right Decisions

Guruji once said: "In this world, our understanding is often shortsighted. When our mental vision is thus impaired, it is impossible to see into the future to know what will be. Being blinded to the potential results of our actions, we frequently do the wrong thing." When we attain divine inner calmness, it is possible to see into the future, which is formulated by the principle of cause and effect. So much of what has happened in the world since Gurudeva's passing he predicted back in the 1930s and '40s. He had that clarity of perception which is the result of complete evenness of mind. Like a divine mirror, a mind that is spiritually calm captures a perfect reflection of Reality. In that mirror we can see clearly any situation, and perceive where the alternative courses available to us will lead, so that we can choose the right one to pursue.

The inner calmness necessary for that intuitive understanding comes only through daily, deep meditation. Never make excuses to neglect your practice of meditation. When I hear that a devotee has fallen away from the habit of meditating, I become very sad, because that is the beginning of nonunderstanding from which his mistakes will proliferate.

Make Truth a Part of Your Daily Life

"With all thy getting, get understanding." You should write that on a piece of paper and put it on your desk or someplace else where you will see it often during the day. Every time you are tempted to get angry or to say something unkind or to indulge in a mood, remind yourself: "With all thy getting, get understanding."

Whenever I would come across an inspiring passage from any scripture, or when Master gave us guidance, I didn't just memorize it; I made it a part of my daily *sadhana.** No matter how inspired we may be by a spiritual truth, it has little meaning unless we put it into practice. Do not become one of those psychological antiques who says, "That was a wonderful talk Daya Ma gave. Aren't Master's teachings marvelous!" But soon they settle right back into their old moldy habits.

Christ described how some scattered seeds may fall on barren, rocky soil; others are sown where weeds will choke out the little plants that sprout; but those that will grow and bear fruit are the ones that land on fertile soil.† The soil of your consciousness must be fertile with receptivity and zeal, and cleared of doubts, moods, and indifference, so that the seeds of Truth may take root and blossom into your own realization.

Guruji used to tell us very candidly what we needed to do to correct ourselves and grow in God-awareness. He was always so direct and sincere, and

* Practices that constitute one's path of spiritual discipline.

† Mark 4:14–20.

that is the way I try to speak to all of you. I want to preserve on paper or tape all the ideals that Master held before his disciples, for it is the understanding and practice of those lofty principles that will keep his teachings pure for countless future generations of truth-seekers.

The Unconditional Love of God and Guru

When I look back on those years with Guruji, I see how blessed we were. Very few people in this world have someone whom they know will always understand them. For us Master was that someone. We knew his unconditional love for us. Yes, he could be fiery when he was not satisfied with how we behaved; but no matter how we had erred, no matter what discipline he gave, in him we had one who would never forsake us.

That spirit of divine friendship and understanding should be cultivated among all the members of our large spiritual family—between wife and husband, parent and child, friends, ashram residents. I feel that bond with so many of you. When we are loyal to Guruji's ideals, we have absolute faith in and give support to one another. That is the fruit of an understanding heart. When we have gathered that fruit with those of like mind, we then have an abundance we can share with all.

It takes effort, my dears. Such unity does not come automatically. When the behavior of others causes inharmony, try to be a peacemaker. Be fair by seeing all points of view. This makes us more understanding of human nature. We become more forgiving, more compassionate.

Do we not expect these qualities of the Divine? I certainly do. We expect Someone who loves us in spite of all our flaws; Someone who understands us even when we do not understand ourselves; Someone who is steadfast in loyalty and always comes to our aid; Someone who is a constant source of strength on which we can draw. That divine beloved Lord is within us; we have a responsibility to Him to try to reflect to each other His love and understanding.

Let Every Day Be Christmas

From a talk at Self-Realization Fellowship International Headquarters

The message of Jesus Christ is as important and vitally applicable today as it was twenty centuries ago. Christmas should remind us of this timeless message and inspire us anew with the recollection of his blessed life.

When I entered the ashram here at Mount Washington, shortly before Christmas in 1931, I had a deep craving to understand Christ. From an early age I had sought answers to the profound and perplexing questions of life: Why are we sent into this world? Why is there so much suffering and tragedy? Why so many seeming contradictions? I had attended Sunday school, and had listened to the ministers, hoping to find answers. They were sincere, pious men—very much in earnest—but still I always went away feeling empty.

Then I met Paramahansa Yogananda, and the impact of his message and his love for God completely transformed my life. Everything he said appealed to my reason and, above all, to my heart. Inwardly I made a sacred vow: "Him I shall follow."

I had been at Mount Washington about a month when I celebrated my first all-day Christmas meditation.* For over eight hours that day Gurudeva meditated

* A spiritual custom begun by Paramahansaji in 1931 and observed annually in the Self-Realization Fellowship ashrams, temples, and centers throughout the world.

with a group of Self-Realization devotees, remaining continuously in communion with God and Christ; it was my first experience with long meditation. As I sat in the afterglow of that memorable day, I remember thinking about Gurudeva: "Here is a man from the Orient, of Hindu origin, one whom the Christian world might call 'heathen'; yet such is his love for Christ that he has seen him and communed with him. It is he who has shown the West how truly to celebrate Christmas."

Guruji predicted that one day this spiritual observance of the birth of Christ would be followed worldwide. Indeed it is so—not only in Self-Realization centers and temples in the West, but in India as well.

Humanity Is Suffering From "Spiritual Starvation"

The world today is in a dismal state. Humanity is suffering from "spiritual starvation," as one minister has said. In man's efforts to achieve great scientific and material progress, he has forgotten to nourish his spiritual nature—the inner eternal Self, the soul. In religion, also, followers have become lost in the external aspects. Mankind has not grasped what Christ's life was meant to mean to each one of us. Even his followers, in large measure, seem to have forgotten what he taught. The concentration is on ornate buildings, beautiful choirs, social activities, charitable works—much of which may be important and even in keeping with the example set by Christ. But above and beyond these, Christ's message was: "Thou shalt love the Lord thy God with all thy heart, and with all thy soul, and with all thy mind, and with all thy strength: this is the first commandment."* The way to cultivate love for God is

* Mark 12:30.

to know Him through meditation. "Know ye not that ye are the temple of God, and that the spirit of God dwelleth within you?"* And in Psalms we read: "Be still, and know that I am God."†

Let me share with you some Christmas thoughts expressed by Guruji. When he was in India in 1935, he wrote to us:

> Beloved devotees and friends of Self-Realization Fellowship:
>
> At this holy season of Christmas, my body is far away in India, and therefore I shall celebrate Christmas with you in Christ-joy, or Krishna-joy as it is called in India, ever omnipresent in your hearts....
>
> My Krishna and Christ, ever one in Spirit, will be born anew in me in my new joy on Christmas morn.
>
> What present shall I give you at this time, but the most precious gift of all gifts, the united Christ- and Krishna-joy which I shall receive Christmas morn and send to you through my deep meditation.
>
> Delve deep into your inner Self, and search in the tangled roots of the tree of your devotion, buried in the soil of meditation, for my hidden gift of all gifts, bound with the golden cords of my ever-burning memory of your love.

May each one of you feel the divine Christ Consciousness‡ in your own consciousness throughout all the Christmas holidays. For as Guruji has said:

> Christmas is intended as a celebration through which the devotee may find the spirit of Christ

* I Corinthians 3:16.

† Psalms 46:10.

‡ God's omnipresent intelligence, and the attractive force of His

manifesting in his own consciousness. In this coming Christmas think first of how you can commune deeply with Christ. The purpose of observing his birthday is to think deeply upon him whose life mankind has come to revere through all these twenty centuries.

The Shining Example of Jesus Christ

Why do we revere Jesus Christ? Not for any worldly achievements usually associated with success on this mundane plane: Jesus had no material wealth, he owned no property, he had no formal education; he knew what it was to struggle and suffer; he was deserted by his friends, and he was crucified. It is because of his God-consciousness, and the shining example of the sweetness and humility of his life, that he has endured like a bright Eastern star lighting up the heavens for all humanity—not merely for those who embrace the external theology of Christianity, but for all souls around the world who deeply strive to know God.

I used to feel that Jesus was a stranger, one to whom it was impossible to draw close because he was too far above my reach. But Master spoke about God and Christ in such a simple, sincere, personal, and devoted way that we felt we too could communicate with Them; we could relate to Them in a personal way. This is the important ingredient that is missing in Christianity today—and in all religions. Man needs to establish with his Creator a sweet and personal relationship; and that can come only by deep, daily meditation.

Throughout his teachings, Jesus tried to help man to relate directly and personally to the Infinite. That

love, manifested in creation; the universal consciousness, oneness with God, manifested by Jesus, Krishna, and other great masters.

ideal meant so much to him that he laid down his life for it. How many in this modern world are prepared to follow that example and lay down their lives for the love of God?

Instead of seeking God, most people devote their lifetime to the pursuit of material happiness and to satisfying their need for food, clothing, shelter—all of which relate only to the physical body. Some people cultivate enthusiasm for intellectual development, and pursue book-learning, reading many volumes in an attempt to gain some understanding. But Self-Realization addresses its message—the message of daily communion with God—to those who have come to the realization that it is not enough to have physical and material security, and that books can never satisfy the soul's deep thirst for truth. Through deep, regular meditation, the devotee begins to experience a personal relationship with God: "He walks with me, He talks with me, He tells me I am His own."* Unless and until we have realized that, we do not know what the teaching of Christ is all about.

The closer we draw to Christ through meditation, the more we want not just to talk about him, but to conduct our lives knowing that he is always near, silently observing us. He never judges or condemns us. If we should err, he is the first to say: "Father, forgive them; these are Thy children. They know not what they do."

But so often we feel guilty or ashamed of our actions, and with a sense of inadequacy we avert our hearts and minds and inner gaze from God and His divine messengers. We feel uncomfortable in trying to relate personally to Them. This is why so many people

* From the well-known hymn, "In the Garden," by C. Austin Miles.

turn away from Christianity, Hinduism, or the other great religions. Unless the love of God becomes one's own personal experience, religion seems dry and rigid. Seekers are not taught how to approach God with humility and trust, as a child would go to his mother.

The only way to find the satisfaction that the soul seeks is through deep meditation. It is only then that we begin to feel the "peace of God, which passeth all understanding."* That is the peace all mankind is craving.

A Worldwide Surge of Spiritual Awakening

Many years ago, Guruji predicted that a great surge of spiritual awakening would sweep the world. We are seeing the beginning of that spiritual power now. Opposing the darkness of the forces of evil is the divine light of goodness and truth. Man is in the middle, so to speak, and neither side, good nor evil, can claim him without his permission. He is endowed with free will, the freedom of choice, to side either with Satan or with God's manifested presence in creation—the universal Christ Consciousness. Blessed is he who uses his discrimination and free will to live, speak, and act in attunement with that Divine Christ.

It is said that when the world is at its darkest and when man's guiding light has grown dim, the Compassionate Lord takes pity on His children and sends a messenger with a teaching that will help to free humanity from its self-created cave of darkness.† Jesus Christ brought such a message. It is not the monopoly

* Philippians 4:7.

† "Whenever virtue *(dharma)* declines and vice *(adharma)* predominates, I incarnate as an Avatar. In visible form I appear from age to age to protect the virtuous and to destroy evildoing in order to reestablish righteousness" (Bhagavad Gita IV:7–8).

of one religion, but a timeless expression of eternal, universal truth, the same as taught by Lord Krishna in India, thousands of years earlier. A revival of this message has been sent to the world, in our own troubled times, in the teachings of our blessed Guru.

The purpose of observing Christmas—as with the birthday of any avatar—is to honor and to resolve to emulate the one in whom God as Christ Consciousness was fully manifest on earth. It is not enough at Christmastime merely to light a candle, or to decorate a tree and exchange gifts. These customs are beautiful and proper; they express the spirit of goodwill, friendship, and love. But if we do these things and forget Christ, then Christmas is empty; we are tired, and glad when it is over.

Rather, during this holy season, let our consciousness revolve around these thoughts: "Lord, teach me to walk in the footsteps of Christ. Let me try to forgive my fellowman, particularly at Christmastime. And let every day be Christmas. Let me remove from my heart all feelings of hatred and ill will. Let me go to those whom I have hurt, and to those who have hurt me, and put forth my hand in loving friendship as did Christ. And help me, O Lord, to strive more earnestly to commune with Thee, Thou who art the Beloved of my soul."

Thus shall we begin to live the life of Christ.

The Universal Message of Christ and Krishna

From a talk at Self-Realization Fellowship International Headquarters

Some of you have asked me to speak on the roles of Christ and Krishna in the Self-Realization teachings. As you know, Self-Realization Fellowship embraces two bibles: the Bhagavad Gita, which contains the teaching of the Lord Krishna; and the New Testament, which contains the message of Jesus Christ. Among the *Aims and Ideals** set forth by our guru, Paramahansa Yogananda, is the following: "To reveal the complete harmony and basic oneness of original Christianity as taught by Jesus Christ and original Yoga as taught by Bhagavan Krishna; and to show that these principles of truth are the common scientific foundation of all true religions." Truth may be called by many names and interpreted in many ways, but Truth is one, even as God is one.

Similarities in the Lives of Christ and Krishna

Krishna was born a prince in India thousands of years before Christ. Just as the coming of Jesus Christ was prophesied in the scriptures, so was the advent of Bhagavan Krishna foreordained. As with Jesus, it was

* See page 325.

In the village of Palpara, West Bengal, 1973

"The time comes when your consciousness remains unbrokenly in the meditative state—always with God....Eventually, you will find that even while you are doing your work, whenever you take your mind within for a moment, you will feel an inner effervescent well of devotion, of joy, of wisdom. You will say, 'Ah, He is with me!' This is the fruit of meditation that can be enjoyed at any time, in quiet communion or in the midst of activity."

Greeting students at YSS school for boys, Ranchi, 1972

With participants in SRF How-to-Live Summer Youth Program for boys, SRF Lake Shrine, 1978

"Children are like tender plants. To grow properly, to blossom into their full potential, they need nurturing....Provide them with the right example and sense of direction that they learn to love God, to accept and carry responsibilities, to be unselfish, to be kind to others—the aggregate of qualities and virtues that is the measure of a spiritual-minded human being."

predicted that he would be a great spiritual destroyer of the enemies of righteousness. When his wicked uncle, King Kansa, heard this, he ordered that the infant should be killed at birth—even as King Herod attempted to destroy the baby Jesus. Krishna's father was divinely warned of this threat, even as was Jesus' father, and he fled with the baby, hiding him in the care of a foster mother. Jesus' parents similarly fled their country in order to save the life of their son. As did Jesus, Krishna grew up in simple surroundings, as a cowherd in Brindaban. (I have visited many places in India associated with his life; the holy city of Brindaban is a wonderful spiritual mecca, where thousands of pilgrims pay their respects to the Lord Krishna.)

The Universal Message of Divine Love

Krishna was an incarnation of divine love. His sublime message was one of love for God, and love for one's fellowman through righteous action. The love he expressed was the highest and purest, as was that of Jesus Christ many centuries later.

At both of those points in history, there was a great need for that gospel of divine love. In the era preceding Jesus, the prevailing spiritual sentiment among his people had been that of Moses: "An eye for an eye, and a tooth for a tooth."* A respect for the law of retribution (that every cause will have an effect) was Moses' contribution to the people of that time and place. He stressed morality, for moral principles are the laws of God and Nature by which we ought to live if we would find physical well-being, mental peace, and spiritual freedom in this world.

* Exodus 21:24.

But by the time of Jesus, people had become too immersed in the letter of the laws brought by Moses, and had forgotten the spirit behind them. Jesus taught the need for tempering law with compassion, forgiveness, and tolerance: "Whosoever shall smite thee on thy right cheek, turn to him the other also";* and, "Forgive seventy times seven."† His vital message has endured to the present day, and has swept the Western world, just as the teaching of the Lord Krishna has continued to flourish among millions of followers in India and the Orient.

Different Aspects of One Truth

Divine incarnations, such as Krishna, Buddha, and Christ, each had a specific message to bring. Lord Buddha emphasized the law of karma, the law that was later stated by Christ in simple terms: "As ye sow so shall ye reap." Buddha spoke of the "wheel of karma" to demonstrate the principle that the effects of any action we perform always return to us as their starting point, just as a circle inexorably completes itself. If we have done something wrong—even if it was long ago, and even if we have kept it hidden from others or have forgotten about it ourselves—the wheel of karma returns to us the unpleasant fruits of that action.

From an understanding of the law of karma we can see why it is so important to remember the words of Christ: "Judge not, that ye be not judged."‡ We see only the external behavior of others; we do not always know why they behave as they do. Instead of criticizing, we should say, with Jesus: "Father, forgive them;

* Matthew 5:39. † Matthew 18:22. ‡ Matthew 7:1.

for they know not what they do."* What a great spiritual science is contained in these words! They mean simply this: "I am not the judge of my fellowman. Let me try throughout my life to exemplify forgiveness, as You, my beloved God, have been forgiving me the countless wrongs I have done throughout many, many lives." We begin to reflect this teaching of Christ's once we learn to overcome being hypercritical of others, and to turn instead the spotlight of our critical attention inward upon our own weaknesses, and thus begin to change ourselves.

The Greatest Commandment

Jesus said that the first commandment is to love the Lord thy God with all thy heart, mind, and soul, and with all thy strength; and the second commandment, like unto it, is to love thy neighbor as thyself. Lord Krishna also taught this when he expressed the Lord's commandment: "Absorb thy mind in Me; become My devotee; resign all things to Me; bow down to Me....Forsaking all other duties, remember Me alone."† And further: "The best type of yogi is he who feels for others, whether in grief or pleasure, even as he feels for himself."‡

If we are to love our neighbors as ourselves, we first have to understand that our true Self is the soul, an individualized reflection of God. We have to forget our little ego-self and its constant preoccupation with "I, I, I." Jesus did not mean that we are to love our neighbor in a narrow, exclusive way, being attached to the physi-

* Luke 23:34.

† Bhagavad Gita XVIII:65–66.

‡ Bhagavad Gita VI:32.

cal form or personality; but rather to love all by seeing in them, as in ourselves, the indwelling Spirit.

Krishna said: "He who perceives Me everywhere and beholds everything in Me never loses sight of Me, nor do I ever lose sight of him."* In a similar metaphor, Christ expressed this truth in these words: "Are not two sparrows sold for a farthing? and one of them shall not fall on the ground without [the sight of] your Father."† That is the promise of the Divine Beloved: "I am never out of sight of that child of Mine who always thinks of Me, and looks for Me everywhere; him do I watch over always."

Truth has echoed down through the centuries, but only rarely does there emerge from the multitudes a soul who fully receives and reflects the divine light. Guruji often said, "One moon gives more light than all the stars in the heavens. Likewise, one moonèd soul who loves God deeply and walks in the footsteps of the great ones gives off more light in this world than thousands who simply preach from the pulpits about the dogma and externals of religion."

Gurudeva's approach to God was so beautifully simple and childlike. That appealed very much to my heart; it is what drew me to this teaching of Self-Realization. Even when he spoke before the multitudes (and he often addressed thousands), he did not lecture, but talked to souls as one of them. There was divine communion between him and the audience, as he communicated what he was perceiving within his own consciousness. That personal experience of God is the ideal of Self-Realization; it is why all the monks and nuns of

* Bhagavad Gita VI:30.

† Matthew 10:29.

this Order are taught first and foremost to feel God within by *living* the ideals and principles of the spiritual life.

The Answer to Every Problem

In my early days in the ashram, I had the notion that since Guruji was a master, he would give us a ready solution for every problem—just as he had healed my body of a very severe illness by merely a touch. I expected that every time I approached him with some difficulty, he would just touch me and I would suddenly be illuminated! But that wasn't so. I had to go through many years of hard self-discipline, and many years of deep soul-searching, and longing for God, in order to cultivate my own personal relationship with the One who is the Answer to every problem.

Our suffering in this world is not a punishment; it is the Divine saying: "You are wandering away, My child. Come back!" Learn to develop such a sweet relationship with God that every time you are disappointed, every time you find some frustration in your life, you realize that it comes from God to remind you not to forget Him. It is His love that makes Him want to protect us from that forgetfulness, which is the primal cause of all our suffering and torment—physical, mental, and spiritual.

It is because humanity has lost sight of God that this world is in such a terrible state today. Materially, there is abundance; but some have much while others have nothing. Mentally, there is confusion, doubt, and fear. Spiritually, the world is starving. It almost seems as though mankind is at last bankrupt in every way.

These conditions will continue until we have received so much suffering that people will have to turn back to God. All of us must eventually discover that the happiness and security we seek are not to be found in this world. We reach up and grasp a cloud, but find that we have nothing in our hand—that is what earthly life is like. So long as we seek happiness in external things, it is ever elusive. But when we find true happiness through contacting the Divine Bliss within, no amount of difficulty in the world can affect us; and when we have divine love in our hearts, no amount of ill will from others can disturb us.

Trouble in our relationships—with husband or wife, or children, or others—comes because we are constantly demanding that they satisfy our need for happiness. And we in turn think that just giving material things to our loved ones will be enough to satisfy their longing for fulfillment. That will never be enough, my dears—never! The more we depend on outer things for fulfillment, the more we create an ever deeper hunger within ourselves—a hunger in our souls that only God can satisfy.

The lives of Christ, Krishna, and all the great ones serve to remind us to turn our thoughts more deeply to God: "Lord, my life is flying by, and I do not yet find You in my heart. Let me make the effort now, that I may begin to know You and to relate to You; that I may find in You that peace, joy, and love for which my soul has been craving and my heart hungering. I have been like a beggar in this world, begging for a little affection from human hearts. Let me beg no more, but turn my attention within and commune with You, my Beloved—You who are the Fountain of all joys, all life, all peace, all love. May I then reflect in my life Your divine light. As I pass through this world, may I be a peacemaker."

World Peace Starts in the Family Unit

Many people are busy striving to bring peace in the world, yet they haven't even achieved peace within themselves and their own family. They may be, as Master used to quote the saying, "street angels and house devils." Peace can never come through the efforts of peaceless individuals.

One must begin by being an angel first in his own home, among those whom God has drawn to him. Each of us is in the particular environment that is necessary for our own spiritual growth, so it is not right to run away just because it is difficult. Instead, we should strive in our family unit to be an instrument of harmony, kindness, thoughtfulness, and love—not necessarily by preaching it, but by living it. This is the right way to bring a Christlike spirit back into the world.

We have within us the power to change this world. We must begin with ourselves, through daily, deep meditation. At night, seek a secluded corner of your home where you can be alone. Whether you are heavy-hearted, or filled with cheer and peace of mind, sit quietly and commune with God in the language of your soul. If you persevere, you will definitely find His response; it cannot be otherwise. The more you talk with Him—not in stilted, parroted prayers, but personally relating to Him in the depths of your heart—the more you will see that in the most unexpected ways you begin to feel His response within. We *can* know God; we *can* commune with Him and feel His love in our lives. That is the universal message of Christ and Krishna.

The Skilled Profession of Child-Rearing

Compiled from satsangas *in which questions about child-rearing were asked*

Bringing children into the world is not only a nature-given right, but also carries with it a God-given responsibility. Society demands training if one is to be a lawyer, accountant, or mechanic. But how few are prepared for parenting—the most demanding of occupations!

I believe that ideally no one should graduate from school without having taken classes on how to be a responsible adult and a good parent. Children are taught how to cook, to sew, to keep books, even how to operate computers today. This is all good, but they also need to be taught how to deal with life.

Training of Children Begins in the Home

The proper training of children begins in the home. The schools have "gone to pot," so to speak. But the deteriorating environment there is not entirely the fault of the schools. We must lay the blame where it belongs—lack of right education in the home.

I admit that raising children is a hard task in this day and age. But no parent has the right to bring a child into the world and then abdicate his or her responsibility to guide that child. Who would plant in their garden a seed or a little tree and leave it to develop by itself, without some kind of care and protection? If you want it to grow healthy and straight, you have to put beside it a strong support, so that it does not bend over or break when the winds come. We have a responsibility to our young ones, and it is a shame when parents neglect that responsibility. If God had not intended that parents guide their children, babies would be hatched from eggs, produced and then abandoned by the parents—left to hatch and grow by themselves. That is what turtles do!

Children Need Loving Discipline

Children need discipline. I do not mean beating them; please understand that. Violence should never be used on a child! You have to guide children with firmness, but there must also be love. My point of reference is to look back to our years with Master: We young devotees on the path were, in a sense, children. He guided us with reason, and with firmness when necessary, but also with great love. That is the ideal.

I remember thinking years ago what a grave mistake it was that so many parents were following the advice of a well-known doctor who advocated no discipline—just allowing the child to be free to exercise his own will, to "do his own thing." Common sense told me that this method of child-rearing would lead to trouble. These fresh souls in little bodies (we won't call them "young" souls because no doubt they have already gone through many lives) cannot express discrimination and understanding, even though these qualities are innate in the soul. Children are like tender plants. To grow properly, to blossom into their full potential, they need nurturing and pruning—the guidance, the love, and the understanding that only parents can give to them. Every child needs to have dialogue with someone who has that understanding which he has not yet gained, but will develop if he is given the right guidance.

The present trend of permissiveness needs to be turned around, and one way is to provide proper training in the formative years. Children should be taught right moral attitudes and right behavior—not only through words, but example as well. Lack of such guidance is a major factor in the tragic breakdown of moral standards and behavior in this country, which has done more than anything else to destroy the family unit. And what has that brought forth? Emotionally crippled children. And emotionally crippled children generally become emotionally crippled adults, who have developed a feeling of rejection, which leads to bitterness toward society as a whole. They feel that the world has not given them their just due. If not corrected, this breakdown of morale can result in a deterioration of moral responsibility such as that which led to the decline and fall of past civilizations.

Parents Should Share the Responsibility of Child-Rearing

Mother and father each have different roles in the upbringing of children, and both are very important. The mother is the principal one to nurture the children in their infancy. I do not mean that she is the only one; but she is the logical parent to give most of the early care, and to instill in the children the training that is so necessary in the primary years. It is she who nourishes the infant from her own body. But the father should not abdicate his share of the responsibility. As the child grows, it needs the companionship, nurturing, and understanding of both parents. It is the common duty of both father and mother to attend to the raising of the children.

I very much believe in the equality of the sexes. Gurudeva Paramahansa Yogananda was one of the first to stress that equality. While everyone else in the West was giving leadership to men only, he went against that tradition, making me one of the first women to be leader of a worldwide spiritual organization.

What does it matter whether one is called Mr., Mrs., Miss, or Ms., when every individual is essentially neither male nor female, but a soul made in the image of God? This is rather like little children quarreling over toys. The real issues are on a larger scale. The soul within is what really matters. Each one of us has an essential role to play in this world. If that were not so, God would have made us all the same. And in the ultimate sense, no role is more important than any other: The significant point is that we play our part well, whatever it might be.

It is not right that a mother should be tied down to a stove all her life. That is not fair or necessary. Obviously, mothers also need to have other challenges in their lives. But in the child's tender early years, the mother's influence is most important; and I believe her place is at home with her children. (In some cases, of course, a working single parent may have to send the children to a day-care center.)

Cultivating a Close Relationship With Your Children

It really is a skilled profession to bring up children, to understand the needs of the child. Each one is different. In the sight of God, we are all souls, possessing the same qualities as the Divine. But because each one has free will and independent intelligence, we have developed in different ways, with unique patterns of karma. Each child must thus be understood as an individual.

I was one of four children in my family. We adored our mother, which I think is what happens when the mother tries always to be understanding. She never had to punish us physically, because we wanted to please her. When we displeased her, we suffered, because we loved her. We could always talk with her; we could always count on her understanding. But she did not treat us all alike. She saw what each one needed, and that she gave to us. This comes instinctively, I think, when a mother spends time with her children. Give your love equally to all your children, but realize that you have to give in a different way to each one. Some children are born with great stubbornness, some are flighty, some are moody, some are always happy and cheerful. It is a matter of getting to know your child and then guiding him, in a way he will understand, when he is going the wrong way.

It is important that parents cultivate the right relationship with their children. Do not try to be like your children. You are their parents, not their brothers and sisters. Teach them to love and respect you as parents. I don't think the "buddy-buddy" relationship is healthy, or helpful to a child. A mother wanting to become a sister to her children is merely trying to nourish her own ego. She doesn't want to grow up. She should be a responsible mother. And the same is true for the father.

Keep the Lines of Communication Open

In order to train your children properly, you must establish effective communication with them. Let them feel they can confide in you. Encourage them to be truthful by allowing them to say whatever is in their minds. If you turn a child away because he has told you something you do not like, that child will become evasive, trying to mask his true feeling and to hide behavior of which he knows you will disapprove. He will instead seek out someone else as his confidant. It is far better that you be that friend, the one to whom he can always turn. In that healthy relationship with your children, they will not feel a need for drugs or to go elsewhere for understanding.

Take time to talk with your children. Answer their questions and explain your guidance to them in language they can understand. You cannot just say, "Don't do it." You have to reason with the child in a way that will get him to listen. One learns by listening, even if one does not agree with everything that is said. Encourage the child in willingness to listen. Constructive words will remain etched in his consciousness. He may be grateful for them when one day he himself becomes a parent. Good rapport with your children has to begin in the early years. If you wait until a problem arises, it will be far more difficult to open those lines of communication at that time.

One thing I would caution about: Never force your own spiritual views on your children. Don't say to your child, "Because I'm meditating, you're going to meditate." Children are like flowers; allow them to grow up and develop their own personalities. There is nothing wrong with that. Your part is to provide them with the right example and sense of direction—that they learn to love God, to accept and carry responsibilities, to be unselfish, to be kind to others—the aggregate of qualities and virtues that is the measure of a spiritual-minded human being.

In my own childhood, at a very early age we children learned to pray at our mother's knee. It was part of getting ready for bed. We knelt around her, said a short prayer, and then prayed for the different members of the family. It was so sweet. We were never forced to do it. A child who is taught to pray loves it. By the time I was seventeen and came into Self-Realization Fellowship, I was so busy praying for others that my prayer at night seemed never-ending—there were so many to add to the list. Praying for others teaches one to feel for others. Children should be taught to be caring and unselfish.

Introduce Children to a Sense of Responsibility

It is important also to teach children to accept responsibility. I am always appalled when I see families in which the parents do everything—all the cooking, dishes, cleaning, gardening—and the child sits in front of the TV or goes off to visit his or her friends, and has no chores. This is not right. Why do parents feel they must do everything? Why aren't they giving the child the kind of guidance that will help him to develop skills and responsibility? The child grows up to be a careless and unreliable man or woman who doesn't know how to train his or her own children. These habits are passed on from one generation to the next, so today many young people are the victims of our having failed in our duty to them.

Children should learn at an early age that nothing comes without effort. One has to work; he has to merit what he receives in this world. This principle is important. If a child is given everything he wants, he does not learn the value of anything. Teach the child that he should contribute his part to the family, to his circle of friends, to his community. That prepares him to cope with what others will expect of him as an adult.

Parents are often too indulgent with their children: "I want to give my child everything I didn't have." Nonsense! Give him a chance to unfold, to achieve, to meet the challenges of life with your help and support so that he becomes a strong individual. You cannot protect him from everything, nor can you assure his happiness by catering to his whims. And in the long run, it will not help him if you try to do so.

One thing I do believe in: If you give a child an assignment, see that he fulfills it. If you tell him to pick up his clothes and put them on a chair at night, insist that he does as you have said. Do not spank the child, but insist. Once good habits have been formed, the child will automatically do what is right.

Young ones will do what is asked of them if they feel they are helping, contributing. Make them feel they are sharing. Give praise and encouragement; make them want to do it. Be sure that the responsibility is not greater than the capacity of the child. And when he does his best, give a reward; if he does not, no reward. That is not necessarily the best practice; it is better that the child obey out of instinctive good behavior, but unfortunately, in most cases a reward seems to help a little!

When I was a child, we did not receive rewards, other than the appreciation of our parents for a job well done. We all had our duties, and we knew we were expected to do them properly. If, for example, we had wiped the dinner dishes and the glasses were not spotless, we had to get out of bed and come down to wash them over. I am grateful for that discipline. I really appreciate it. Had I not received that training as a young girl, I might not have been as able to accept Master's discipline when he placed upon my shoulders increasing responsibilities, culminating in those I carry today.

Should parents choose their children's careers?

It is my experience that if someone else tells us what to do with our lives, we may follow that suggestion for a while, but sooner or later, if we are to be happy, our latent inner inclinations must be fulfilled. When anyone asks me, "Shall I marry or remain single?" the first thing I want to know is, "What do you want in your heart?" Because if I suggest that someone become a renunciant, that life will not necessarily wipe out all other desires. The desire to follow a particular course in life must start within, and then that inclination can be strengthened by outer guidance.

For example, there have been many, in East and West, who have followed the monastic path because their parents expected them to, and raised them to become monks or nuns. But such devotees do not make very good monastics, if this vocation is not the foremost desire in their own hearts. After maybe five, ten, or fifteen years, other desires assert themselves, and they seek another way of life.

Only you can say what you really want. When devotees seeking my advice say, "I want to know what God wants me to do," I come back to the same point: What do *you* want? Start with that first, and then objectively analyze what way your life is karmically destined to go.

Sometimes we are reluctant to assume responsibility for our own lives. We want God to tell us what to do—provided that what God wants for us is in harmony with what *we* really want! I am not against seeking the will of God; in fact, I am all for it. But no amount of saying, "I want to follow God's will," will suffice if while trying to follow this we are inwardly tormented by desires for something else. We have sown the seeds of desires, have harbored them within, perhaps for many lives. So it is not enough to accept reluctantly what we think God wants of us, or what our parents or friends would choose. We must follow what we feel is right for us, and then strive to move onward from that point.

Each of us has within him intelligence endowed by God with which we are to accept responsibility for ourselves, and to learn how to make the right choices in life. When we do that, while at the same time meditating and trying to keep in tune with the Divine, we fulfill our individual destiny. The duty of parents is to help guide their children along these lines, while giving them the freedom to follow their own natures.

My boys are fourteen and sixteen. They want to date, but I come from the Indian culture, and I don't approve. As you know, in India marriages are arranged. I know that this is not the custom in America, and that I must have a balanced attitude. But I still feel they are very young, and right now their energies should be invested in studies and sports.

First of all, let me say that you cannot make a general rule, because everyone is different. Some are more mature than others of the same age. Secondly, I do agree that the dating system in the West is too permissive, but I also think that the custom in India could be improved. I have seen some tragic consequences of arranged marriages in India. So both systems have their flaws.

Guruji very much believed that in the early years the sexes should be educated in separate schools. The attention of the children should be focused on academic and character training, development that will equip them for a better life as they become mature, without the undue stimulation of the awakening senses involved in boy-girl relationships. Unfortunately, moral standards have deteriorated in today's society. In an atmosphere of permissiveness it is a mistake to have dating at an early age. The growing problem of teenage pregnancies is ample evidence of this.

I counseled one young girl whose father, having been raised in Guruji's ideals, was strict with his children. He did not permit them to date at the early age at which many of their friends were going out. They adhered to that. Even so, when they were permitted to go out on their own, peer pressure caused the young girl to get involved with the wrong type. It was then that the matter was brought to my attention. It took several meetings, talking patiently with her and pointing out that the important thing was that she become a responsible, capable adult who would then be able to make the right choices in life. Fortunately, she listened, and today she is extremely happy, having married a very fine young man; and they have a lovely child.

You are from a different culture, and you have to determine which country's customs you want to follow. Many Indian parents in this country do continue to choose the life-companions of their children, and I don't quarrel with that if they have carefully studied the characteristics of the young people concerned to be satisfied they are compatible. It can be a good custom when it is done with proper consideration of all character traits, interests, and such questions as: Do they get along? Will they continue to be harmonious as they mature, sharing concordant goals and ideals?

On the other hand, if you choose to follow the customs of the West, then I think the best thing, when you decide they are old enough, is to let them first invite their friends to your home, rather than meet outside, so you can get to know with whom they are mixing. They might not always behave quite as you think they should, but make allowances for their age and interests, as long as you are satisfied that moral principles are being observed.

Let them come on a Friday afternoon after school is out, to stay for a few hours, play records, have little parties, or other types of recreation they enjoy. I think it is important for parents to open their homes in a warm and friendly way to their children's friends, so that the children feel that home is a place where their friends are welcome.

You have a right and a duty to be strict regarding the non-use of alcohol and drugs. If necessary, seek professional counsel and help in enforcing this. I have seen too many minds and bodies tragically destroyed by these substances. I am sure this does not apply to your children, but I am saying this because it does happen in some homes.

About fifteen or sixteen would be the age that is generally acceptable to responsible parents in this country for their children to begin social association with the opposite sex. Eighteen is a little late if you are going by the accepted standards of the West. I am not saying this is right or wrong; I am simply stating that your children are in an environment where the general trend is to have close friends of the opposite sex at an earlier age. You will be in a position of great disadvantage if you appear to be unreasonably strict.

So many parents do not even know the friends

with whom their children are associating. And frankly, the children then think, "My parents don't care." Very often children are glad that the parents care enough to "put their foot down" and establish rules. But you have to begin at an age when the children respect the training. Do not wait until they are teenagers, because by then it may be too late. They will have become accustomed to more independence than you will want them to exercise.

My neighborhood is really bad. Many of the parents don't seem to care what their children do. Is it all right to let my children play with these youngsters? Should we stay there, or should we move? The area was all right when we bought the house.

If you live in an area where the children are unruly, I would be inclined to be cautious. I would want to know whom my children were playing with, and what they were doing—but without making them feel that they were not being allowed any freedom.

The strongest influence in the lives of children comes from their companions. Children are imitators and pick up the tendencies of those they mix with. If in your neighborhood the other children are not the kind that you feel will help the development of your youngsters, or who might even lead them into trouble, then I would take some steps.

It is important to understand how much children respond to the environment they are in. Be careful that you are not discriminating according to color, religion, or nationality, but just according to the quality of individuals. There is nothing wrong with living in any kind of neighborhood; but the vital point is, what is the quality of the people there. You cannot spend your life worrying about your children because you live in a rough area; better to move to a district where there is not that kind of problem, and have peace of mind.

In summary, I would leave you with one vital point: The best chance for success in raising children is if the parents themselves set the right standards by their own example. Children need to see that the results of those standards imposed on them are beneficial. When guidance is given by example, and with love and understanding, it will enhance the karmic good already present in the children from their past lives, and provide opportunity for further growth. To thus nurture inherent good tendencies and to plant seeds of new ones in young lives given into their care is the God-given duty of parents—a skilled profession, indeed!

When Is Physical Force a Rational Defense?

From a satsanga *in which this question was asked*

In his interpretation of the Ten Commandments, Paramahansa Yogananda has written the following about the commandment *Thou shalt not kill:*

> The meaning is that one should not kill for killing's sake; for then you become a murderer. One should not take another's life in a moment of violent emotion. But if your country is attacked and goes to war, you should fight to protect those whom God has given to you. You have a righteous obligation to defend your family and your country.*

I have been asked if Guruji would then disapprove of those who do not want to go to war. No; he came on earth to increase understanding, not to condemn. He understood the feelings of those who become "conscientious objectors" and serve their countries in other capacities. During the Second World War Guruji often spoke of the millions who were killed. He explained that souls who are thrust out of the body suddenly, as when death occurs on the battlefield or in aerial bombing, return much sooner to earth than those who have

* From "The Ten Commandments: Eternal Rules of Happiness" in *Man's Eternal Quest.*

been able to live out that incarnation. He said that many of these souls would return with such revulsion toward war that they would in future refuse to fight. And isn't this what has happened, with many absolutely refusing to be sent to war? Guruji could see ahead; he perceived the cause and effect of actions, not only of individuals but of nations.

We cannot simply say that all killing is evil, that all war is wrong. If one nation is threatening another, the second nation is justified in defending itself. Bear in mind that we are dealing with a world of duality, of good and evil, where few have realized the highest state of consciousness. It is appropriate, and common sense, to defend one's self, or one's loved ones, or one's country, even if that necessitates killing.

If you see a person about to hurt someone you love very much, you would not stand by, saying, "I forgive you." Your natural instinct would be to defend the loved one. If you can do so without harming the attacker, well and good. If you cannot, then use whatever degree of force is necessary. When the attack is stopped and there is no longer a threat to the innocent, if the aggressor has been injured, then do what you can to help him.

God Judges the Motives Behind Actions

Remember that God is watching the motive in each individual action. This is why we should always try to analyze the real intention behind our actions, and to discriminate as to the correctness of their projected end results. And this is also why it is difficult for man to be a fair judge of man. Emotion often clouds the judgment of reason. For example, it would not be correct to condemn as evil all killing of animals. If a man has a gun and shoots birds and harmless creatures for sport, or because he gets a certain thrill out of it, that is wrong. If, on the other hand, that man sees—as occasionally happens in India—a wild tiger attacking a human being, or a snake about to strike a child, it is fitting at that time to use the gun to defend the higher form of life. In both cases, God judges the motive rather than the action.

Different Gradations of Evolution

Because of the law of evolution, there are different gradations of life. The highest intelligent form of life is man, and below man are the lesser forms. Science tells us that plant and animal life began in the sea, then moved to the land, and increasingly higher and more intelligent forms gradually evolved.

Now, if to protect a higher form we must take the physical life of a lower manifestation, this may be justified. It would be highly impractical and unwise *not* to destroy such disease-carrying insects as mosquitoes, which spread life-threatening illnesses. There is no sin in that, because in doing so we are protecting higher forms of life.

The same principle applies, for instance, to rabid animals. Here in the Mt. Washington area there are a number of wild animals, and occasionally one may become rabid. If it becomes necessary to protect human life by destroying a rabid animal, then that, too, is right action, and is not a sin. It is also an act of compassion to put that suffering animal out of its misery.

Discrimination, and Reverence for All Life

One ought always to use discrimination. There should be a reverence for all life. I have said that killing for sport is wrong. So is killing for convenience. If there is a fly in my room and I see that it is in distress, or if it is disturbing me, my first instinct will be to open a window and let it out. There is no need to destroy the fly. But on the other hand if I am in a country where insect-carried diseases are endemic, or where there are vermin such as rats, which are a threat to health and life, then it is not wrong to deprive those insects or rodents of their existence, without malice, knowing full well that the spark of life within them will evolve to a higher form in its next existence.

So it is not wrong to take the life of something that threatens human life or the higher forms of animal life. If you saw a rattlesnake threatening a helpless little puppy, what would you do? It is obvious that you should protect the puppy by taking the life of the snake. Also, if that snake is in a densely populated area, discrimination will tell you that you must destroy it, for it might not only kill the puppy, but perhaps some human being as well.

On the other hand, if one is out in nature and sees a rattlesnake in an uninhabited part of the desert, I don't believe that under those circumstances one should kill. That is where God put the snake; it is doing no harm, and is part of the natural ecology. So leave it alone. In its natural environment it will not have the opportunity of harming domesticated animals or humans; that is the point.

Communication Is the Key

While I believe a person should defend himself and others against real danger, it is foolish for two people to fight each other over differences. There have to be reasons for what people do, and I believe in getting to the cause of fights rather than just exchanging blows!

Children should be taught by their parents not to fight. They must understand that this will not change others; that the best way is through discussion, communication, understanding. Some children bring with them naturally aggressive tendencies from past lives, or develop those tendencies in their present environment. They will become worse if they are allowed to use violence to get what they want. They need to be encouraged to communicate, to develop understanding of others and of themselves.

Now, saying "You did this," or "You did that," is not communicating. If you are accusatory, the other person will always resent it. The way to communicate is to say, "We are having problems. Please help me to understand." Then first let him express what he feels you do that causes him to act as he does. After he has expressed himself, then say, "Now, may I?" Try that. It is the way understanding and friendship are developed.

Going back to my childhood: I was a little older than some of the children in the neighborhood, but my younger sister was occasionally picked on by some of the other youngsters. That disturbed me, because I was born with the consciousness that it was my duty to be everybody's defender! If I struck back at those who were hitting her, nothing was accomplished. (Gangs are developed that way.) But I found that by talking, harmony was achieved, and so that became my way.

Master said of me later, "She's a peacemaker." That started in my childhood, with my mother's training. We always had dialogue with her. She took the time to explain things to us, and I never felt that I had to hide anything from her. All parents should try to create such an atmosphere of trust, so that their children naturally come to them for help when in need.

So first ask people why they do what they do. Instead of reacting with anger, try to understand the "why" of the other person's behavior. I have practiced that all my life. Analyze; it helps you to grow in understanding of yourself and others.

I am not suggesting that if someone is being attacked, one should not try to help the victim. I am saying that one must use his common sense to decide what action will be of the greatest help. Some people have such short tempers that they wade right in, then and there, and fight. But that is not the best way. Pour oil on troubled waters; try to lessen the tensions. Once emotions are calmed, then it is possible to create understanding faster.

After emotions have calmed down, and some time has elapsed, it is possible to see that even in the person who has acted evilly, God exists. The God I profess to love is just as much in an erring individual as He is in me: the same God is in all of us. The only difference is that the image of God in the wrongdoer is temporarily clouded by the darkness of evil behavior. But that does not mean that the *person* is evil.

Such thinking lays the foundation so that later, when you are meditating, or when you are free from emotional reactions, you can feel a sincere love in your heart for that person, and begin mentally to send your love to him. This practice is a tremendous force for changing others. I have seen it work time and again. Use the power of prayer and thoughts of love whenever someone misunderstands you and you cannot communicate with him in any other way—but also keep on trying to communicate; never give up.

Strengthening the Power of the Mind

From a talk at Self-Realization Fellowship International Headquarters

Gurudeva Paramahansa Yogananda strongly emphasized the principle of positive thinking. Many medical doctors and other health specialists have expressed the view that perhaps as much as ninety percent of our physical problems may originate in the mind. Knowing the powerful influence wielded by the mind, Master felt very deeply the importance of developing positive thinking, of keeping the mind strong even when the body is having difficulties. When he founded his work here and in India, he included as one of its basic aims and ideals: "To demonstrate the superiority of mind over body, of soul over mind."

Devotees should apply this in their lives more and more, with reason and common sense. Master did not teach us to be rash; but on the other hand, there are some people whose endurance level is nil. They cannot stand the slightest pain. Don't be so pain-prone; don't accept illness; don't accept defeat: develop greater mental strength. How? While trying to help yourself, do not dwell on the problem, do not talk about it; practice greater faith in the power of God. That is what Guruji taught us to do.

To help keep the mind strong and positive, use Guruji's *Scientific Healing Affirmations** daily. When I

* Published by Self-Realization Fellowship.

first came to Mt. Washington, we included one of his affirmations as a part of our group meditation every morning. In Guruji's teachings we have everything we need to develop ourselves. Apply the teachings; use them to increase your stamina and faith.

Strength begins in the mind. Faced with adversity, we become fearful of what might happen to us. Guruji said, "While trying to remove the cause of trouble, have full faith in God." To reason, "Well, if it is Thy will that I die, then I'm going to die," is not positive thinking! There is a time to exercise the philosophy, "What comes, let it come," but until it happens, be strong-willed. "Never say 'die'" is what Master used to tell us.

Always be positive in your thinking—not just about your health, but everything. Positive thinking and faith are essentially the same, and it is a disgrace to our divine potential when we do not exercise them. I am not advising you to be foolhardy. Have common sense: If your leg is broken, don't just sit down and say, "God will heal it." Use the healing sciences that God has enabled man to develop; but while doing so, have complete faith that everything will be all right.

Sometimes what we want may not be what God wants. That is when our faith is tested. But we must go on trusting that He knows best: "Very well, Lord. If it is Your will, I accept it. My faith, my trust in You, is unshaken. I know that whatever You will is for my highest good. Help me to see the positive side of this experience, that I may learn from it and thus grow nearer to You."

I have always had a very strong belief that anyone who makes a devout pilgrimage to a place made sacred by the Guru's presence—such as these grounds at Mt.

Washington, or where his body is*—and prays with faith, will receive a direct response. I have seen this work in my own life and in the lives of others. The idea is to link our faith with the divine blessings.

On one of my trips to India, I had an attack of bronchial pneumonia. I traveled from Singapore to Bangkok with a temperature of a hundred and four degrees. When we reached the hotel there, the devotees with me could see I was ready to collapse, and they called a doctor. He sent me to a hospital, and had X rays taken; and after studying them, he said, "You have tuberculosis. You will have to go back to America."

I was stunned. Then came the reaction, "That's impossible! I won't give up!" Before his passing, Master had asked me to look after his work in India, and I was not willing to accept defeat. You see, when you have developed faith, by practicing positive thinking and trust in God, it sustains you in times of emergency. In such a crisis, the first thought of the average individual would be, "I'm going to die if I don't get home and into a sanitarium!" Inwardly I said, "No, Master, you didn't bring me this far only to send me back."

I consulted with the doctor to see what else we could do. "Well, let's keep you in the hospital," he said. "I'll give you further examinations and some treatments. This climate is good for you, so we'll just keep you here for a while." I did everything they asked of me, holding the thought that it was God and Master who were looking after me through the doctor. Then they took more X rays, which showed there was no tuberculosis! I went on to India.

* Many disciples of Paramahansaji make pilgrimages to Forest Lawn Memorial-Park in Glendale, California, where the Guru's body is interred.

I had, however, developed a very uncomfortable rash, probably from some of the medication given to me. One afternoon, one of the devotees in the ashram asked if I would like to visit Tarakeswar,* outside Calcutta. At the time, Master's experience at the temple there did not come to mind. However, I went, not as a sightseer, but with devotion—which is the only way to approach any place of worship. Many devotees were there, milling around; but I sat down to meditate. I remember thinking, "Lord, I know You are here. Give me some sign: remove the rash from this body." Then I began to meditate and the thought of my ailment completely left my mind. When I got back to the ashram that night, there wasn't a trace of the rash. That is the power of faith. That is why Christ said, "Thy faith hath made thee whole."† It is faith we need, plus common sense. The two go hand in hand.

I'll give you another example: For years my tonsils became periodically infected. I learned to live with them, but finally they became so bad that Master sent me to Doctor Kennell,‡ a throat specialist. He looked at my tonsils and said, "Good heavens! They should come out." So he removed them, and then advised: "Now,

* Hindus regard the Tarakeswar Temple with the same reverence that Catholics feel toward the Grotto of Lourdes. Many miraculous healings have taken place in Tarakeswar. And, as many know from reading Paramahansaji's autobiography, his Uncle Sarada was healed as a result of prayers offered there on his behalf by his devoted wife. Paramahansaji himself had a remarkable vision there of the Cosmic Lord.

† Luke 8:48, 17:19.

‡ The late Dr. Lloyd Kennell was a devoted and beloved disciple of Paramahansa Yogananda. He assisted in conducting services and meditations at the Self-Realization Fellowship Temple in San Diego from 1942 to 1952.

just eat and drink cold things, and take it easy. It might be good if you were to go to bed for a couple of days, so that you don't overdo."

Doctor came to the ashram that night to see Master, along with other devotees who had been invited to dinner. I was helping with the cooking. Generally, Guruji also asked me to serve the food. When I entered the dining room, Doctor Kennell looked at me with surprise and said, "What are you doing? Didn't you go to bed at all?"

"No," I answered, "I didn't need to. Besides, Master said it's not necessary."

"Develop your mind," Master used to say. "Don't be controlled by your body. Strengthen your mind and let it control your body." That's how we were taught to rely more on mind power. In that sense, we lean very strongly toward the principle of mind over matter; but we do not go to extremes. I don't want any fanatics among you!

What Master urged all of us to do, taught us to do, insisted we do, is develop the strength of the mind, realize the power of mind over matter. When you cultivate that mind power, you will be surprised at the amount of energy it brings into your body. As you meditate more, you will be aware of the tremendous energy that surrounds these physical forms; we are living in a sea of God's cosmic energy. That energy can be drawn on by a strong mind.

There is no question about it, as the body gets older its capacity to store and use energy begins to wane. But even then, do not give up exercising mind power. Let us hope that to the last day of our lives we will all be usefully active. A strong mind will help to make it so.

At SRF Lake Shrine, 1988

"If we consciously look for the best in every situation, that positive spirit and enthusiasm acts as a wonderful stimulant to the mind and feelings, and to the body. Right attitude is a tremendous help in removing the mental and emotional obstructions that cut us off from the divine resources within us."

At Yogoda Satsanga school for girls, Ranchi, 1972

(Above) Greeting devotees after *satsanga* at YSS Ashram, Ranchi, 1967; and *(below)* at SRF Mother Center, Los Angeles, 1982

"The way to receive love is to give love. Yet how few in this world know how to love sincerely, deeply. By meditation, as we learn to love God more and to feel His love, it becomes possible for us to love, even without asking anything in return."

With His Holiness Sri Jagadguru Shankaracharya Bharati Krishna Tirtha of Gowardhan Math, Puri, during a visit to Yogoda Math, headquarters of Yogoda Satsanga Society of India, Dakshineswar, May 1959. His Holiness was the ecclesiastical leader of millions of Hindus and senior head of the ancient Order of Swamis as apostolic successor of Adi Shankaracharya (India's renowned ninth-century philosopher).

In 1958 the Jagadguru ("world teacher") became the first Shankaracharya ever to travel outside India, speaking at leading universities in the United States on the value of India's eternal principles of truth. This historic visit was sponsored by Self-Realization Fellowship.

(Left) With Swami Sivananda, founder of the Divine Life Society, at his headquarters in Rishikesh in the Himalayas, 1959. With them is Sister Revati of the SRF Mother Center.
(Above) With Ananda Moyi Ma, the "Bliss-permeated Mother," at the latter's ashram on the Ganges at Banaras, 1959.

"The greatest lovers this world has ever known are those who have loved God. Down through the ages they remain an inspiration to all mankind. To produce true lovers of God, true knowers of God, is the purpose of India's teaching; this is what her scriptures have proclaimed to mankind."

Our minds remain strong if we are anchored in God. Guruji always brought our minds back to God. When we went to him with problems, there were times when he gave definite advice or discipline; but as a general rule, his answer to every kind of difficulty would simply be, "Just keep your mind with God," or "Just put your mind on God."

His mind was always absorbed in and one with God, wherever he was or whatever he was doing. Often in the midst of a conversation—he might be talking about something mundane—he would suddenly close his eyes. I could tell that he had focused them at the Christ center. We would all become silent around him, while he remained within. After a short time, he would come out of that state and ask, "What was I saying?" and get right back into the subject again.

That is the way to live in this world: make God the center of your life. Why make the body, personal ambition, or anything else but God the guiding light of our lives?

I often look upon the spiritual path as a challenge. To me, it is a thrilling accomplishment to be engrossed in something and then have the ability to pull back instantly the wild horses of the mind; that is how to keep the thoughts always inwardly on course. Make God the supreme goal, the one central thought around which all actions of your outer life revolve regardless of the difficulties you face. That is the ideal of the true yogi.

Anchoring Your Life in God

From a talk to nuns at Self-Realization Fellowship International Headquarters

In his *sadhana,* or practice of spiritual discipline, the devotee must be wholeheartedly bent on attaining the state of continuous awareness of God. In my early years, because I believed in what our Guru [Paramahansa Yogananda] taught, and in applying it, I used to reason: "If I use my time rightly, and learn to practice Gurudeva's techniques and teachings correctly, then surely, as the years go by, those high states of consciousness about which he speaks can be mine also."

The purpose of the Self-Realization Technique of Concentration is to completely interiorize the mind, so that no disturbances resulting from messages carried by the five sense-telephones can penetrate the inner awareness of the withdrawn consciousness to distract the attention and pull it outward. The resultant peace is the first proof of God's presence. When you feel that peace, practice Kriya Yoga meditation long and deeply, remembering that depth of attention is of the utmost importance.

Train the Mind to Be Aware of Truth

Actually, if you could but realize it, that Divine One whom you seek is within you and all around you. It is not God who is lacking in awareness of us; it is we who must rise above this finite world in an increased awareness of Him.

We live, in a sense, in a very false world. Guruji once spoke on the subject: "This World Is Not As You See It." How true! Because of *maya,* cosmic delusion, which clouds our perception of truth, we behold as reality this world of solids, liquids, and gases. We accept as true the illusions of our senses and emotions, and our moods or different attitudes through which we pass each day. But the more we become anchored in our real Self, the more we immerse ourselves in God's presence within, drunk with one drive, one hunger, one desire—God alone—the more we understand what Reality is. The entire being becomes absorbed night and day in one thought: God.

There is a saying: "As he thinketh in his heart, so is he."* It is not how a man behaves outwardly that determines what he is, but how he thinks in his heart. If externally the devotee observes all the spiritual laws, but inwardly his mind hungers after things of this world, then sooner or later those thoughts will express themselves outwardly. Similarly, the devotee whose mind is completely absorbed in God, who is always thinking of Him, always dwelling in the thought of Truth, of Love Divine—that individual's thoughts also are sooner or later reflected in his life through his habits, words, and deeds.

It is in attitude that we begin to know God. If we had right attitude, in this instant each one of us would be directly communing with God. Right attitude means that we behold life as it really is, that we are constantly aware of truth. And the truth is that God alone is real, and everything else in this universe is unreal.

If we were to see truth, we would behold nothing

* Proverbs 23:7.

but that great, divine, intelligent, loving Force manifested in everything on earth, even a grain of sand. But we do not yet have that realization and so have to train our minds to think in these terms. We should begin with strengthening our control of the mind and discipline of the body. The soul should be in command at all times. The body and its appetites are to be rendered subservient. Even in the face of sickness, the soul should assert its authority.

"Just Give It to God"

When there are struggles with the body, give them to God. I remember an occasion when this body was giving much trouble, and it was hard to keep my mind on my work. I complained to Gurudeva: "It is so difficult, Master, to be with God. It is difficult even to carry on my duties when there is so much discomfort."

How wise he was! He did not sympathize. In such a casual way he said, "Just do your best, and give it to God."

At the time, I was thinking, "He doesn't understand; I feel like I'm dying!" But when I left his presence, I began to reason that his intention was for me to learn something from his not sympathizing, not in any way encouraging me to cater to this illness. That lesson was: "Don't pay so much heed to the body." I recalled what Christ said: "Take no thought for your life, what ye shall eat, or what ye shall drink; nor yet for your body, what ye shall put on."* And the counsel of Swami Sri Yukteswar, which Master often quoted to us: "Why not throw the dog a bone and then forget it?" In other words, give the body its just due, and leave the results in God's hands.

* Matthew 6:25.

No matter how well we care for this body, fill it with vitamins, vegetables, fruit juices, and all the things that are supposed to make it healthy, some day it may nevertheless be stricken with illness, and the time will definitely come when we will have to cast it away. So do not give it supreme importance. That is what Master meant by his words: "Just give it to God."

On one particular occasion, Master himself, having taken on the karma of others,* was in great physical pain. I could not bear to see him in such discomfort over so many, many weeks. In my distress I said to him, "What is the point in seeking God if you, whose life is so completely dedicated, who have not a single thought for self or self-comfort, suffer like this in order to help others? I don't understand it. Where is the justice of God?"

Master looked at me with a great fire in his eyes; I could see in those eyes the power behind the whole universe as he said to me:

"You must not speak that way. You don't understand. In this struggle, despite the pain, Divine Mother is showing me worlds upon worlds of understanding. You don't know what tremendous scenes She is showing me through this physical illness. *Never* criticize

* Explaining the process by which God-knowing souls can lighten the karmic burden of disciples, Paramahansa Yogananda once said: "If you saw that a man was going to hit another, you could step in front of the intended victim and let the blow fall on you. That is what a great master does. He perceives, in the lives of devotees, when unfavorable effects of their past bad karma are about to descend on them. If he thinks it wise, he employs a certain metaphysical method by which he transfers to himself the consequences of his disciples' errors....Because saints are conscious of God as Eternal Being and Inexhaustible Life Energy, they are able to survive blows that would kill an ordinary man. Their minds are unaffected by physical disease or worldly misfortunes."

Divine Mother. *Never* find fault with Her, even though outwardly something may appear to be unjust."

I hung my head and thought how foolish I had been to speak in that manner, even though it was out of love and a longing to see him free from pain. Thus, even in sickness his attitude was right, untouched by the suffering.

In our lesser ways we can also express right attitude. No matter what the problem, do not let the mind waver. There comes a time when you see yourself as the soul, always in perfect command of your whole being. The soul is the charioteer who holds the reins of the mind and guides the chariot of the body. Never is the soul controlled by physical or mental pains, moods, emotions, and habits.

That is the state we are all striving toward. It is attained by meditating. Master said, "I want you to use your time here rightly so that you can get to God in this life." I am so pleased whenever I learn of devotees spending extra time in meditation—and I am always aware of it. Wherever I am, I constantly ask Divine Mother to bless you all. I know that if you devoutly and sincerely call on Her in deep meditation, then without doubt—perhaps when you least expect it—you will feel Her divine response.

That Divine One is every moment just behind your thoughts. To me, this is the most thrilling truth. Even if my meditation is only for a brief time, that awareness comes over me. Now, in just an instant my mind can go within. I say, "Divine Mother, just behind these closed eyes Thou art; just behind this mind Thou art; just behind the life in this body Thou art." Let your mind become immersed in that consciousness, by affirming it, by again and again mentally diving deeper into that thought. Then see how sweetly that Divine One blesses you.

"Full of Life and Joy"

This is something Master said that I love; it is so beautiful: "In the spiritual life one becomes just like a little child—without resentment, without attachment, full of life and joy." Stop and think of that: Just like a child, absolutely trusting, absolutely devoted to the mother or the father, absolutely innocent, guileless—with a pure heart. You give a child a toy; he plays with it enthusiastically for a little while, but then drops the object and forgets about it. We should be like that: whatever comes, we should live life free from attachment.

"Let nothing hurt or disturb you," said Master. "Be still within, and calm outwardly. Spend your leisure time in meditation. I have never known any pleasure of the world as great as the spiritual joy of Kriya Yoga. I would not give it up for all the comforts of the West or all the gold in the world. Through Kriya Yoga I have found it possible to carry my happiness always with me."

Developing Inner Strength

I have often said to you that if you were to take even one truth Master has taught and devote yourself to realizing it, you would become saints in this life. Take some principle of truth each day and live by it. You might say to yourself, "I'm so burdened by my duties that I have no time to keep my mind on that thought." But I cannot accept that. I know the spiritual path is hard; it is difficult to know God. But I also know that your tests and duties are the very ones that will give you the inner strength with which to find Him. Doubt it not, because that is exactly what happened in my own life and what I have seen occur in the lives of many.

Know for certain that, because you are a child of the Divine, you have within you all the power you need to conquer your weaknesses. Master emphasized that. He never permitted us to whine, weep, or moan. He filled us with divine strength.

You may think, "Well, if I had freedom to devote all my hours to meditation, I could get there." But such a life would not teach self-discipline. It is in meeting problems every day that we develop inner strength, and learn how to discipline this unruly self. If you never lifted your arm, its muscles would soon atrophy. The limb would become weak and useless, because never used. Strength, will power, faith—all these "muscles"—are developed when one is forced to use them. So never think that if life were less difficult for you, it would be easier to know God, because that is not true. The ways in which God is disciplining you are what you require now for self-unfoldment. Always remember that.

My reason for emphasizing this is that when you develop a healthy attitude of surrender to the will of God, you progress very quickly on the spiritual path. You race toward your divine goal. But when there is resistance or unwillingness, you become bogged down. Take life in stride. And have faith that when it is Divine Mother's will, when the lesson in a particular experience is learned, She will remove that corresponding test or trial from your path, because the need for it is no longer there.

"Solitude Is the Price of God-Realization"

Above all, as I urge you again and again, develop love for God. Hunger for just one attachment—to God.

There is nothing more wonderful than solitude, wherein one's mind is uninterruptedly watchful of the Divine Beloved within. That is what Master stressed: "Be alone more. Solitude is the price of God-realization." My spiritual duty is to encourage you to be alone more with God. Get in the habit of communing with Him. Walk out of doors more, talking with God. Guruji said, "I want to see you with your minds always fixed in God." If you do not practice this in your *sadhana,* you will never understand what I mean; you will never know the value of that spiritual solitude wherein God becomes the Divine Companion. When He is with you, then you can enjoy the companionship of all.

Do not indulge in idleness. Become drunk with God, with the pleasure of talking with Him. Churn the ether until you feel His response within. That is the foundation on which I nurtured my *sadhana*—I would cry in the night for God. If I could shake you out of your lethargy and make you hunger for God every moment, night and day—so that no matter what your duties, you are craving the fulfillment of your longing for love by seeking God within—you would see how wondrously different your life becomes. The day will come when you will remember these words, and say, "How right she was! She tried to stir our hearts as Master stirred hers." I can only urge you; you yourself have to eat the food in order to benefit from it.

There is nothing in the world, there is no companionship, that can match the joy of God's presence. Guruji used to say to us, "When I don't like this world, I go into the other world." When conditions were too troublesome, he would just switch off his sentient consciousness and become absorbed for a time in the revitalizing bliss of the Divine Consciousness. Without such an inner awareness of God I do not think I could possibly carry on—physically or mentally. But one must first develop the ability to "switch off," to lift oneself to those higher states of consciousness. That comes by self-discipline and deep meditation—the training each one of you is receiving through Guruji's teachings and through the circumstances that come into your daily life. Know for certain, beyond any doubt, that Divine Mother and Master are looking after your life: "To those who think me near, I will be near," said Guruji. That nearness means constant blessing, constant watchfulness over your spiritual life.

The Divine Covenant is there between you and God and Guru. As Master said, "Success on the spiritual path is twenty-five percent the devotee's effort, twenty-five percent the guru's blessing, and fifty percent God's grace." So think how little you have to do! But your twenty-five percent must be done one hundred percent. You must do *your* part; that is the point.

Whenever anything goes wrong in your life, inwardly cling to God. Cry to Him. Try to straighten things out—I am not saying you should not make an effort to correct the situation—but while doing so, keep your mind always calm and resting in God.

Sri Gyanamata* said: "God first; God alone." Let that ideal be constantly uppermost in your mind, no matter what you are doing. Once your mind becomes pinpointed in that consciousness, you will see it is much

* Sri Gyanamata ("Mother of Wisdom") was one of the first *sannyasinis* of the Self-Realization Fellowship monastic order. Paramahansa Yogananda often praised her saintly spiritual stature. She entered the ashram in 1932 when she was in her early sixties; Sri Daya Mata had entered the ashram a year earlier, at age seventeen. Paramahansaji often left Gyanamata in charge of the younger devo-

easier to carry your responsibilities; you are no longer unreasonably troubled by them. You fulfill your duties conscientiously, but the mind is so deeply anchored in the ocean of God's presence that it cannot be tossed about by the waves on the surface. That is how the divine ones carry on. That is how Christ was able to withstand his supreme trial. No matter what difficulties confront you, remain anchored in God through the practice of deep meditation. Be untouched by outer circumstances. Remember Master's prayer: "When boisterous storms of trials shriek and worries howl at me, I drown their noises, loudly chanting: 'God! God! God!'"

"Nothing Can Touch You if You Inwardly Love God"

How sweet it is to recall Master's words to me, "Always remember, nothing can touch you if you inwardly love God." I have clung to those words throughout these many years. And I say to all of you: "Nothing can touch you if you inwardly love God." So love Him that you are fully aware of the strength within you, which is of God; the faith within you, which is of God; and that you are fully united with the Love within you, which is God.

This is the secret, and I speak from my own experience: No matter what my duties, the moment my mind stops concentrating upon any particular activity or making decisions about the work, it doesn't turn to useless, distracting things, but rests in the thought of God. He is the center of my life. The mind is with Him, nowhere else. Where else will it go? My whole being becomes immersed, as in an effervescent fountain of

---

tees when he was away from Mt. Washington. Her inspiring spiritual counsel is presented in *God Alone: The Life and Letters of a Saint.* *(Publisher's Note)*

joy. The waters of divine love inundate my heart, mind, and soul. You can learn to practice this wherever you are. When riding as a passenger in a car, or at work, whenever there is a moment of inactivity, for that instant let the mind rest in God: "My Beloved, my Love. No matter how busy I am outwardly, my Love, I am always thinking of You."

Never be satisfied with less than awareness of God. The moment you find yourself becoming dull, slothful, or lazy about your spiritual life, pray to God to shake you out of that state. I always say to Him: "I don't care what You do with me, whether You visit me with trials or with happiness, only let my mind always be in You. I ask nothing more. Do with me what You will. It is all the same to me. I only know that in my mind I must be with You constantly."

You will be amazed how Divine Mother responds to such longing when the thoughts come from not just the lips, but from the heart. She is watching your heart. You must mean what you say. Hold on to this inner flow of devotion no matter what you are doing: keep the background of your mind always busy with God. It is possible. The more you practice it, the easier it becomes. In the worldly sense, that is exactly how someone in love behaves: in the midst of all his activities and duties, the mind of the lover is on the one he loves. The devotee is he who is in love with God; and he is the wisest, because he chooses the true Eternal Lover, the one Beloved who will never disappoint him. That Love never fails; it is always new, always true, always constant.

Everyone seeks ideal love, ideal joy. That love, that joy, is God. Everything we grasp in life ultimately produces disillusionment, misery, and unhappiness, except God. He alone is all-fulfilling. That is why Christ said: "Seek ye first the kingdom of God, and His righteousness; and all these things shall be added unto you."* "All things" includes the fulfillment of everything the human heart has ever desired or craved. We are inclined to doubt, but be not doubtful; have faith.

In the beginning, when the path would get difficult, and I occasionally felt a little discouraged or doubtful, I would say to God, "All right, Lord, I'll settle it this way with You: I will use this lifetime to try to find You; and I will put my whole heart, mind, and soul into it. I will keep on, no matter what happens." If you make that kind of resolve, you will see that the Divine makes no false promises. When He says, "All these things shall be added unto you," you *will* find in Him all fulfillment—no craving will be left.

The Indian scriptures teach desirelessness. This is not a negative state of consciousness, but one that gives constant ever new happiness. It means that state wherein there is nothing more to crave—you have everything! When we are filled with material desires, yes, there is a pleasurable anticipation at the prospect of having them fulfilled; but if there is no hope or probability of fulfillment, then there is constant frustration. The consequence of unfulfilled desires is unhappiness. The spiritual state of desirelessness means that Gain, having which, there is nothing greater to be gained. Having achieved the highest fulfillment, there is naught else to desire. The devotee rejoices, "I am fully satisfied."

I often think inwardly, "I am content. I am satisfied. I thirst no more, for I am drinking unceasingly from a Well that is endless." That is the wonderful state of desirelessness.

* Matthew 6:33.

Please pray with me: "Divine Mother, teach me to be like a little child, trusting, filled with faith—seeking Thee, sharing with Thee my joys, my troubles, my problems. No matter where I go and no matter where I look, may I behold Thy blessing, in both light and darkness, showering upon me. Divine Mother, help me to realize that Thou art the nearest of the near, dearest of the dear, closer than the closest to me. Bless me with the consciousness of awareness of Thy Presence just behind my thoughts, silently speaking to me through my conscience, silently guiding me in my practice of mental attunement with Thee."

The Perfect Joy

Resurrecting Your Consciousness by Perfecting Your Attitude

Compilation from talks given during Easter-season satsangas *at Self-Realization Fellowship International Headquarters and SRF India Hall, Hollywood*

As the blessed season of Easter draws near, I have been thinking about what I could share with you of the inspiration of the divine life of the Lord Jesus Christ, and of what his resurrection means to us in our everyday living. Gurudeva Paramahansa Yogananda often extolled St. Francis of Assisi as one of the great lovers of Christ, an exemplar of what a follower of Christ should be. In this very room [the chapel at SRF International Headquarters] Guruji had a vision of Saint Francis, and from that vision came the poem we all love so much, "God! God! God!" And I can never forget the great inspiration that flooded my being when we visited Assisi, on our way back from India in 1959, and saw the places that are so permeated with the spirit of this beloved saint.

There is one incident in particular in the life of St. Francis that to me highlights the very essence of the spiritual life. During my early years in the ashram, our revered Sri Gyanamata gave to us younger devotees a book on the life of this saint.* I would like to read to you today extracts from it.

* *The Little Flowers of Saint Francis.*

One winter's day, as St. Francis was going from Perugia with Brother Leo to St. Mary of the Angels, suffering sorely from the bitter cold, he called Brother Leo, who was walking before him, and spoke thus, "Brother Leo, even if the Friars Minor* in every land give good examples of holiness and edification, nevertheless write and note down diligently that perfect joy is not to be found therein."

And St. Francis went his way a little farther, and called him a second time, saying, "O Brother Leo, even if the Friar Minor gave sight to the blind, made the crooked straight, cast out devils, made the deaf to hear, the lame to walk, and restored speech to the dumb, and what is a yet greater thing, raised to life those who have lain four days in the grave, note that perfect joy is not found there."

And he journeyed on a little while, and cried aloud, "O Brother Leo, if the Friar Minor knew all tongues and all the sciences and all the scriptures, so that he could foretell and reveal not only future things, but even the secrets of the conscience and of the soul; note that perfect joy is not there."

Yet a little farther went St. Francis, and cried again aloud, "O Brother Leo, little lamb of God, even though the Friar Minor spake with the tongue of angels and knew the courses of the stars and the virtues of herbs, and were the hidden treasures of the earth revealed to him, and he knew the qualities of birds, and of fishes, and of all animals, and of man, and of trees, and stones, and roots, and waters; note that not there is perfect joy."

And when this fashion of talk had endured two good miles, Brother Leo asked him in great wonder: "Father, I pray thee in God's name tell me where is perfect joy to be found?"

* The name for members of the order of monks founded by St. Francis.

> And St. Francis answered him thus, "When we are come to St. Mary of the Angels, wet through with rain, frozen with cold, and foul with mire and tormented with hunger; and when we knock at the door, the doorkeeper comes in a rage and says, 'Who are you?' and we say, 'We are two of your brothers,' and he answers, 'You tell not true; you are rather two knaves that go about deceiving the world and stealing the alms of the poor. Begone!' and he opens not to us, and makes us stay outside hungry and cold all night in the rain and snow; then if we endure patiently such cruelty, such abuse, and such insolent dismissal without complaint or murmuring, and believe humbly and charitably that that doorkeeper truly knows us, and that it is God who makes him to rail against us; O Brother Leo, there is perfect joy.
>
> "And if, compelled by hunger and by cold, we knock once more and pray with many tears that he open to us for the love of God and let us but come inside, and he more insolently than ever shouts, 'These are impudent rogues, I will pay them out as they deserve,' and comes forth with a big knotted stick and seizes us by our cowls and flings us on the ground and rolls us in the snow, bruising every bone in our bodies with that heavy stick—if we endure all these things patiently and joyously for love of Christ, write, O Brother Leo, that in this perfect joy is found.
>
> "And now, Brother Leo, hear the conclusion. Above all the graces and the gifts that Christ gives to those who love him is that of overcoming self, and willingly to bear other pain and buffetings and revilings and discomfort for love of God."

This story expresses the ideal to be followed by everyone on the spiritual path, the ideal made manifest in the highest way in the crucifixion and resurrection of Jesus: Spirituality lies not in the power to heal others, to perform miracles, or to astound the world with our wisdom, but in the ability to endure with right attitude whatever crosses we have to face in our daily lives, and thus to rise above them. This spirit bestows all-conquering strength and supreme happiness.

Rising Above Painful Experiences

To each of us come times of great tribulation that we feel are impossible to endure. We ask, "Why has this happened to me? It seems so unfair and unjust." Whenever I am tempted to reason in that way, I remember this story from the life of St. Francis. Every experience—whether joyful or painful—comes for one reason: that through it we might draw closer to the Divine Beloved. Perfect joy lies in selflessly striving for the best outcome, and then humbly accepting whatever God gives.

When human relationships bring disappointment, most people become bitter. Never allow that to happen to you. Turn to God, like a child who runs to his mother for solace. In the companionship of true friends, we enjoy the love of the one Divine Friend. And from those who misunderstand and misjudge us, we have equal opportunity to experience the perfect joy of turning to God for strength and comfort. In that relationship with God, you cannot feel bitterness toward those who mistreat you. You regard your feelings of hurt or loneliness or inward emptiness as a reminder to deepen your relationship with that One who will never fail you.

This I learned in my early days in the ashram. There was a certain group of residents here who made it a practice to exclude me from all of their activities. I felt left out, rebuffed. In the beginning, it hurt me very much (I was still an immature young girl), and I wondered, "Why? Why do they reject me?" But there was no resentment within me. I reminded myself that I had not come to the ashram for human companionship, but to seek God. I used to go out on the grounds, especially at night, and oh, how my heart would cry out in yearning for the Divine Beloved.

When we make the sincere inner resolve, "Lord, I want You, only You," in that instant the Divine is fully conscious of our affirmation. From then on, our part is to strive to accept all circumstances as coming to us with the permission of God. We learn to see our ordeals as God's love exhorting us to be nonattached to everything but Him. By facing and overcoming painful experiences, we break the chains that imprison the soul in this little cell of pain-racked flesh and petty emotions.

What Makes Us Suffer?

I do not know how people endure their problems without that understanding, without love for God. So many individuals come to me asking for help, and my heart bleeds for them. But we must ask ourselves, my dears, what makes us suffer? Not other people; not the circumstances we are in; not God. It is we who hurt ourselves when we make the mistake of relying on external things for fulfillment.

When we are filled with upsetting emotions, hurt feelings, and restless desires, do you know what is really wrong? At the root of these sufferings is the loneliness and inner emptiness that comes from not knowing God. Our souls remember the perfect love we once tasted in complete oneness with the Divine Beloved, and we are crying in the wilderness of this world to have that love again.

Why do we feel jealousy, anger, and possessiveness in our human relationships? Because each one of us is hungering to possess that something which is uniquely ours, secure in the knowledge that nothing and no one can take it away from us. We look for a singular condition or environment that will give us that sense of security, a special friend we can cling to, a love we can call our own. The urge of every human being is for perfect love, perfect union with another. But God is the only one we can possess in that way. All human relationships eventually end in loss or disillusionment unless they are anchored in the Divine; it has been so since the beginning of time.

Why do we criticize? Because our true soul-nature is perfection, and we instinctively look for it—in outer conditions, in other people, in organizations. We become resentful when these inevitably fall short of our expectations. The soul yearns for its lost divine heritage; but so long as we depend on the world for the happiness we seek, we will never know perfect joy.

Outer conditions are never going to be perfect; I always keep that in mind. Possessions, social position, the praise of others—all these are so transitory. What we have or do not have in this temporal world is not as important to us as our inner attitude toward whatever comes to us each day. It is through perfecting our attitude that we find strength, joy, and realization of our innate divinity.

What Is Right Attitude?

Each year, on New Year's Eve, we in the ashram would gather in the chapel to meditate with Master from 11:30 p.m. until after midnight. At the close of the meditation, he would often give us a particular thought or quality on which he wished us to dwell in the coming year. On one such occasion, he said to us: "Be humble; don't criticize; learn to be sympathetic." These three are essentials of right attitude for every devotee.

Humility has nothing in common with putting on an outward show of piety; it means being able to take all of life's experiences with the right attitude, even when we are reviled with unkind words. St. Francis, whom I would call a saint of perfect humility, expressed it beautifully: "Learn to accept blame, criticism, and accusation silently and without retaliation, even though untrue and unjustified." In trying to defend ourselves against criticism, we become mired in self-pity and self-righteousness. Real humility, on the other hand, enables us to stand strong, because it is God we are seeking to please, not man. In being true to Him, we will become the kind of person whose qualities may also be more pleasing to man.

Root Out the Cancer of Criticism

The next point Master stressed was that we should not be critical. A fault-finding attitude is like a cancer, eating at the very roots of your peace within. You cannot be a happy individual if your mind is filled with negativity and carping.

Once I was present when one of the devotees in the ashram came to Master and sharply criticized another individual. Master listened patiently for about three minutes. Finally he smiled at the fault-finder and said: "Now let me hear you talk about your own shortcomings for an equal amount of time." The devotee was shocked, and I doubt that he ever again expressed himself in a critical way to Guruji!

Of course, constructive criticism—sincere suggestions for improvement—can be valuable. But it is easy to become overly analytical and negatively critical. If we find that the mind is constantly being tossed about on the waves of restless dissatisfaction and ill-will, we can know that our attitude is not right. So long as we are filled with any kind of negation, whether or not we feel that our attitude is justified, we cannot experience God. Darkness and light cannot coexist in the same room; likewise, wisdom and ignorance, love and hate, cannot coexist in the consciousness. The less we indulge in or listen to gossip and criticism, the more peace we will enjoy within.

In Giving We Receive

The last point Master put before us that New Year's Eve was this: Learn to be sympathetic. People usually think this is something everyone else lacks; we all wish others would be more sympathetic toward us. But it must begin with us—forgetting self, thinking less of our own welfare, and being more thoughtful of the needs of those around us. As St. Francis said, "It is in giving that we receive."

In one respect only should we be selfish, and that is in zealously guarding our relationship with God. From Him we draw unconditional love and understanding to express in our relationships with others.

The greatest joy of my life comes from this: I am in love with God. I have not followed the path that most people in the world pursue in seeking human love and companionship. But I feel so much loved, *so much loved.* The Beloved of the Universe never disappoints me.

Even in times of trial I know that His blessing is just behind those painful experiences, urging me to sunder all limiting attachments and draw closer to Him. The devotee with the right attitude feels a sweetness even in pains and trials, which he recognizes as the love of the Divine. Learn, oh, learn, my dear ones, to accept all of life's experiences with that attitude. And know also that the blessing of Guru is always there to help you. That will never fail you.

As Easter approaches, let us strive to resurrect ourselves from the lack of spiritual zeal into which we tend to fall when life becomes too burdensome or when we get too involved in materiality. Strive to unite your heart with others in a deeper sympathetic understanding. Help others, but avoid being critical. Reach out to others with a sincere love; but above all, love the Divine Beloved. To be drunk with longing for God is to clear our consciousness of the negative attitudes that separate us from His perfect joy.

Steps Toward Emotional and Spiritual Maturity

From a talk at Self-Realization Fellowship International Headquarters

As I look back over the years of discipline, guidance, and training that our guru, Paramahansa Yogananda, gave to those of us who came in his contact, I see how it so wisely led us toward mental and emotional maturity. One of the basic problems of mankind is immaturity. We have wars because we behave like spoiled, thoughtless children. Youngsters pick up rocks and throw them at each other; grown children do the same, only they throw bombs. We fight, we quarrel. If someone has a "toy," we want it—like a child. In other words, everyone grows up in years, but very few grow up mentally and emotionally. Who can we say really reached maturity? A Jesus Christ, a Buddha, a Mahavatar Babaji, a Paramahansa Yogananda—any great saint. It is what we all ought to strive for.

Here are some criteria of emotional maturity:

The Ability to Deal Constructively With Reality

1. *The ability to deal constructively with reality.* Think upon that. If we are immature, we do not want to face reality when it is not to our liking. We would much rather turn and run away from it. We don't really want

to be confronted by truth when it contradicts our convictions. We would rather hide; we would rather not hear it. For instance, we do not want our Guru or our spiritual counselor to tell us things about ourselves that we don't like to hear. We do not want our family to tell us something critical about ourselves, even though they may be right. Criticism makes us want to strike back. If a wife says to her husband, "You smoke too much," the first thing he wants to do is to say something mean to her—emotional immaturity: "You hit me, so I'm going to hit you." Children do that. He who is emotionally mature will hold his calmness, and first think: "Is it so? Yes, it's true. I do smoke too much. Well, I should correct this, because it is harmful to me." He may not respond this way to his wife; he may keep silent. But at least he will not say anything mean in retaliation. He will look at the truth and be mature about it.

Millions end up in mental institutions or under the care of psychiatrists because they do not really want to know themselves, to face themselves and their flaws. But this is the first growing-up step everyone must take.

Do you know the reason we are averse to acknowledging our faults? As souls, we have a concept of ourselves as being perfect. It is basic to our understanding. We *are* perfect, no question about it; but as the soul, not as the ego, which assumes the limitations of this physical form and gathers imperfections through incarnations of wrong habits. It is the ego that does not want to accept corrections from anyone.

Isn't it true, however, that when anyone criticizes us, if we take it with the right attitude, we benefit? It doesn't really matter whether it is said in a mean or unkind way, or in an understanding way. It would be nicer and to the critic's advantage to speak kindly; but in the ultimate sense, a person's unkindness is his own problem. Your problem is how you react.

Let me refer to Saint Francis of Assisi. This is what he said, and what he lived by: "Learn to accept blame, criticism, accusation, silently and without retaliation, even if untrue and unjustified." This is a statement of an emotionally mature being. If we can do one-fiftieth of that, we will be regarded with much admiration and respect—not only by everyone else, but by our own selves.

The Capacity to Adapt to Change

2. *The capacity to adapt to change.* I am grateful for the training in adaptability that we received from Master. We were taught to adjust instantly to any change in our duties or in the conditions around us. We picked up at any time of the day or night and traveled from one ashram to another. We had no time in which to gather everything together. We would get to Encinitas, and there were always guests there (we had no retreat for them in those days). We gave up our rooms and went into the living room and slept on the floor with just a blanket. I loved it. It is human nature to get terribly fixed in our ways. But the nature of the world is anything but fixity. So the ability to adapt to change is essential.

Find Happiness in Giving

3. *The capacity to find more happiness and satisfaction in giving than in receiving.* Cultivate a generous, open heart. Develop the habit of finding joy in giving, giving. It doesn't matter what you give. Find ways to make others happy. Do not give thought to whether you will receive anything in return. Take Christmas-

time, for example. You exchange gifts with someone; but then you think, "Well, this isn't equal to what I gave him." Disgraceful! What does it matter? The more freely you give, the greater your satisfaction will be. It *is* more blessed to give than to receive.

Your giving does not need to be of material things. Give of your heart, give of your understanding. Even if your own body is causing you difficulty, when someone comes to you depressed, discouraged, negative, it is wonderful if you can send that person away uplifted by having said something encouraging to help him along his way. Master often cited the example of Saint Francis: though he was blind and suffering, yet he gave strength and healing to others. He has inspired millions down through the centuries by his words, his sweet humility, and his love for God.

Learning to Love

4. *The capacity to give love.* Love for others is a crowning feature of emotional maturity. This does not refer to giving pleasure through sensual love. We are talking about divine love, which is without condition and which asks nothing in return. The relationship we have with our Guru, the relationship we have with God—the kind of relationship we should develop with all—is based on divine love.

Learn to love. Avoid the word *hate.* And avoid those kinds of thoughts and actions that do not reflect love. When you have to speak to somebody about something unpleasant, do it with love. What an indescribable joy it is to be truly in love. You do not wear your heart on your sleeve; that isn't necessary. But to feel genuine love for people, to feel love for all living things, to have a reverence for all life—this is an integral part of the idealism of a mature being. This we saw so perfectly embodied in Guruji.

How we respect and love the individual who always has a kind word to say about everyone. We may not always have peace and understanding with others, because not everyone will understand us. Christ had his enemies, but from his side there was always the giving of love. He had the patience to wait for their understanding. And for those who gave him hatred he was able to pray, "Father, forgive them, for they know not what they do." This was not just a noble sentiment uttered to impress mankind. He meant it! Can we not practice this too? We must. It is the way to peace and happiness and emotional maturity—divine maturity. Let us get into the habit of using the word *love* more; and feel it. I love the birds; I love the trees—I love all nature. I love to look up into the vast blue sky. I love people; I separate them from their flaws.

We all have irritating defects, yet God endures us. Can we not endure one another? It is ourselves we should strive to change—to scrape away the dross of imperfection and ignorance that covers our brilliant golden soul—while being very, very tolerant of the flaws of others. We should not feel that we have a duty or right to go around correcting everyone "because I am practicing yoga, therefore I know what is best." This is what we call spiritual egotism. The best way to influence others is by our understanding hearts, our kindness, our compassion, and our love.

Guruji often reminded us: "Fools argue, wise men discuss." Well, we all tried not to be fools! We made sincere effort to discuss openly with each other our differences.

We are all divine children sharing this path to God with thousands and thousands of Guruji's disciples throughout the world. "Lord, thou hast given this monk a large family," as Guruji has said in his *Autobiography of a Yogi.* We are united in divine love, divine brotherhood, divine friendship; and one common goal: seeking God together and serving Him in whatever way we can as we reach out to our greater family of all living beings.

Overcoming Character Liabilities

From a talk to monastics at Self-Realization Fellowship International Headquarters

The all-round spiritual guidance of our Guru [Paramahansa Yogananda] included not only the principles of meditation and right action, but also the necessities for balanced psychological health. Because I feel responsible for helping you to understand the spiritual life, I want to point out to you the negative qualities that destroy our peace and happiness and our relationships with others, and keep us away from God.

The spiritual path is like a razor's edge. Without adherence to the straight and narrow principles of the path, it is very difficult to find God. We cannot attain that most priceless Treasure without making the maximum sacrifice: the giving up of all the character flaws that identify us so inseparably with this physical form and its ego, and thus stand between us and God.

Train the Mind to Be Objective

Self-pity is one of the indications of immersion in the little ego-self. If we harbor self-pity, our attitude is always subjective, taking everything personally. We cannot be objective about anything. As a result, we constantly feel sorry for ourselves. To be objective is to think in terms of what is the best attitude to have toward our work, in our relationships with others, and above all, in our relationship with God.

When we are wallowing in subjective consciousness, we are extremely touchy. No one dares to approach us with any constructive criticism, because we are always on the defensive. Defensiveness is a symptom of self-pity. Train the mind to stand aside and impartially analyze a situation, and your reaction. Acknowledge what is true when it is pointed out to you.

If you become sad, moody, or "go to pieces" because someone has criticized you, know that this is one of your weak links. God tests each of us in those areas where we need to develop strength. He will not appear to any of us out of the clouds and say: "Now, My child, these are the things that are wrong with you." Rather, He brings into our lives those circumstances that give us opportunities to recognize and heal all of the psychological weaknesses in our consciousness.

The twin of self-pity is self-justification, the urge to always defend and justify our behavior. Resist the compulsion to explain yourself every time you are confronted with your faults and mistakes. If, for example, someone says to you that you gossip too much, or always look on the dark side of things, hold back and silently introspect. Maybe that person is right, and is acting as a true friend.

Self-Esteem Comes From Within

Another flaw of the ego is self-importance: "I did this; I did that; I originated that idea." False pride comes from attaching too much importance to our accomplishments, forgetting that God is the Doer, and that He alone deserves credit for any success we may achieve. The saying, "Pride goeth before a fall," is very, very true. The moment you indulge in false pride, you are headed for a fall.

Guruji used to quote: "Full many a flower is born to blush unseen/And waste its sweetness on the desert air."* It really does not matter whether or not we receive credit for our deeds. The need for human recognition can be a pitfall on the spiritual path; it can carry us away on the wings of flattery, because it appeals only to the ego.

Spiritual progress lies in doing what is right, not in receiving recognition for it. You may say, "Well, then, I would lose my motivation; I *want* to be appreciated!" The appreciation that really means something comes from within, when we know we have *God's* approval. Many people have attained world fame, but have still ended their lives in suicide. The adulation they received became empty for them, because they did not have that inner satisfaction. But if you know in your heart that you have won the grace of God, that you are pleasing in His sight, your mind will not be ruffled by either the praise or the blame that may be heaped upon you.

Whenever anyone praised Gurudeva, such a dear, sweet, humble smile shone on his face. He would lay that tribute at the feet of the Divine with some simple words of appreciation: "I look for nothing from anyone; but I am very happy if in some way I can please my God." He was a truly humble being, always the same, even-minded in all circumstances.

Balanced Attitude Toward Mistakes

The opposite extreme of self-importance is self-

* Thomas Gray, *Elegy in a Country Churchyard.*

After a period of devotional chanting performed by Sri and Srimati (Brahmacharini Mirabai) Sachinandan Sen, devotees of YSS ashram and noted teachers of Indian classical music, Ranchi, 1964

"Learn to cultivate and express love and friendship for all. We begin by loving those whom God has sent to us as our family; and then expanding that love to include our neighbors, our country, and eventually all nations...until ultimately we do come to feel and accept the whole world as our family. Then we are expressing the universal love of God."

With statue of St. Francis of Assisi received as Christmas gift, December 25, 1973

Conducting *satsanga* in Rome, 1969, during three-month speaking tour of Europe, which also included classes and Kriya Yoga initiations in London, Munich, Stuttgart, Cologne, Berlin, Vienna, Zurich, Milan, and Paris

"It is a joy to be used by God in whatever way He wants. You only wish that you had a thousand million voices to speak His name, and that you had a thousand million hearts to express and to receive His love."

condemnation, which is equally destructive. Many years ago there was a person living here who was a veritable devotee of self-condemnation. He was always thinking or talking about how unworthy and imperfect he was—I am the least of the least, I am so undeserving, I have so many faults, I, I, I—until those around him wanted to say, "Will you just forget the 'I' for a while? Think of yourself as dust if you want to, but don't talk so much about it!" Self-condemnation and humility are not the same. The ego is strong in self-condemnation, and wholly subdued in humility.

Do not be too quick to condemn yourself. Everyone makes mistakes, and I do not think God cares even a little about them. He is concerned only that we desire and strive to be better. He seeks from us the resolve: "Lord, I may falter again and again, but I'll go on trying to the last breath within me."

Be Honest With Yourself and With God

Dishonesty is a serious flaw. It is an outer indication of a deep psychological conflict within. You cannot be dishonest and have your mind with God, who is Truth itself. It is impossible to have your feet in two different boats, one leading toward Truth, and the other in the opposite direction toward untruth.

But should we always speak the truth even if hurtful to others? Master explained it in this way: "If you see a blind man going down the street, and you are determined to be honest, and therefore call out to him, 'Hey, blind man, wait a minute!' that is cruel." Use discrimination to understand what it *means* to speak the truth.

In one incident, someone had said something unkind about another, and it was brought to Master's attention. He questioned that person, who said, "Well, I was asked a question, and I thought I ought to give an honest answer." Now, this individual had no right to judge someone else, as the matter was not his responsibility, and he did not have all the facts. After explaining this, Master gave an illustration to help him understand the principle of spiritual honesty. He said: "Suppose someone is being chased by a thief with a knife in his hand. You are a bystander. The thief asks you in which direction the fleeing man went, and you reply, 'He is hiding in that tree.' You were honest, but your answer will cause great harm. Therefore, that kind of truthfulness is not right. It would be far better to remain silent, or even to point in another direction, than to do something that promotes an evil result." Discrimination must be our guide in this world of relativity.

Try first and foremost to be honest inwardly with God. Never pretend, before Him, to be anything but what you are; He already knows you. Endeavor to be in tune with His evaluation of you. Instead of trying to defend yourself, surrender your errors to Him: "Lord, I was impatient; I lost my temper. I know it is wrong, because I am no longer at peace within my heart. Forgive me."

If you are sincere, you will feel better for having gone to God as to a father, mother, or any other loved one. When you hide from God or from yourself, it gradually builds up deep feelings of guilt within. The time comes when you really don't want to face God; you really don't want to turn your mind within and look at yourself, because you feel ashamed of the ugly and unattractive things you think are there. Such people often need psychiatric treatment, because they lose the ability to be objective about themselves.

Meditation gives the right understanding about

God and His great compassion, and your relationship with Him. Gradually you begin to pull away all layers of psychological problems that separate you from Him. Through meditation, you will be able at last to look at yourself honestly, with all of your weaknesses, and feel no guilt or fear of God. You take your faults one by one and transmute them into soul virtues.

Patience and Determination

Impatience is another character flaw. We are all guilty of becoming impatient at times, especially when we are under great pressure. This is a normal, human reaction. But this trait can become a real stumbling block in getting along with others and in making spiritual progress.

An individual who does not know how to exercise patience will not remain steadfast in his pursuit of God. We need to have the divine determination expressed in Gurudeva's chant, "In the valley of sorrow, a thousand years or till tomorrow, but I'll wait to see You, You, You—just You."* That is patience: "It doesn't matter, Lord, whether You come to me now or a thousand years from now, I'll go on seeking You just the same." That patient, loving determination will draw God to you. But if you threaten to give up if He doesn't respond within what you consider a fair amount of time, you have already determined your failure. God will not be dictated to. He will come when He is ready. Above all, He will come when He determines that *we* are ready. If we put any time limit or other condition on our seeking, there is no hope of His response. Patience must be exercised.

* From *Cosmic Chants,* by Paramahansa Yogananda.

Gurudeva helped us to acquire patience by making us exercise it. Once he left me and another devotee waiting for several hours on the Golden Gate Bridge in San Francisco. When we became too weary to stand up any longer, we decided we didn't care what people thought, and sat down on the bridge curb. The wind became bitterly cold before Master and the driver returned in the car to pick us up. The thought occurred to me that I was turning blue and might be freezing to death! But I did not allow myself to complain or show irritation. On another occasion, Master took a small group, including my brother Dick Wright and me, to the Chicago World Fair in 1933.* He went off with my brother and told me to wait. It was four hours before they came back! He had said, "Don't wander off," so I saw nothing of the World Fair except the building in which I was waiting, which happened to be the Ford Motors Building—not very interesting to me!

One could become critical of such training, and say that it was unreasonable. I think most people would have become impatient and angry. Anyone who had such an attitude and lack of spiritual understanding did not remain long around Guruji. What was important to our Guru was that we develop the qualities needed to find God, not that we be always comfortable or that our lesser desires be satisfied. I am profoundly grateful for all of Gurudeva's discipline and molding of my character; without it I would not know the inner fulfillment, strength, love, and joy that bless my life now.

* Paramahansaji had gone to Chicago primarily to address the World Fellowship of Faiths on September 10, 1933, during the time the World Fair was in progress.

Hatred and Resentment Corrode Your Inner Life

Hatred is a dangerously corrosive character trait. It is impossible to feel attunement with God if there is hatred in the heart. Hatred is a tremendously powerful force; only one is greater, the power of love. When the heart is attuned to hate, that negative emotion gnaws at the very vitals of the spiritual life. It is one of the greatest tests of human nature.

Jesus could have reacted with intense hatred when his body was being so cruelly destroyed by his enemies. But he did not. He exercised the large-heartedness, compassion, and divine love that are of the soul, the real nature of every being.

If there is hatred in your heart toward anybody, no matter how justified you may feel, know that you will be tormented inwardly until you overcome it. No one whose heart is a channel for that malignant vibration can know God.

Resentment is a cousin of hatred. It is a natural human reaction when we feel we have been injured or wronged—such as when something we have said returns to us distorted, or when somebody says something about us that we believe is not factual. Like hatred, resentment also will destroy your spiritual life. The moment you allow yourself to become afflicted with resentment, in that instant you lose your awareness of God. Eliminate it from your consciousness. As often as it tries to enter, throw it out.

Overcoming Jealousy and Envy

Jealousy is a result of a deep sense of insecurity. When we feel attunement with God, we no longer find any cause for jealousy. We are content with what is our own, because we recognize that it comes from Him. We do not want anything anyone else has because we are fulfilled; we do not need anything more. Jealousy is common among worldly minded beings, but it too cannot remain in the hearts of those who are seeking God. Master gave an illustration related to jealousy, one I never forgot. He said to some of the devotees, years ago, "Here is my hand, with my five fingers. This finger cannot take the place of that finger, and that one cannot take the place of the next. I need all of them to do my work. Each one of you has his rightful place in my heart, and in the love of God." And each one will find his rightful place within family or community if he gives the best of himself. So there is no justification for jealousy.

Closely akin to jealousy is envy. Guruji would sometimes deliberately give something to one disciple and ignore others. Those who understood Master knew that he did this to bring to the surface any tendency toward envy, so it could be recognized and removed.

I'll give you an example: Throughout the years Guruji used to give little gifts to us disciples at Christmastime, but he always gave the least to me. The first time, I wondered why. I thought, "Well, maybe he doesn't really like me as much as he does the other devotees." Then I became very much ashamed of that thought, realizing it was a disgrace to think that way. It is human—but I did not like to see that smallness in myself or anyone else. So I analyzed it. "Do you really care? You have never wanted material things. What you want is that he care for you, and he doesn't need to show that by giving you special Christmas gifts." Then and there I learned what it was to overcome envy. I have never since allowed myself to feel that emotion.

Master was absolutely intolerant of jealousy and envy; he would not permit such self-centeredness in disciples who wished to be close to him. He used to say: "Keep your eyes on your own plate, and do not be concerned with what is on anyone else's plate. You can have only what is your own, and that will surely come to you." That was a great lesson to me—that it really did not matter what Master's relationship was with any of the other disciples. What mattered was whether I was deepening my own relationship with God and my Guru.

Motivating Yourself to Seek God

We get out of life exactly what we put into it. Therefore, laziness is one of the negative qualities we must overcome if we are to succeed in our search for God, or in any other endeavor. Guruji has said, "I can forgive the physically lazy man, but not the mentally lazy man." There may be health reasons for physical laziness, but mental laziness means a lack of willingness or enthusiasm. There is no excuse for anyone on the spiritual path to have such a dull, uninterested mind that he will not make the effort to deeply seek God. If we do not perform our work, our meditation, and our other responsibilities with wholehearted enthusiasm, with divine motivation, we will never find God, nor the real happiness we are looking for; it can't be done. No one else can give us that spirit; we have to change our mental attitude.

As a young disciple in the early days of Master's work in America, I often analyzed my own motives, because I noticed that those who lived here halfheartedly, as though just to get by, were missing something. They were not changing for the better. They were not drawing closer to God. I realized, however, that it was not my responsibility at that time whether anyone else had come for God or not. I had come for God, and I resolved not to waste my time, to be selfish in this respect: I would remain by myself if the company of others did not inspire me. I kept my mind with God. That is the way I lived, and from that seclusion and steadfast enthusiasm came great understanding and strength.

Procrastination is a tenacious offshoot of laziness. The procrastinator says, "I will try hard tomorrow, but today let me be what I am." That can go on all the days of your life. One who keeps putting things off never achieves his goals. Do your very best now, today—and every today.

Overcome Negative Conditions by Positive Thinking

Negative thinking is a cancer on the soul. Master wrote, "Though my sea is dark and my stars are gone, still I see the path through Thy mercy."* Positive thinking is absolutely essential to success in any endeavor, and particularly so on the spiritual path.

In this world of relativity, there are two sides to everything. One side of a hand or a coin, for example, could not exist without the other. Similarly, there are two ways to look at every situation: positive and negative. Always be very sure that you look on the positive side. Never allow yourself to wallow in negation; for if you do, you will have no inner peace, and you will find it very difficult indeed to commune with God.

Sometimes people say, "I try to meditate and feel God, but it seems I am not getting anywhere." I ask them, "Do you really keep your mind filled with the di-

* From *Cosmic Chants*, by Paramahansa Yogananda.

vine power of positive thoughts?" The minds of negative people are always restless and discouraged. Master once said that positive thinking makes the difference between the ordinary man and the divine man. Certainly there are innumerable things wrong in this world. But we should not feel helpless. We must refuse to allow our minds to be dragged down by outer circumstances.

Where Do Negative and Vulgar Thoughts Come From?

The worst kinds of negative thoughts can sometimes arise from the subconscious mind. As an example, someone wrote to me recently: "Whenever I sit to meditate, vulgar, trashy thoughts pour into my mind. Why does this happen when I'm trying to meditate?" My response to that question is this: For the simple reason that you are not yet really meditating. For the first time in your life, perhaps many lives, you are learning to go within to know yourself. The mind is a repository of all past experiences, including negative thoughts, gossip, worldliness. If there is a preponderance of these unspiritual impressions, naturally, when you first look within, this is what you see.

The consciousness of the beginner at meditation is like a glass of muddy water. But as you discipline yourself to still your mind, gradually the mud of dark thoughts begins to settle or vanish, and the clear water of divine perception is revealed. The nature of water is clean and pure. It only appears dirty when mud has been mingled with it. The nature of man's consciousness is also pure; but negative thinking, trashy thoughts, gossip, jealousy, envy, hatred, all the negative qualities we have noted, obscure its purity. When you learn to still the mind in meditation, you will find that the waters of your consciousness again become purified.

Concentrate on Perfecting Your Relationship With God

It is good to review spiritual guidelines. Master used to call us together on occasion to speak on those qualities that are essential to spiritual success. At the foundation of these requisites is our duty to concentrate on perfecting our relationship with God, our love for God. We will not be able to do so, we will have no time to think of Him, if our minds are filled with negation, and busy catering to any of these other psychological liabilities. Tell the Lord, over and over again, "I have come into this world to change myself. Help me. Give to me whatever discipline You know I need. All I know is that I love You, I want You. I want to perfect myself so that I can find You."

We cannot live without loving something. Let that something be God—not our self, not our passions and habits, not our desires, but God. Direct all your concentration and yearning toward Him. Even if at times the body and mind and ego try to drag you down, do not be dismayed. Go on calling to Him silently: "Give me love for Thee. Reveal Thyself, reveal Thyself."

Pray for that intimate relationship with God in which you know that He is real and that He does respond to you. It will transform your life. Master said to me many years ago: "Some day, Faye,* your life will be so different, your consciousness will be so different, you will not recognize yourself as you are now. It will be like another birth for you." That is what happens. You know only one thing, that like the Apostles of old, you have one wish: "I will lay down my life for You, Lord." There is such joy in it. It is not a tiresome, tedious task. It is a joy to be used by God in whatever

* Daya Mata's given name.

way He wants. You only wish that you had a thousand million voices to speak His name, and that you had a thousand million hearts to express and to receive His love.

Never cease to keep on trying to do better, to spiritualize your life in every way. Remember, the only difference between a saint and a sinner is that the saint never gave up trying.

Humility: Perpetual Quietness of Heart

Compilation of two talks at Self-Realization Fellowship International Headquarters

Someone here has written to me, "In a *satsanga,* please speak to us about the desire to be known. In what ways does this wish interfere with spiritual progress? How does one achieve a healthy balance between natural self-confidence and true humility?"

The desire to be known is in every human heart. It is part of our basic nature, in this sense: As God is eternal and infinite, so man's soul or *atman,* made in God's image, has those same divine qualities—and it is ever conscious of its everlastingness and of its oneness with all things. So it is understandable that this inherent immortality and omnipresence expresses itself as an urge to have a place in history—to be remembered and appreciated not just within one's little circle of acquaintances, but universally. The problem is that most people erroneously look for satisfaction in worldly recognition.

Human fame is shortlasting and leaves us unsatisfied; the renown of even the greatest artists or writers is temporary. Even if it persists after their death, they won't remember in their next incarnation that that acclaim once belonged to them. The only way man can feel the fulfillment of an extension of his being is through realization of himself as an immortal soul, one with God.

Analyze the craving for fame. You want to be appreciated, you want the security of knowing you have the approval and esteem of others. The highest way to satisfy this yearning is to erase from your mind the egoistic desire for human acclaim, which is notoriously fickle, and seek recognition from Him whose blessing is eternal. When you commune with the Divine, the desire to be cherished is satisfied completely and everlastingly.

The Meaning of Humility

Even the desire for spiritual attainment should be put in its proper perspective. To seek the stature of becoming a saint because one craves the adulation of others is a false notion. Gurudeva Paramahansa Yogananda often cautioned that many high-souled beings fall as a result of such entrapment by the ego. To want sainthood because that is the state in which one humbly loves God and communes with Him is the right attitude.

Humility is not expressed by someone's saying, "I am a humble being." The very fact that he says, "I am humble" means he is not. It is a contradiction, because he thinks much of himself to say that. To think you recognize some virtue within yourself, and then tell the world about it, is not humility. He who is truly humble does not speak of it—he is not even aware of possessing this great virtue.

Pray to God for humility. Ask Him in your meditations to show you what true humility is. Without this basic quality one can go very far on the spiritual path and then suddenly be plunged into the depths of delusion. The first thing Master looked for in those who came to live in the ashram was whether they had the right motive. When anyone thought his place in life was to become a great teacher, a savior of mankind, and expressed that conviction to Master, he would just smile and say nothing. No one with a sense of self-importance can become truly great.

One of the ways Guruji fostered humility in his disciples was that any time he saw someone inclined to want to take over, to want to put himself or herself forward, or to demand attention from him, he immediately began outwardly to ignore that individual, or to keep that person at a distance. He knew it would not be good for that soul if he responded to the conscious or unconscious self-centered demand: "Take notice of me! Give me your time! Give me your attention!" From such training the receptive devotee learned to step back, to be content in being the least in the group.

The way to practice humility is to relate everything to God: "Lord, Thou art the Doer, not I." Whenever you are praised, remind yourself that all of your abilities have been borrowed from Him, the Source of all power. In truth, there is only One who empowers our brains, throbs in our hearts, works through our limbs—and that is God. How can we accept praise? Of ourselves we can accomplish nothing. Awareness of our total human insufficiency should not produce in us an inferiority complex; rather, it teaches us a joyous dependency on the love of our Creator. The more we rely on God, the more we understand what true humility is, and the more His strength and power and confidence fill our lives.

True humility is not weakness. It is to be always resting in the thought of God, to live in the consciousness: "Lord, let not my will be done, but only Thine." If we are sincere in affirming this, we are able to set aside instantly our personal desires and the frustration of their nonfulfillment, remaining content in the greater desire to do whatever God wants of us. That is true humility: to put God and God alone uppermost in our lives.

Strength to Withstand Criticism

The moment we feel we have to defend ourselves when we are criticized, we are practicing egotism. Certainly, when principles are offended, we have a duty to make a stand; but there is no need to retaliate against personal criticism. Look within to see if there is something that needs correcting, but don't become upset. I often remind myself: I am what I am before God and Guru, no more and no less. I make no claims to being perfect or to possessing great talents or abilities; my endeavor in this life is to perfect one thing—my love for my God.

When we strive for that humility which puts God ahead of our personal desires and ambitions, we develop tremendous inner strength. We become able not only to withstand criticism but to bear any cross in life.

"A Blessed Home in Myself"

For years I have had this inspiring quotation on my desk:

> Humility is perpetual quietness of heart. It is to have no trouble. It is never to be fretted, or vexed, or irritated, or sore, or disappointed.
>
> It is to expect nothing, to wonder at nothing that is done to me, to feel nothing done against me. It is to be at rest when nobody praises me, and when I am blamed and despised.

> It is to have a blessed home in myself, where I can go in and shut the door, and kneel to my Father in secret, and be at peace as in a deep sea of calmness, when all around and above is troubled.*

Such security and peace can be attained by keeping the mind fixed in God. After years of practicing this, it happens that even in times of greatest difficulties or pressure, by taking my mind within for just an instant I feel such joy, such devotion.

What a vast world of love and joy is within the soul! We do not have to acquire it; it is already ours. We have only to remove the dark curtain of ego, to tear away the covering of egotistical thoughts and behavior that hides the divine brilliance of the soul. When we entertain any form of selfishness or self-centeredness, we cannot know that sublime state; we are held prisoners in the confining consciousness of "I, me, and mine." The escape from that prison is through the door to the Divine.

Be drunk with love for God, and the little self will be lost in Him; then He will use you in ways more magnificent than you ever dreamed possible. God Himself works through the humble, receptive devotee.

Receptivity means to be always inwardly surrendered to God: "My Lord, Thou art my life; do with me as You will. Place me in a high position or use me just as fertilizer for Your work. It matters not to me. I want to so perfect my love for You, my Lord, that in seeking Your guidance I will never try to dictate how You should use me. All I know is that I love You."

That is the attitude of a humble being, one who sincerely wants to know God. He strives to do every-

* Canon T. T. Carter (1809–1901).

thing with the greatest enthusiasm, so that in carrying out difficult menial tasks he is as much absorbed in divine love as when he is speaking before appreciative multitudes. When we truly love God, there is no other craving. We do not care for fame or for acclaim from anyone, because we have found Joy within ourselves.

The Guru: Guide to Spiritual Freedom

From a talk given in Ranchi, India

The devotees of Paramahansaji have asked me to record the various experiences that have been mine through the twenty-one years I was blessed to be with Gurudeva. So many, many remembrances of those years are coming to my mind. What a divine relationship! founded upon reverence, respect, justice, and above all, unconditional love. To me, the relationship between guru and disciple is the sweetest and most pure that can exist between souls. A true guru, one who has fully realized his Self, has no thought of the ego-self. He has no desire to draw the adoration of others. Whatever love the devotee gives to him, he lays at the feet of the Divine Beloved. Guruji often used to say to us: "The guru's sole purpose is to bring the disciple to God; God is the true Guru."

The Purpose of a Guru

For the average person to find God, the help of the guru is essential. Some will argue, "Yes, but there have been many who have found Him without a guru." It may seem so, but those souls came to this world already highly advanced. In order to reach such a lofty state, they would have to have had a guide in previous lives. If someone wants to be a doctor or a scientist, he cannot gain adequate knowledge thereof simply by reading books or hearing lectures. He must have direct experience. A would-be doctor must go through intensive training and internship, guided by someone who has already succeeded on that path and can show him the way. Only then will he know how to care for others' physical bodies.

Similarly, you cannot know the Divine by reading books about Him, or by hearing sermons and discourses about truth or the Infinite. You have to have someone competent to guide you. We become so accustomed to our own habits and behavior that we cannot see our flaws. Only when someone with love unconditional offers to help us and says, "My child, correct this," do we receive the clarity of understanding and the incentive to really change our lives.

The guru is like a crystal-clear mirror, and everyone who stands before that mirror beholds himself exactly as he is. When the disciple sees himself thus revealed, he then knows what he must do to remove all the imperfections that have covered his flawless soul.

The guru's duty is to probe deep within the consciousness of the disciple and point out all "tender spots" of weaknesses, so to speak. I'll give you an example. As a child, I used to be very sensitive, and extremely shy. So, one day, shortly after I had come to the ashram, Guruji was sitting with a group of the devotees. He was toying with a piece of newspaper, and was laughing and chatting with the disciples sitting around him. But I didn't join in; I stayed in the background. I saw he was making a hat—they call it a "dunce cap" in America—a three-pointed cap. I said to myself, "What is he going to do with it? He's got something in mind."

Reason said to me, "It's obvious that he is not going to put that dunce cap on any of these older disciples. He has it in mind to place it on the head of his youngest one; that means Daya Ma. Now I have just finished taking my vows, and I promised unconditional obedience to my Guru; but that does not mean I have given him the freedom to make fun of me before all of his disciples." That was my line of reasoning. I thought, "This is where I draw the line."

When he finished making this paper cap, he looked around at all the disciples. I should have been in the same lighthearted mood that they were. But I was holding on to sensitivity. As he motioned to me, saying, "Come here," I shook my head, "No." I thought perhaps he would just pass me by and call one of the other devotees.

I found through the years that Guruji did not do one thing without a deep-seated reason behind it; such was his divine understanding. So he said again, "Come."

"No."

Finally, once more, but he was losing his smile: "Come!"

I became more determined. The more he coaxed, the more determined I was. "No, Guruji, not this."

Finally, his smile evaporated, and he became very quiet. I can see him now, sitting there, his eyes withdrawn and stern. Whenever he looked that way, the disciples would begin to wonder, "What is he thinking; something is coming."

He said to the devotees, "All right, you go now." I quickly got up to go, too, because I thought, "Now is the time to get away."

He said, "No, you stay." Then I knew I was in for it; but I was still quite determined.

"Do you think that was the right way to behave before all of these people?" he said to me.

I was still angry. "Master, is it right"—see, I was trying to match wits with him—"for the guru to make fun of a disciple before all of the other disciples?"

He answered, "To be bound by the ego like this will not take one to God."

I was still quite fiery, and said, "Master, I cannot accept the notion that one should be scolded and ridiculed before others."

By this time, Guruji's words were becoming stronger. "All right, until you understand what I am trying to teach you, go stand in the corner."

I can still see myself, a young seventeen-year-old devotee, being told to go stand in the corner. That had never happened to me before.

Only a few weeks earlier Guruji had said to me: "When I went to my Guru, he told me, 'Learn to behave': and so I say the same thing to you. The way to know the Infinite is to learn to behave." At the time I thought: "I don't have much of a temper, and I get along well with people. I don't think there'll be any problem in my learning to behave. This will be simple." But it is much deeper than one thinks!

"Go stand in the corner." I went.

"This is easy," I thought, "I can obey that."

"Turn your back and face the wall." I did that. "Now, stand on one foot."

By then, I was shocked at this first taste of discipline; and still a little fiery. You know the natural reaction of human beings. When we have trouble with one another, first we're fiery. Then, as a rule, we move from the emotion of anger to the emotion of self-pity; we dissolve into tears. Notice this the next time you get angry:

first, anger; then tears, which are nothing but self-pity unless they're shed for mankind, for another human being, or for God.

And so I dissolved into tears, and began to feel sorry for myself: "I have never seen him make fun of others or scold any of the other disciples in front of me. Why does he pick on me before the rest of them?" This was my reasoning: "Poor Daya Ma, you are being mistreated."

But the longer I stood there by the wall, the clearer my understanding became. I thought, "Now let me ask myself: Why did I come here?" If you always honestly question yourself and your motives, it will bring you back to the basics of right behavior. Most of our problems in life are caused by the fact that we keep missing the point. Patanjali refers to this pitfall. We start toward some goal—whether spiritual or material—but the first thing we find is that somewhere along the way we have missed the point.

So there I stood, reasoning with myself. "Why have I come here? It's obvious; I came because I wanted God." I asked myself, "Are you going to get what you came for if you behave like this? Do you really care what people think of you? If you do, you'd better go back to the world. This behavior doesn't belong here."

The moment I understood this truth, I said, "I am wrong." I turned and went to the Master. "Forgive me. Put the cap on my head."

"It isn't necessary now," he said. "I wanted you to learn, to understand. Be absolutely untouched by what someone says or thinks of you. If the whole world is pleased with you, but God and Guru are displeased, you have failed in life. But if the whole world turns against you—criticizes and blames you—but you have won the praise, the approval, of God and Guru, know you have succeeded in this world." That is truth! Look at the world; study it. The very people that lift up a man and adore him become disenchanted in the next instant and cast him down.

Then I knew what Guruji was trying to teach me. He knew that I was very sensitive as a little girl, and saw it as something Daya Ma must overcome. From that time on, through the years, he freely scolded me before everyone. I admit there were times when I went to my room and shed tears. But I didn't let him know it, because I knew he was right. Every time Guruji disciplined me in all those twenty-one years I was with him, I never could find fault with his judgment. I always knew he was right: I must correct *myself.* That is the lesson I learned that day.

Be a Pillar of Strength That Others Can Lean On

One time, when I was feeling sad that I had disappointed him, I said, "Master, am I really so much worse than the other disciples that you must scold me so much?"

He said, "Not at all. I give you this kind of discipline because you must become like steel inside." Oh! How those words ring in my ears: "You must be like steel inside."

"But Master," I said, "I don't like hard, callous people."

Guruji said, "Don't misunderstand me. I did not say 'hard.' You must become like steel, bendable but unbreakable, so strong that nothing can hurt you."

Then I understood that to be like steel is to not let life crush you; but to be gentle and compassionate, and a pillar of strength that others can lean on, if necessary.

In other words, it was basically what he said to me another time: "So love God inwardly that nothing will ever be able to touch you outwardly." If you take such a thought and meditate on it, what strength it gives you!

In the later years, he scolded me one day before a large group of disciples in the ashram. It didn't faze me, because I had learned never to let my feelings interfere with truth. I said, "He is right; I have done that. I must correct myself." That is the right way to take discipline.

When I had left the room, he sweetly turned to the other disciples and said, "You see how she behaves? It's been like that for years. No matter how I speak to her, she remains always calm and receptive inside. You all should learn from her." When I was told this, many years later, tears filled my eyes. I said, "That was Guru's blessing. I am eternally grateful for the strength and understanding he gave me."

The guru is a spiritual doctor. Master used to say, "The duty of the guru is to see and heal the psychological sores deep within the consciousness of the devotee." The ordinary doctor removes disease from the body through surgery or medication; the divine doctor removes spiritual and psychological disease through his wisdom and discipline. If Guruji had not given Daya Ma strength through his wise discipline, how on earth would she be able to carry on today? Know for certain, my beloved ones, when you have the responsibility of leading, your head is a little bit above the crowd, so to speak, and you become the easiest target for others. If Guruji had permitted me to cater to my sensitivity, I would be lost today. But through his wise and wonderful discipline I learned to look always to please my beloved God. That is where my gaze is fixed. If I can please man in pleasing God, I am happy. If I cannot, I will not sacrifice pleasing my Beloved in order to win the praise or the approval of mankind.

Master once said to us: "I have given you all such training that you will never, never have to bow down to any individual." He meant: No one will ever be able to "buy" you by flattery or anything else. And that's the way we live and serve Guruji's work. As I say to devotees all the time, if you would win Daya Ma's love, love my God. That intoxicates me. When I see devotees who love my Beloved, I am drunk with joy. Nothing else can reach Daya Ma's heart, in that sense—nothing personal. I love those who love my Beloved; I love those who are seeking my Beloved. I love those who are striving on the path. I don't care what their weaknesses are—a thousand million weaknesses can be there. That is not important to me, for I know that if they are sincere in their efforts to love God and follow the Guru's guidance, they will surely overcome those impediments and find the perfect freedom that is our birthright as souls.

Paramahansa Yogananda—As I Knew Him

Compilation from writings and from talks given in India and America

As the years roll by, the mind gathers new experiences while time generally dims the memory of those long past. But events that touch the soul never fade; they become an ever-living, vibrant part of our being. Such was my meeting with my guru, Paramahansa Yogananda.

I was a young girl of seventeen, and life seemed to me one long empty corridor leading nowhere. An unceasing prayer to God revolved within my consciousness for Him to guide my steps to some purposeful existence in which I could seek and serve Him.

The answer to that yearning came in an instantaneous realization when in 1931 I entered the large, crowded auditorium in Salt Lake City and saw Paramahansaji standing on the platform, speaking of God with an authority I had never before witnessed. I became absolutely transfixed—my breath, thoughts, time, seemed suspended. A loving, grateful recognition of the blessing pouring over my being brought with it an awareness of a deep conviction rising from within me: "This man loves God as I have always longed to love Him. He *knows* God. Him I shall follow."

Upholding the Ideals of Honor and Integrity

I had a preconceived ideal of what a spiritual teacher ought to be. You might say I had in my mind's eye fashioned a pedestal on which to enthrone such a person. In reverence I mentally placed my Guru there; and never in those many years I was privileged to be in his presence did he once, in character or deed, step down from that lofty height.

Although in our era integrity, honor, and idealism have seemingly vanished under a tidal wave of self-seeking, Gurudeva lived uncompromisingly by the eternal spiritual values, and kept them ever before the disciples' vision. I am reminded of a time in 1931 when funds were urgently needed. During this period, the financial resources were so meager that the Guru and disciples subsisted on thin soup and bread, or totally fasted. The mortgage was due on the Mt. Washington property, our Mother Center. Paramahansaji went to the home of the mortgage holder to ask her for an extension of time to meet the payment. This understanding woman graciously extended the deadline. Even so, it seemed impossible to gather the necessary funds in time.

Then one day a business promoter came to Gurudeva's classes and became interested in his teachings. The man saw in the teachings not only their spiritual value, but a lucrative potential as well. "Let me take charge of promoting your society, and within a year I will put you on the map. You will have tens of thousands of students and will be rolling in dollars," he promised Paramahansaji.

He outlined his plan for commercializing the sacred teachings. Gurudeva listened politely. It would indeed mean the end of his financial worries and would forestall the hardships he knew still faced him. But without a moment's hesitation he thanked the man and replied, "Never! I will never use religion as a business. I will never compromise this work or my ideals for a few paltry dollars, no matter what the need!"

Two months later, while teaching in Kansas City, Missouri, he met his exalted disciple of many former lives, Rajarsi Janakananda, who was destined to play an important role in Self-Realization Fellowship. This great soul, embracing the Guru as his own divine teacher, and the Guru's teachings as his everyday way of life, gave the funds with which to pay off the entire mortgage. Great was the rejoicing when, down by the Temple of Leaves at Mt. Washington, a bonfire was made and the mortgage thrown into the flames. Being very practical-minded, Gurudeva took the opportunity to roast potatoes among the embers. The devotees gathered around the bonfire with the Guru and enjoyed the potatoes while the mortgage continued to roast—until well done!

Assurance of the Divine Mother's Presence

There are other incidents that stand out in my memory, and other aspects of Guruji's divine strength. Feeling the weight of a growing organization with many disciples to feed, house, and support, and having a desire to be free of distractions from his single-hearted longing for unbroken communion with God, he fled to the desert in Arizona. There he remained in solitude, meditating and praying to his beloved Divine Mother for freedom from the burdens and distracting duties of organizational responsibilities. One night while he was meditating—"as though my heart would burst with such longing for Her response," he said—She appeared to him and spoke these soothing words:

> Dance of life or dance of death,
> Know that these come from Me, and rejoice.
> What more dost thou want, than that thou hast
> Me?

Joyously overcome with this assurance that his adored Divine Mother was ever with him, in the midst of life or death, he returned with peace and all-surrendering love in his heart to take up again the mission She had laid upon his shoulders.

Gurudeva had great spiritual powers, a natural manifestation in one who has God-realization. Paramahansaji explained such powers as simply the workings of higher laws. In the early days of his ministry he sometimes publicly demonstrated those laws to encourage the faith of a skeptical society. I was one of the many he healed instantaneously.

Gurudeva was to say in later years, "If I were to display the powers God has given me, I could draw thousands. But the path to God is not a circus. I gave the powers back to God, and I never use them unless He tells me to. My mission is to awaken love for God in the soul of man. I prefer a soul to a crowd, and I love crowds of souls." Gurudeva withdrew from the masses and began to concentrate on qualitative rather than quantitative growth. He sought out in the crowds those "souls" who responded to the high ideals and spiritual goals of his teachings.

Service, Wisdom, and Divine Love

A newspaperman once asked me during an interview, "Would you say that Paramahansa Yogananda was a *bhakti, jnana,* or *karma yogi?"** I replied, "He was many-sided. It took one of such a nature, stature, and understanding to reach the hearts and minds of the American people. It enabled him to bridge the gap between life in India and life in America; his teachings express a universal quality, as applicable in the West as in the East."

As a *karma yogi,* Paramahansaji worked for God and for the upliftment of mankind with a dedication rare in this world. We never saw him spare himself when he had an opportunity to serve or help another. He cried for those who suffered, and worked tirelessly to eradicate the root-cause of all suffering—ignorance.

As a *jnani,* his wisdom flowed forth in volumes through his writings, lectures, and personal counsel. His *Autobiography of a Yogi* has been acknowledged as an authoritative textbook on Yoga, and is used for both teaching and study in various courses in many colleges and universities. This is not to say that Paramahansaji was merely an intellectual. To him, intellectualism without realization was as worthless as a hive without honey. He stripped religion of its veils of dogma and theoretical analysis and revealed the heart of truth: those essential principles that give mankind not only an understanding of God, but the way to realize Him.

To his followers, Paramahansa Yogananda is known, above all, as a *premavatar,* incarnation of divine love, a supreme *bhakta.* Outstanding in his character was his overwhelming love for God, whom he reverenced as the Divine Mother. This, said Jesus, is the first commandment: "Thou shalt love the Lord thy God with all thy

* *Bhakti yoga, jnana yoga,* and *karma yoga* are three of the main paths to God, emphasizing, respectively, devotion, discriminative wisdom, and selfless service.

heart, and with all thy soul, and with all thy mind." Paramahansaji demonstrated such love, whether he was speaking before multitudes, as witnessed in his early days in America; or administering to the worldwide needs of his growing Self-Realization Fellowship/ Yogoda Satsanga Society; or guiding those who had come to him for spiritual training.

Paramahansaji was capable of great fire when spiritual discipline was called for, but always there was boundless compassion, and patience when patience was needed. Well do I recall his words to us when we became indignant over an attack by a few hostile critics of his work: "Never speak an unkind word against other teachers and societies. Never try to appear tall by chopping off the heads of others. There is enough room in this world for all, and we should respond to unkindness and hatred with goodness and love."

He gave to the world a "Universal Prayer," whose theme was the very heart of his life: "Beloved God, may Thy love shine forever on the sanctuary of my devotion, and may I be able to awaken Thy love in all hearts."

"Only Love Can Take My Place"

Near the end of Gurudeva's life, he was preparing to receive the Indian ambassador, Dr. Binay R. Sen (who was to come the following morning to visit Guruji at our Self-Realization headquarters). Guruji called the disciples into the ashram kitchen and said, "Today we will prepare curries and Indian sweetmeats for the ambassador." We cooked all day long, and Guruji was in a state of great joy.

Late that evening, he called me to him and said, "Come, let us take a walk." The ashram is a large three-story building. As we walked down the third-floor hall, he paused in front of a picture of his guru, Swami Sri Yukteswarji. He gazed at that picture for a long time—eyes unblinking. And then very quietly he turned to me and said: "Do you realize that it is just a matter of hours and I will be gone from this earth?" Tears flooded my eyes. Intuitively, I knew that what he said was to come to pass. A short time earlier, when he spoke to me of leaving his body, I had cried to him, "Master, you are the diamond in the ring of our hearts, and of your society. How can we carry on without you?" With such sweet love and compassion, his eyes like soft pools of divine bliss, he answered: "When I am gone, only love can take my place. Be so drunk with the love of God that you will know nothing but God; and give that love to all."

On the final day, he was to speak at a banquet for the ambassador in downtown Los Angeles. We who served him arose in the early dawn and went to his door to see if we could do anything for him. As we entered, he was sitting very quietly in the chair in which he frequently meditated and was often in ecstasy. When he didn't want us to talk, he would put his finger to his lips, meaning, "I am in silence." The moment he did that, I saw the withdrawal of his soul, that he was gradually severing each of the hidden ties that bind the soul to the body. Sorrow filled my heart, and yet strength too, because I knew that no matter what happened, through my devotion to him, my Guru would never leave my heart.

All day long he remained in that interiorized state. Toward evening, we went with him to the large hotel where the banquet was to be held. Arriving early, Guruji waited in a little room upstairs, quietly meditat-

Paramahansa Yogananda

"With such sweet love and compassion, his eyes like soft pools of divine bliss, he answered: 'When I am gone, only love can take my place. Be so drunk with the love of God that you will know nothing but God; and give that love to all.'"

At the feet of her guru, Paramahansa Yogananda; SRF International Headquarters, New Year's Day, 1937. Daya Mataji is seated in the middle, in a light-colored sari. The large group of disciples and students had gathered to welcome Paramahansaji home after his seventeen-month trip to Europe and India.

ing. We disciples sat around him on the floor. After some time, he gazed at each of us in turn. I remember thinking, as he looked at me, "My beloved Guru is giving me a farewell *darshan.*"* Then he went down to the banquet hall.

There was a large audience, which included city, state, and Government of India officials. I was sitting some distance from the speakers' table, but my mind and gaze never left the blessed Guru's face. Finally, the time came for him to speak. Gurudeva was the last to do so before Ambassador Sen was to address the gathering. As Guruji rose from his chair, my heart skipped a beat and I thought, "Oh, this is that moment!"

When he began speaking, with such love for God, the whole audience was like one person; no one stirred. They were transfixed by the tremendous force of love that he was pouring from his heart upon all of them. Many lives were changed that night—including some who later entered the ashram as monastics and many others who became members of the society—because of that divine experience. His last words were of the India he loved so much: "Where Ganges, woods, Himalayan caves, and men dream God—I am hallowed; my body touched that sod."†

As he uttered these words, he lifted his eyes to the *Kutastha* center, and his body slumped to the floor. In an instant—our feet seemed not to touch the ground—two of us disciples were by his side.‡ Thinking that he

* "Holy sight," as of one's guru; i.e., the blessing bestowed by the sight of a God-realized being.

† The final lines of "My India." This inspired poem by Paramahansaji appears in *Songs of the Soul* (published by Self-Realization Fellowship).

‡ Sri Daya Mata and Ananda Mata. A faithful disciple of Para-

might have gone into *samadhi,* we softly chanted *Aum* in his right ear. (Over the years he had told us that when he went into ecstasy, if after some time his consciousness did not return we could bring him out of that state by chanting *Aum* in his right ear.) As I was chanting, a miraculous experience took place. I do not know how to describe it to you, but as I knelt over my blessed Guru, I could see that his soul was leaving the body; and then a tremendous force entered my being. I say "tremendous" because it was an overwhelming blissful force of love, peace, and understanding. I remember thinking, "What is this?" My consciousness was lifted up in such a way that I could feel no sorrow, I could shed no tears; and it has been so from that day to this, because I know beyond any doubt that he is truly with me.

Death Had No Claim on Him

Someone has asked me, "Has our Guru appeared to you since he left his body?" Yes, he has. I will speak more of this as I continue my story. Thousands came to see Guruji's mortal form for the last time. His skin was golden, as though bathed in a golden light; and the sweetest, most benign smile was on his lips, like a benediction on everyone. For twenty-one days after Guruji left his body, that form remained in a state of perfect preservation. There was not the slightest sign of decay. And even in the very matter-of-fact western hemisphere, the newspapers were emblazoned with headlines and reports on this miraculous event. The morti-

---

mahansa Yogananda since 1931, and sister of Daya Mata, Ananda Mata entered the ashram in 1933 at the age of 17. She was an officer and member of the Board of Directors of SRF/YSS until her passing in 2005. *(Publisher's Note)* cians who observed his body stated that "the case of Paramahansa Yogananda is unique in our experience."

Not long after that the full responsibility for leadership of Gurudeva's work fell on my shoulders.*

When a great teacher leaves this world, it often happens that some different opinions arise as to how the mission begun by the guru should be guided. Questions arose during discussion of the work on the morning after I became the leader. Should the guidance of the work be in the hands of the householders or monastics? Guruji had told us it was to be with single-hearted renunciants like himself; but that directive was being challenged by some of the members. True, Guruji's love for all devotees was the same. I also felt no distinction; why be bound by externals? A devotee is a devotee because he loves God, not because he wears an ocher cloth. But my mind was troubled.

That night, I sought Guruji's answer by meditating deeply and praying to him. It was very late and I was still meditating when suddenly I saw my body get up from the bed, walk down the hall, and enter Gurudeva's room. As I did so, out of the corner of my eye I saw his *chuddar* (shawl), fluttering as though in a slight breeze. I turned, and there stood my Guru! With what joy I ran to him and knelt to take the dust of his feet, holding them close to me.† "Master, Master," I cried, "you are not dead—you are not gone! Death has no claim on you." How sweetly then he reached down and

* Rajarsi Janakananda, who succeeded Paramahansa Yogananda, served as President of Self-Realization Fellowship/Yogoda Satsanga Society of India from 1952–1955.

† Such is India's regard for her saints, that even the dust of the feet of a holy personage is considered sanctified and filled with blessing for the one who touches it.

touched me on the forehead. As he did so, in that instant I knew the answer I must give at the meeting the next morning. Guruji blessed me, and I saw myself once again sitting upon my bed.

The next morning, I met with the directors of the society, and gave the answer Guruji had conveyed to me; and his work has been united and growing and growing and growing, ever since. Such is the blessing of God.

The Ever Living Guru

Paramahansa Yogananda will always be the Guru and supreme spiritual head of Self-Realization Fellowship/Yogoda Satsanga Society of India. All of us who carry on the work begun by him serve humbly as his disciples. Our only wish is to turn the attention and the devotion of all who come to this path toward God, and toward our divine Guru, who can introduce them to God. Gurudeva was always quick to remind us that in the ultimate sense, it is God alone who is the Guru. Gurudeva's one wish, as an instrument of God, is to draw us to the Divine Source from which we can receive, as from none else, what our souls seek. To be loyal to Guru is to be loyal to God. To serve the Guru and his work is to serve God, because it is God to whom we give our first allegiance. Guru is the divinely appointed spiritual channel through whose blessings and inspired teachings we find our way back to God.

I used to think that it would be very hard for devotees to understand the guru-disciple relationship after the Master had gone from this earth plane. I never voiced this doubt to Guruji; but he often answered our unspoken thoughts. I was sitting at his feet one evening, when he said to me: "To those who think me near,

I will be near. This body is nothing. If you are attached to this physical form, you will not be able to find me in my infinite form. But if you look beyond this body and see me as I truly am, then you will know that I am always with you."

I did not fully comprehend the truth of that statement until some time later. One evening, while I was meditating, the thought came to me: Consider all of the disciples who gathered around Jesus Christ during the few years of his ministry on earth. Some thought much of him; some served him selflessly. But how many out of the crowds really understood and followed him all the way? During his great trial, and at the moment of his passing, how many stood beside him and supported him? Many who knew Jesus, and had the opportunity to follow him, forsook him during his lifetime. And yet, twelve hundred years after Jesus Christ had left this earth, there came a humble, sweet, simple devotee who, through his beautiful life and perfect attunement and communion with Christ, exemplified everything that Jesus had taught, and thereby found God. That humble little man was St. Francis of Assisi, whom Guruji loved so much. I realized that the same spiritual law by which St. Francis could be perfectly in tune with his guru, who had appeared on earth centuries before him, still works for us today.

A true God-appointed guru is ever living. He knows his own and helps them whether or not he is incarnate on the same plane as the disciple. All of those who strive to keep themselves in tune with Gurudeva through devotion and deep guru-given meditation will feel the assurance of his guidance, his blessings, as much today, or any time in the future, as when he was with us in physical form. This should be a great comfort to all who have come since Paramahansa Yogananda's passing, and who lament that they did not have the opportunity to know this blessed one during his earthly incarnation: you *can* know him when you sit silently in meditation. Go deeper and deeper with your devotion and prayer, and you will feel his hallowed presence. If we who have been left to carry on in his stead did not realize and experience this, we would be helpless to serve his work. It is because we feel his blessings and guidance, because we know he is as near today as when he was with us in the fleshly form, that we have the strength, determination, enthusiasm, devotion, and conviction to do our part in spreading the message of Self-Realization Fellowship.

Paramahansaji's life and work have already done much to influence the course of history, and I am convinced that this is only the beginning of that influence. He joins the conclave of divine souls who lived on earth as incarnations of the light of Truth to illumine the pathways of mankind. The world must sooner or later turn toward that light, for it is not the will of God that man should perish by the hand of his own ignorance. There is a better tomorrow, just waiting for mankind to open its eyes and see the dawn. Paramahansa Yogananda, and others who have reflected the Divine Brilliance, are the light bearers of that new day.

Love Will Be the Savior of the World

Compilation from talks given in India and America

Paramahansa Yogananda's message, as he predicted, is spreading rapidly around the world, in every land. Thousands are following this path of Raja Yoga, and practicing Kriya. What is needed today, more so than for many centuries past, is for the law of love to be not only preached, but lived. The world teeters on the brink of destruction. This is no idle statement. Just one word from one leader in a powerful nation could precipitate disaster. Doesn't it shock you to realize that? One man has only to give the order, and his word destroys. Such is the power of hatred. There must be some in this world who will cry out against the ungodliness of animosity. The only way is by the positive giving of love. That is why this message of Self-Realization/Yogoda Satsanga is here today.

Everything is interdependent upon everything else; nothing stands alone. The very balance of the universe is affected by the thoughts of human beings. Unless and until people in all nations begin to think in terms of love and unity, there is little hope for peace in the world. Because of the evil in people's hearts and actions, we see many, many kinds of catastrophes. The counterbalance of good against evil is being shaken. To stabilize it, we must change ourselves. Love is what is needed.

The Need for Forgiveness

So many people are compelled by emotional reactions, going through life with their hearts filled with bitterness against others because of something they said or did. This is wrong. There should be forgiveness in our hearts.

Once when Guruji was meditating, he prayed: "Divine Mother, Jesus said that the number of times one should forgive another is seventy times seven.* But isn't this a little too much? When an offender repeatedly does the same thing, are we supposed to keep on forgiving?"

Divine Mother replied: "My child, I have been forgiving My children every day since the beginning of time. Can you not forgive seventy times seven?"

There is never a time when the Divine does not forgive us. For our human weaknesses God has much compassion. Frailties of the flesh are the result of the compulsions instilled in us by Nature. In the ultimate sense, therefore, they are not of our making. God created this mortal flesh and gave it the capacity to interact with its material surroundings; from this propensity arose the inclination to satisfy all of its desires and demands. When, in these pursuits, we transgress God's laws, we bring suffering on ourselves; and then God sorrows for us.

But no matter how wicked one's deeds, and how

* "Then came Peter to him, and said, Lord, how oft shall my brother sin against me, and I forgive him? till seven times? Jesus saith unto him, I say not unto thee, Until seven times: but, Until seventy times seven" (Matthew 18:21–22).

momentarily painful the consequences, there is no such thing as eternal punishment. How could there be when we are all made in God's image? How audacious of anyone to ascribe to God the cruelty of condemning His children to eternal damnation. The dogma that "You are a sinner, and if you don't change your ways, God will plunge you into hellfire and damnation," is not what Christ taught—though some may misinterpret his words in this way. The very idea casts a wrongdoer into such utter depression and sense of futility that he feels there is no hope for him. When Christ hung on the cross, he had the courage and love to show divine forgiveness: "Father, forgive them; for they know not what they do."*

Sin is a wrong concept: Human beings err through ignorance, as Jesus acknowledged. As an eight-year-old child, I rebelled at the idea of hellfire and damnation for sinners. This was not the God that I would seek. My concept was of a compassionate Deity who would look at each of His children—all of whom have made many kinds of mistakes—and say, "My child, let Me pick you up; let Me wipe away your tears;† let Me soothe your conscience and give you peace." That God I could follow. Isn't a mother like that? Could a parent be more loving and compassionate than God?

I'll tell you a pertinent story. Master was once talking to a man who had very dogmatic notions about truth. He said to Master, "Do you not believe in hellfire and damnation?"

Guruji said, "No, except that man creates a hades right in the here and now. He makes out of this world

* Luke 23:34.

† "And God shall wipe away all tears from their eyes" (Revelation 21:4).

and his own life a heaven or a hell, depending upon his behavior; and this is where we suffer."

The man persisted with his dogmatic arguments. Guruji was very intuitive; he changed the subject, and then after a while he said, "Isn't it true that you have a son who is causing you great suffering because he drinks and carries on in a very bad way?"

The man's jaw dropped. "How did you know? Yes, this has been the greatest sorrow of my life."

"Then may I make a suggestion to you?"

"Yes." The man was eager for a solution.

"All right, take your son out some day for a walk in the hills, and have two trusted friends waiting there for you. When you pass by, have those friends pounce upon your son and bind him. Then let them build a fire; and when it is good and hot, throw your son into the flames!"

The astounded man looked at Master. "Are you mad, to make such a suggestion to me? This is outrageous!" Guruji had made his point.

"Exactly so! Yet you ascribe such behavior to God, who created you and instilled in you that love for your child. How dare you attribute to Him feelings so callous and punitive that He would take all of His children who have done wrong and cast them into eternal flames?"

That is how Master shook dogma with truth. How dare we, indeed, ascribe to God brutal behavior that even we wouldn't dream of? He is a God of compassion; a God of infinite love.

How Love Changes Others

For the endless forbearance shown to us by that Compassionate One, can we not love and forgive one another the mistakes we make? The moment we do, the heart becomes free; never allow it to remain bound by hard feelings toward anyone—I don't care who it is or what he has done. We should ask ourselves: "With whom have I to do? Only God—to please Him. Can I not show unconditional love to those souls whom He sends to me, His children? Can I not try to help them through my example, through my love?" I know it works. I have seen it work.

Some years ago, shortly after becoming president, I spoke at a function at one of our Self-Realization Fellowship temples. During the banquet that preceded my talk, a woman I had never seen before was seated near me. She was not a Self-Realization member, but had decided it was her duty to be the critic of our society and its administration.

All evening my mind had been absorbed in the joyous love of Divine Mother. Suddenly, though, this person caught my eye. It was an absolute shock to see what was in her gaze. I realized, "This person hates me!" For a moment my mind was shaken. But I turned within and asked myself: "Of what value is my love for God if it is so shallow that my mind can be dragged down by the unkindness of others? Can I not practice what I have preached? Of course I can!" In that instant the blissful consciousness of God's presence returned.

As the meal progressed, this woman busied herself in making disparaging remarks about me to those around her, loud enough to be sure I could hear her. As Gurudeva taught us to do, I began sending to her waves of love from my heart.

Because I had not allowed my mind to be affected, when the time came for me to speak, the words flowed from the inspiration that was in my soul. Afterward, as the members of the audience gathered around to greet me, this woman suddenly burst forward with tears in her eyes, and said, "Please, I must speak with you." I agreed to see her after the function, and these were her words to me: "I beg you to forgive me for what I have done to you tonight. I know now that Paramahansaji chose the right one to lead his society." I embraced her with the love that was in my heart.

Love for God Keeps a Spiritual Teaching Alive

I never wanted position. When it was made known to me that the Board of Directors was going to select me as the leader of Guruji's worldwide work, I said, "I cannot accept it; please free me from this obligation."

They said, "No, it is Master's wish; he told us."

I went to my room; and for one week I meditated, wept, and prayed to Divine Mother to please not give this responsibility to me. I didn't want to lose my ideal of being just a humble disciple of Gurudeva, loving God and serving His work in the background of the organization. I didn't want anything but God.

As I was praying, I was telling Divine Mother, "I am no administrator. I have had no such training. All I know is what I have learned here in the ashram. I am not the one to lead this great worldwide organization."

Suddenly my sweet Divine Mother said to me, "Let Me ask you just one thing: Do you love Me? Do you love Me?" That thought filled my consciousness, sweeping away everything else.

I burst into tears and cried, "Divine Mother, that is all I have to offer You. I am nothing and I have nothing—no special qualities—to offer. But I know one thing: I love You. And in this life I am trying to cultivate ever-increasing love for You." And with that Divine

Mother replied, "That is enough. That is all I ask."

"All right then," I said to Her, "I accept."

The experience was so beautiful, so divine, that it cannot be conveyed adequately in words. From that day to this I have carried on in that thought. Love for God is what keeps a spiritual teaching alive. A divine man and an ordinary man may utter the very same words, but one will move you and the other will not. Why? Because the Spirit is living in the words of one who loves God.

When I became president, there were inevitable little misunderstandings. My heart was sore at the inharmony, and I used to pray, "Divine Mother, why? I am only trying to do Your will."

During my visit to India in 1964 I had many marvelous inner experiences. One day I prayed to Mahavatar Babaji: "Show me the way; I will do anything, whatever you command." In that instant I received the answer. Love is the way to reach people, to change people. It may take a long time and patient persistence to bring about the desired effect by love alone, but the effect is lasting. The person comes to understand that you have nothing but love and kindness for him, and that you want nothing from him but his love and goodwill.

For example, during my first trip to India (in 1958–59), there were many obstacles to be faced. Owing to Guruji's absence from India for so many years, those who had taken charge were well ensconced in their own ways. As I had served as Guruji's secretary in all India matters, his wishes were well known to me. But certain of these individuals looked on me as an intruder and a threat to their positions. The vast majority of devotees received me with open hearts, eager to hear about Master's teachings; but in the eyes of those few, Daya Ma was an American (and a woman at that!) and had no right to teach Indians about their own religion and traditions. But I made up my mind that no matter what was said about me, I would never retaliate. That is not my way, and never will be.

One day, after a severe confrontation from one of these individuals, I was scheduled to address a gathering of devotees. Before the meeting, I sat to meditate in front of a picture of Master. As my prayer deepened, his living form emerged from that photo image. Guruji blessed me, and my soul was overwhelmed with the divine inspiration of his presence.

In that state of consciousness I addressed the gathering that evening. The leader of those who had been trying to thwart me decided to walk out, possibly thinking the others would follow him. But a wonderful thing happened. Looking at him, I could not see him at all; there was only the Divine manifesting in that form. Then I knew what God was trying to teach me: "Behold Me in all—not only in those who love you." That consciousness has remained with me.

From that moment, the attitude of those other "enemies" completely changed. One of them came forward at the end of the *satsanga* and *pranamed* before me, saying, "Forgive me." I was humbly thankful, for the sake of unity among Guruji's followers in India. Since then his Yogoda Satsanga work has grown tremendously.

The moral is simply this: Empty the heart of wrong feelings; let it be loving and forgiving. Don't reason, "But that person has mistreated me." Everyone has had someone who persecuted him; we must expect that. But never allow the ill feelings or actions of others to embitter you. If you do, then you are lost. You will not be able to help yourself or them. Keep your heart free of malice, no matter how anyone treats you, no matter what others do. If you give love, you will have peace in your soul.

We hear about these principles and read them in our scriptures, but so few practice them. How many wars have been fought in the name of religion. We think we must fight; but nothing lasting is won in that way. Jesus said: "All they that take the sword shall perish with the sword."* The real conquerors of mankind were not those who grabbed a little bit of land—the "Napoleons." The conquerors of hearts have been the truly great leaders of the ages. These in truth win mankind and change the destiny of the world.

Stand Up for Principles, But Without Enmity

There are times, of course, when we should speak up firmly, when it would be wrong not to take a stand. But there should be no feeling of enmity. Guruji used to tell a story that illustrates this:

In a village, there once lived a cobra whose bite had taken the lives of many of the people. The leader of the community went to a wise man and said, "We can't go on like this. The snake is killing off all the villagers. Won't you please do something about it?"

The wise man agreed to help. He went to the cobra and said, "Look here, you must not go on killing these people. It is unnecessary and wrong. Leave them alone."

The cobra said, "All right, I will follow your advice. I will practice nonviolence."

A year went by. The wise man was passing through the village again and wondered what had happened about the cobra. He went to look for the snake,

* Matthew 26:52.

but it was not in its regular nest. He finally found the hapless creature, its lacerated body stretched out in the sun, just about to breathe its last.

"What on earth happened to you?" the wise man asked.

The cobra answered, "This, Mister Wise Man, is the result of following your teaching of nonviolence. Look what the villagers have done to me. I lie here quietly; and because they no longer have cause to fear me, they come and stone me!"

The wise man said, "You didn't understand. I told you not to bite, but I didn't tell you not to hiss!"

When necessary, when principle is involved, we shouldn't hesitate to "hiss." One should not become a doormat. Stand for truth, but never "bite." That is the divine law.

It is not difficult to give love, because the very nature of our souls is Love. If at times we cannot give love to others, it is because we do not find it within ourselves when our consciousness is on the surface, operating through our senses and emotions. If we turn our consciousness within in deep meditation, communing with God—even a little bit every day—we begin gradually to experience that Love which is our real nature. Feeling love within ourselves, it is very easy to give it to others.

Living a God-Centered Life

From a talk given at SRF International Headquarters just prior to Sri Daya Mata's departure for an extended visit to Paramahansa Yogananda's Yogoda Satsanga Society ashrams, centers, and meditation groups in India

While I am away in India, everything concerning the work of Self-Realization Fellowship should continue as usual. To whom should questions on counseling and spiritual matters be directed? To Divine Mother, as always. She is not going anywhere! Don't think that just because Daya Mata is away, everything will collapse. No human being in this world is indispensable. We sustained the greatest loss we will ever know when we were bereft of the physical presence of our Guru. By comparison, no other loss is really serious.

I remember Master's assurance to us: "When I have left this world, only love can take my place. Whoever reflects truly that divine love—that love of God and the Gurus—such a one will always be at the head of this society. Babaji has long ago already selected those who are destined to carry on this work." Such was the prediction of Master. So there need never be any concern about that.

The life of the president of Guruji's society has but one meaning: not to draw souls to his or her personality, but to draw souls to the feet of God, the Divine Beloved. The greatest gift you can give to me is to give your heart to Divine Mother. That will make me happy.

Because when you give your heart to Her, then I know that no matter what path your life follows, you will be saved. That is my sole interest for you; that is what Gurudeva wants for you.

"Divine Mother, Let Me Win Hearts for You"

While I was meditating last night, I had a most marvelous experience. (One doesn't like to speak of these things, except to inspire others with the message of God.) I was conversing with Divine Mother, deeply praying to Her, when suddenly my whole being was flooded with such intoxicating, sweet love. She gave to my heart this message: The only meaning of life is to love God; that is the sole reason for which man was created. I said to Her: "O Divine Mother, let me win hearts for You. That is my only desire in this world. Let me win hearts for You."

When we set our feet firmly on a path that enables us to seek and to love God, we begin to fulfill the true purpose of life—we know then that we have really begun to live. I can truthfully say that the only time I know I am fully alive is when I am communing with God. Everything outside of that state is just a part of God's cosmic drama. We are here today playing a particular role. But throughout how many years and how many incarnations has this drama of life and death been repeated? How many times in past lives have we crossed one another's path? In lives to come how many times will we meet again? What is the purpose of these constant comings and goings, passing in and out of the "room" of this finite world, and those of the astral world?* Only that from the lessons our experiences

* "In my Father's house are many mansions" (John 14:2). The high

teach us we might gain Self-realization, the full and complete realization that we are part of the One—God alone.

As often as we become lost in this play, we must shake ourselves out of that delusion. Do not shed tears for things of this world. Most of us cannot remember what we cried about five years ago—even one year ago. Weep for only One; weep for God. So long as we allow ourselves to be tossed about on the waves of change, we will be subject to the disturbing contrasts of temporary pleasure and painful sorrow. But when we take our consciousness beneath the waves of change, diving deep into the ocean of God-consciousness, then those external fluctuations no longer affect us. That is why Lord Krishna said, "Be anchored, O Arjuna, in That which is changeless."* When we make the effort to reach that state, then true realization begins to come.

Whenever you become troubled, remember these words: "Why are the saints saints? Because they were cheerful when it was difficult to be cheerful; they were patient when it was difficult to be patient; they pushed on when they wanted to stand still; they kept silent when they wanted to talk; they were agreeable when they wanted to be disagreeable. That is all."

In other words, as Guruji used to say: "Learn to do

---

and low astral spheres, composed of subtle light and energies of lifetrons, are the heaven (or hell) to which souls go after death of the physical body. The length of stay there is karmically predetermined. So long as one has unfulfilled material desires or earthly karma (effects of past actions not yet worked out), he must reincarnate on earth to continue his evolution back to God.

* "O Arjuna, free thyself from the triple qualities and from the pairs of opposites! Ever calm, harboring no thoughts of receiving and keeping, become thou settled in the Self" (Bhagavad Gita II:45).

the things you ought to do when you ought to do them." That is saintliness, and that is freedom.

Serving the Guru

One of the devotees has asked me to discuss the subject of serving the Guru. I would love to dwell on that for a little while, but not with an answer you might expect. Serving the Guru can be summed up in these few words: Keep your mind with God. That was the first order of service to Master. During his lifetime, there was always much work to be done, and Master was grateful for assistance, but he would not accept service from any disciple whose mind was not with God. Guruji's mode of training was to deal directly with what we were thinking rather than with what we were saying, for one's thoughts are the true test of the state of one's consciousness. If a devotee were not making the effort to keep an inner attunement with God, that disciple would have a very difficult time keeping his emotional equilibrium around Master, because of the Guru's strict subtle discipline. One had to be constantly watchful, lest his mind express negative thoughts.

The slightest sign of jealousy in any disciple was the quickest way to be eliminated from Master's presence. He would not tolerate around him that kind of worldly self-centered emotion. Jealousy, anger, hatred—the Guru felt that these negative human emotions can be and should be overcome. He had numerous ways of helping us to remove such flaws from our nature.

Overcoming Negative Moods

In my early days in the ashram, one problem I had, which was with me since childhood, was moodiness. They were not very deep dark moods, but mental changes—one moment happy and the next wondering, "Why am I unhappy?" You see, I had always loved the sunlight and happy, smiling faces, and whenever I would find myself in an atmosphere of gloom, inharmony, or sadness, it affected me. Moods are karmic in the sense that they are the result of habits from past lives that have returned with us in this life. This karmic burden is one of the first things of which we must rid ourselves on the spiritual path. I agree with those who have said, "A sad saint is a bad saint." Why be a spreader of gloom in this world? My unhappy moods troubled me, because my goal was to keep my mind with Divine Mother. I resolved that I would never let Master see me in a mood.

When I woke up one morning, the sky was cloudy; everything seemed gloomy and meaningless. Master called for me, and I thought to myself, "Good heavens, I don't feel so good today. I must do everything I can to keep him from finding out I am in this unhappy mood." I put on a big broad smile—feeling very proud of myself that I was keeping this mood locked up inside me, and Master wasn't going to see a single furrow crossing my brow. I had barely entered his room when suddenly, out of the clear blue, he pointed his finger at me (as he sometimes did with us when he wanted to emphasize a point) and said vehemently, "Don't come in my presence anymore when you are moody!" I was stricken right where it hurt the most: my Guru was displeased with me.

I spent three days struggling with this mood. Do you know what happens when we are moody? We feel self-pity, hurt, and then we get angry. We become convinced that through our behavior we will punish our loved ones for misunderstanding us. Inwardly I got the stubborn notion, "All right, Master doesn't want me around him, so I'll stay away." The longer I held out, the more I could see that it was *I* who was suffering; my behavior wasn't changing Master's attitude toward me. And so I thought, "Who is responsible for this mood? *You* are! Then who must get rid of it? *You* must get rid of it." By the time I had applied this logic, I knew that there was only one person who had to change. It wasn't Master; nor was it the people around me. It was up to *me* to change.

That was a tremendous lesson for me; and since that day in 1932, I have never permitted myself to be dragged down by any mood. I learned that one *can* control and conquer moods. As Master used to say to us, "Remember, no one can make you happy if you have made up your mind to be unhappy, and no one can make you unhappy if you choose to be happy." Remember these words, for they are true.

I have always held to the truth, as it is written in the scriptures, that we are made in the image of the Divine; and if God's nature is bliss and love, then my nature is bliss and love. Therefore, it is my duty to disassociate myself from all the dark human qualities that are not part of my true soul nature. When moods, negativity, hatred, unhappiness, try to creep into our consciousness, we must affirm, and strive to manifest outwardly: "This is not me! I am bliss; I am joy; I am wisdom; I am peace."

"Ye Shall Know the Truth, and the Truth Shall Make You Free"

Freedom comes by holding on to truth*—that

* "Ye shall know the truth, and the truth shall make you free" (John 8:32).

which is real—and by denying that which is false. Hatred, dishonesty, darkness, evil—these are false. They are born of delusion and exist in the world of relativity. They are part of that veil of *maya* which covers the beautiful face of Divine Mother. Pull away that veil and behold always the Divine Beloved.

To live free of delusion and its dark qualities is the only way to live in this world. It is so easy for the human nature to be quarrelsome, to hate, to think negatively—because that has been its habit for countless incarnations. But each of us here has come to the spiritual path because of some awakening that has caused us to question, "What is reality?" We may not have used those exact words, but that was our inner longing. If that urge is not deep or is not properly nourished, we may fall back into our old habits and ways; then truths become inspiring words, but are no longer real to us. For some, truth just goes in one ear and out the other, because, as Guruji used to say, there is nothing in between to stop it! We must cultivate the spiritual receptivity that catches truth and absorbs it.

The trouble with the world is that people often fail to absorb the right things. They are busy instead absorbing what others have done to them or said to them, or how people treat them—all of the things that have to do with the mundane world. Who absorbs what the Divine is constantly trying to say to us? Who listens to the sweet, simple, truthful Voice that is right within our hearts? That is the One I love to talk with. That is the One who always responds to the devotee.

Don't worry so much about what other people do. Be concerned more with how you treat others than with how they treat you. This is the mature attitude, the right attitude. He who makes himself mentally vulnerable to hurt by others is a perpetually unhappy person. Instead of complaining, "He has hurt me; she said these things to me; they are persecuting me," one should say, "Lord, it matters not so much what others do to me, but it matters much what I do to others. Let me be kind, even when pierced with the sharp words of others. I lay all the offenses against me at Thy feet. Let me learn from them and have right understanding." When we have complete understanding, we have Self-realization.

Nothing Comes to Us by Accident

Know this for certain: No experience can come to any one of us by accident—even though it may appear that way at times. The Divine is most organized. Just as there is a time and a season for everything in this universe, so there is a time and a season for everything that happens in our lives.* We should never blame any human being or any external circumstance for the conditions that confront us. Just simply say, "Well, Mother, this has happened. What is the meaning of this for me?" And then do not become distraught if She doesn't respond at once.

Part of loving God is to have endless patience. It may sound like a contradiction to say that we must have zeal for God and at the same time have patience to wait for His reply, but it is not. One can be so busy thinking of God and doing for Him that time ceases to be a consideration; time ceases to exist. The devotee's whole life becomes one long pursuit of God and communion with Him—in meditation and in activity alike.

The most effective way to achieve this constant communion with God is to inwardly talk to Him with

* "To every thing there is a season, and a time to every purpose under the heaven" (Ecclesiastes 3:1).

all your heart. And go on talking to Him with endless patience and devotion until that sweet response begins to come. Most people give up because they have the notion that God is not responding; but He does make known His presence in His own time and in His own way. One of the problems is that we forget to listen! Listening is part of conversation with God. As the Bible says, "Be still, and know that I am God."*

If every one of you, from this day forward, were to get in the habit of practicing that silent communion and conversation with God, faithfully waiting and listening, you would see how He answers the call of your heart. It cannot be otherwise. He responds even in the midst of activities. But if you are outwardly so busy chattering, bustling about, catering to the fleshly form, and entertaining restless thoughts, so that you don't have time to listen, you will miss His subtle whispers.

For me, the easiest way to receive response from God is to inwardly call to Him with all my heart, "My Love, my Love." You must go on saying it, even if at first you do not feel it. One day you really will mean it. "My God, my God; my Lord, my Lord. 'Tis all You, You." Nothing else needs to be said.

Practicing the Presence of God

Someone has asked, "How can we most effectively practice the presence of God during our working hours?" The answer is very simple, as Guruji said to me: "When you begin your day, inwardly say, 'Lord, help me to do the right thing in my work.' Then throughout the day, hold the thought, 'Lord, I am doing this for You. I shall do the best job I can, because of the joy I find in

* Psalms 46:10.

doing it for You.'" Practicing the Presence in this way should not make you absentminded. Be alert! Like one who is in love, the devotee does his work magnificently for the Beloved.

If one is sincere in his resolve, there is nothing in his life that he cannot turn in the direction of the Divine. Those things that do not take him toward God—those contradictory desires, thoughts, and actions—he cuts out of his life by the power of discrimination. In time, all worldly tendencies fall away like dried leaves from a tree. They do not have to be forcibly plucked off, they drop naturally because they no longer have any meaning, they no longer give any pleasure. The devotee finds a transcendent joy in God.

If one meditates regularly and practices the presence of God, the thought of the Divine will begin to revolve constantly in the background of the mind. In discussing this point, Master often used the analogy of a cow and her calf. The mother cow lets her calf gambol all over the pasture, and she appears to be oblivious of its whereabouts. But if someone goes near that calf, see how the cow reacts! She was always very much aware of the calf's presence. Guruji used to say that the devotee should be like the mother cow. We go on performing our duties in this world, but always in the background of our minds is the awareness of God. We let nothing distract our attention from Him.

When my mind is fixed upon the Divine Mother, everything runs more smoothly. My heart does not feel burdened by anything; I am carefree, peaceful, enthusiastic. No matter where I go or what I do, Divine Mother goes with me. It is so because I have trained myself in this way for many years; this consciousness comes solely through practice. It is possible for you also to develop this kind of intimate relationship with God. Think of the Divine Mother; make Her your own. I know She is there.

If you follow what I am suggesting, the time comes when your consciousness remains unbrokenly in the meditative state—always with God. The devotee eventually becomes like Brother Lawrence: Whether he was sweeping the floors or worshiping God before the altar, his mind was constantly engrossed in Him.* That is the state you want to come to; but it requires effort—it does not come by imagination. Eventually, you will find that even while you are doing your work, whenever you take your mind within for a moment, you will feel an inner effervescent well of devotion, of joy, of wisdom. You will say, "Ah, He is with me!" This is the fruit of meditation that can be enjoyed at any time, in quiet communion or in the midst of activity.

Finding the Guidance and Strength You Need

Someone has asked me: "Is it not a form of temptation when one is habitually 'inspired' to shorten or miss a meditation in order to perform some service?"

Yes, it is a sort of temptation. It is from meditation that we find the guidance and strength we need to perform well our service for God. So why should we give it up? Often our trouble is that we tend to live too much in the consciousness of time—the mind constantly feels rushed and worried—and this affects our meditations. When I am meditating, I do not think about anything but my meditation. If a thought of some aspect of work

* "The time of business does not with me differ from the time of prayer; and in the noise and clatter of my kitchen, while several persons are at the same time calling for different things, I possess God in as great tranquility as if I were upon my knees...." Brother Lawrence, in *The Practice of the Presence of God.*

comes into my mind, I say to myself, "God is my reality. It is He whom I am seeking. Why should I think about anything else? His work will be done after meditation."

For a balanced spiritual life, both meditation and work are necessary. With meditation only, one becomes mentally slothful and physically lazy. With work only, one becomes too restless—he can never sit quietly and turn his thoughts to God. It is possible to combine and balance both work and meditation, although at times this may seem difficult. You have to make up your mind that you are going to do it.

Using Your Time to Best Advantage

Many devotees are of the opinion that they can have either God or work, but not both. I don't agree. I know the two can be combined if you have less "fillers" in your life. Fillers are the idle talk and useless activities that waste the free moments, the gaps of time, throughout the day. If you learn how to use your time rightly and do away with those fillers, you will see that you have plenty of time to meditate on God and to work for Him.

During our years with Master, we were very busy. We would work eighteen hours or more a day—that is no exaggeration—and still we would not miss our meditation. There were some nights when we had no time for sleep, but we didn't collapse or go to pieces. We had the inspiration, the willingness, and the belief that we could do it; and that's why we were able to do it. You see, everything is in the mind. For those who thought it was too difficult, it *was* too difficult: Their minds found millions of reasons why they could never miss sleep, why they could not work too long, why they had to shorten or miss their meditations.

We should grasp this point: The Lord is watching what we are within; He knows when we are sincere and when we are rationalizing and making excuses for ourselves. We should not try to hide our true motives or behavior from God, nor from ourselves. "To thine own self be true; and it must follow, as the night the day, thou canst not then be false to any man."* Self-honesty is one of the primary factors in healing oneself of the sickness of ignorance.

A Program for Longer Meditations

During that period of my life in the ashram I made a vow to myself that in addition to working my full days, I would still make time to meditate six hours one night a week. On that day, I would quit my work at five o'clock, go to my room, and from six o'clock until midnight I would meditate. Each one of you should put this into practice; you have no idea how it will change your life.

If it is not possible for those who have family responsibilities to arrange for six hours of meditation once a week, the next best thing is to snatch whatever time you can, and make the most of it with sincere effort. That is all you can do. God appreciates the devotee who does his best. If our best is only one-half hour of deep meditation, that means as much to God as one whose best is six hours. Whatever free time you have, give it to God; that is what He wants.† Be honest with Him in your heart. If you have only one hour for deep meditation, then let that one hour be spent wholeheartedly with God.

* *Hamlet*, Act I, Scene 3.

† "For the Lord thy God is a consuming fire, even a jealous God" (Deuteronomy 4:24).

Meditation is different from seclusion. Seclusion means setting aside some time to be alone—perhaps on weekends, on a Sunday, or just an hour or two during a weekday. This is a time for relaxation, introspection, and study; it may also include periods of meditation. Master started our Self-Realization retreats to give devotees the opportunity for seclusion—to get away occasionally from all their worldly concerns in order to think of God and to have longer and deeper meditations.*

How to Combat "Dryness" in Meditation

If spiritual "dryness" comes in meditation—when one feels a lack of devotion for God—what is the best way to combat it? There is only one way: Refuse to give up. Maintain continuity of effort in meditation, and eventually you will break through that obstacle.

The weak person's mind would suggest, "Well, I'll give up meditation today because I'm not making any headway, and I have many things to do." But to me, that is false logic. Instead, the devotee should reason, "In an instant life ends! I am never going to make the excuse that I will meditate later; I will do it now. Later may be too late!" It has been my practice that the moment I think "meditation," I meditate. There is no wavering back and forth.

Let me give you an example: In the past few weeks there have been tremendous pressures and last-minute emergencies—many things have happened to impede my departure for India. When I sit to meditate, my mind naturally tends to think about these matters; but with all my will I say to these intruding thoughts, "Out with you!" From experience, I know that all this work

* Information about Self-Realization Fellowship Retreats is available from the international headquarters.

can just as well be done when I am finished with meditation. My efforts in communing with God need not be compromised.

Last night, in my meditation, the overwhelming presence of Divine Mother suddenly stole over me. "Ah," I said, "Divine Mother, with just one brief moment of Your joy, Your bliss, a thousand million struggles cannot take my mind away from You." More and more that joy stays with you; it lingers throughout the day's activities. These assurances from the Divine remain in your mind, so that you feel a constant flow of communion. You live, move, and have your being in that consciousness. That state comes by persevering in meditation, whether you feel God's response or not.

So the next time you experience dryness in meditation, do not give up. Continue to talk inwardly to the Divine Mother; ask Her to give you more devotion. Go on praying to Her every day in meditation for as long as it takes. In addition to periods of meditation, throughout the day cultivate the habit of taking the name of God inwardly, especially when you feel very pressed. No one needs to know. Repeat it mentally again and again, until your whole consciousness churns with one thought: "You, my God; You, You, You." If you do that, you will find that suddenly, when you least expect it, God will respond.

God Is Won Through Unconditional Love

One's search for God must be unconditional—that means "without any qualifications." If one conditions his search to one, three, five years—"Lord, I give You this long, but if You don't respond by then, goodbye"—God will say, "I don't want that kind of love." You could not win anyone that way. Who would want to enter into a marriage contract with someone under similar conditions? The true lover gives his love "for better or worse, till death do us part, and beyond." That is the attitude the devotee must have with the Divine. There must be surrender to God. Trust Him; give yourself to Him. Let Him use you as He will. God will not use you badly—not at all. He will use you wisely and tenderly and with love.

There is so much uncertainty about life that unconsciously we put our faith in the Lord all the time. We are not sure from one minute to the next whether we will still be here on this earth! We should make that unconscious trust more conscious. Love God silently in your heart. Know that He has the power to change any unfavorable situation; and in His own time He will do so, if you believe this.

Every Human Being Can Find God

Question from the audience: "If one is living or working with others who are very negative or materialistic, what is the best way to deal with this?"

When husbands and wives can hand-in-hand seek God together with unconditional love, what wonderful companionship this can be. They become divine friends, each helping the other on the spiritual path. Blessed are those who have such a relationship. But if those of you who are married do not yet have it, don't be discouraged. It is possible to change others—not by words, but by your own behavior. You can conquer by love. But it must be unconditional, not the kind that demands, "I'll go on giving love *provided* he or she responds to me as I wish." Do not be overly concerned about another's response; leave that in God's hands. Trust in the power of His love.

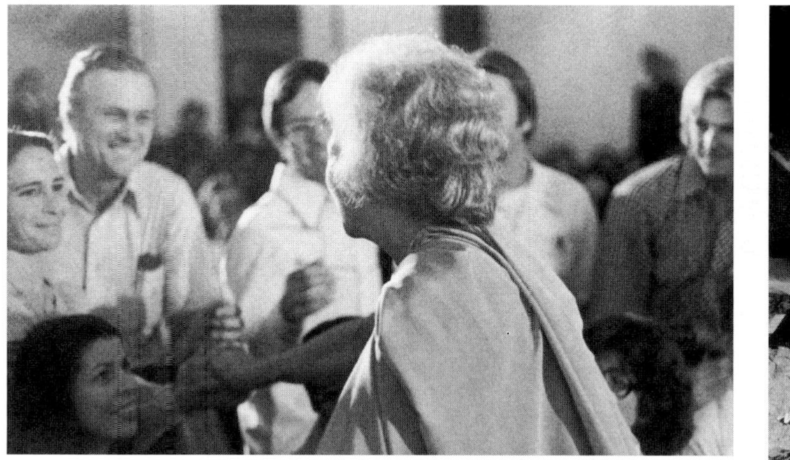

(*Above*) Greeting participants at Convocation, Biltmore Hotel, Los Angeles, 1978; and (*right*) after *satsanga* in Delhi, 1972

"Give of your heart, give of your understanding....When someone comes to you depressed, discouraged, negative, it is wonderful if you can send that person away uplifted by having said something encouraging to help him along his way."

A loving benediction, Self-Realization Convocation, 1983

"The only meaning of life is to love God; that is the sole reason for which man was created....When we set our feet firmly on a path that enables us to seek and to love God, we begin to fulfill the true purpose of life — we know then that we have really begun to live."

If others are critical of our spiritual pursuits, we should continue with our efforts just the same, but quietly and unobtrusively. To those who do not understand, we should not say anything about what we are doing, nor should we try to impress them.

Shortly before entering the ashram, when I lived at home, I would get up in the middle of the night, when everyone else was asleep, and go into another room to sit quietly and pray; and then steal my way back to bed. (I was shy and didn't want the others to know about my deep feeling for God.) If someone noticed that I was up and asked why, I would say, "I didn't feel like sleeping, so I went into the other room for a while." There was no point in making a big show or display of what I was doing. If one really wants God, there is always a way to find time and opportunity to be with Him.

Another means of dealing with the misunderstanding of others is to constantly give them your love—not in words necessarily, but expressing through your behavior the goodness of your soul. Be thoughtful, kind in speech, unselfish, serviceful, understanding. Others need not know your specific religious leanings and personal beliefs; what you are thinking and what is in your heart will be expressed through your actions. This has a beneficial effect on people more than anything.

Yes, it may be difficult to do this. But it becomes easier with practice. It will help you to become stronger if you regularly meet with others with whom you can communicate on a spiritual level—at church, in group meditations, in *satsanga.* We draw great strength from such meetings. This helps us to carry on with the right attitude, knowing full well that in God's own time He can free us from inharmonies in our environment.

There is no human being who cannot find God if

he wants to—regardless of the circumstances. There are no legitimate excuses. It depends on the degree of one's desire. If a person wants something very badly, he will go after it no matter what the obstacles. He has the will to do it. We have been given all the resources necessary to accomplish our goal of finding God. But we must show Him that we mean business. We must reverse the searchlight of our interests and focus our will upon finding God. Then we will receive His response.

An Anthology of Counsel

Words of guidance and inspiration drawn from satsangas *and letters to Self-Realization members*

The Answer to All Problems

What a helpful and inspiring message is conveyed in these words of Gurudeva Paramahansa Yogananda:

> In God are all the answers to your problems. He reveals Himself through divine law, and if you follow the law you will get His answer. Walk in the peaceful valley of faith, then God will walk with you and you will realize that your responsibility lies with Him. Be free forever from the trials and cords that bind you. God is the Father, and you are the child. Union with Him is sufficient for all your needs.

One who practices meditation faithfully learns that it is truly God who holds the answers to all problems. Meditation uplifts the consciousness so that we have a new, broader viewpoint. Petty trials no longer trouble us, and it becomes easier to see the path of right action in everything. As God becomes more real, He becomes not only our main Goal in life, but the center and source of our inner security *now.* We recognize life as a school, and its experiences as opportunities to learn. Spiritual security gained through contact with God in meditation makes it possible to give love, understanding, and forgiveness, unconditionally—and so our relationships with others improve. Secure in God, the yogi does not demand of others that which they are unable to fulfill. More and more he finds God "sufficient for all needs."

So many today are seeking an answer, a solution, to the fearsome troubles of life. But the only permanent resolution to the problems of individuals and of nations is to return to God. With heart and mind fixed in God, face each new day with hope and faith in Him.

The Power of Prayer for World Peace

Thought is the most powerful force in the world. Out of the thought of God has sprung all that we behold in this universe.

"Out of the abundance of the heart the mouth speaketh."* What we are thinking comes out in our speech and in our actions. Therefore, the first step in praying for world peace is to become peaceful beings in our own personal lives. How can we effectively pray for peace, how can we send out powerful thoughts of peace, how can we give peace to the world, unless we ourselves are peaceful beings?

To become a peaceful being requires deep meditation. The importance of meditation is expressed repeatedly in Guruji's writings. We need to take our minds deeply into the practice of meditation.

Guruji told of his aunt in India who came to him and said, "Please help me. I have been saying my prayers on my beads for forty years, and still I find no peace within." He told her, "While you are saying your prayers, your mind is wandering everywhere and

* Matthew 12:34.

thinking about everything else. When you are praying, put your whole attention upon what you are saying; keep your mind on the One to whom you are addressing your prayers."

We should not merely "parrot" prayer. A parrot may repeat words, but it does not know what it is saying. When we pray or meditate, the whole mind and attention should be there, to the exclusion of everything else. That is the real way to pray; and developing such concentration is the purpose of the Self-Realization techniques of meditation.

So, to help bring peace to the world, first strive to become peaceful beings; then concentrate upon doing good, spreading peace. The first proof of God's presence within is peace—that peace "which passeth all understanding."* To achieve that peace is the duty of every human being—the creature God has endowed with intelligence, discrimination, and the ability to think. When we feel that inner peace, we know that we are in tune with the Divine. We can then pray deeply and more effectively for world peace.

I am not saying that you shouldn't pray for the world until you feel peace yourself. I am saying, start where peace begins, in yourself; change yourself so that when others come into your presence, they feel peace and calmness. Then, when you sit to meditate and to pray for others, the power of your attention, the power of your peace, reaches out and can affect the whole world.

Guruji said that the vibrations of words and thoughts produce definite effects, and make an impression in the ether that could be picked up by anyone

* Philippians 4:7.

anywhere if he had a powerful enough instrument. Science has shown this in a limited way through the use of radio and television. But even without these media to broadcast my words, their force and the power of thought behind them are at this moment traveling around the world. With a supersensitive instrument this could be proven. So a strong vibration of peace flowing from our hearts and minds can have a great influence on the world. Doing our part to contribute to this influence is one of the duties of devotees who follow Paramahansaji.*

Why Are Some Children Born With Suffering?

If we believe that God is just—I certainly do, and all great religions teach this—then what can be the cause of children with birth defects, who seem to have come into the world to suffer? God loves every one of us equally; and just as He cares for each sparrow, and is aware of each grain of sand, He cares far more for us. So there is no reasonable answer to this question except the law of karma, cause and effect: What you sow, you reap.

This does not mean that we should be hard-hearted toward the afflicted, saying, "Well, this suffering is his karma." No! God gave human beings the ability to be sympathetic, to be compassionate. No other creature has those qualities. But God gave them to us, expecting us to use them as exemplified by Christ and other great spiritual giants.

What we see in this life is just one link in an eternal chain of existence. The rest is hidden, so we forget that

* To this end, Paramahansa Yogananda established the Worldwide Prayer Circle. See footnote on page 32.

behind the little link of 60, 70, or 100 years is the whole eternal cycle. What we have sown in this life or in previous lives we must reap in this or some future life. Effects, however, may not always outwardly imitate the causes. Many factors of past actions and behavior, physical and mental, interact to create karmic patterns. Only a master can read those indications accurately. Therefore, no one should judge or presume the causes of anyone else's present condition. Karma is not meant to punish but to teach.

So when we see a child with birth defects or anyone who is afflicted, we have a twofold duty. First of all, to understand there is a self-attracted cause, and not blame God for being cruel. Then we have an opportunity to grow—and we do develop greatly through compassionate behavior—through giving of ourselves in sympathy, service, in doing whatever we can to alleviate the condition or suffering and to help that person to bear his affliction.

An Answer to Atheism

There are those who proclaim there is no God. But is it really possible to be an atheist? I can understand someone's rejecting certain orthodox concepts of God because he has had some disillusioning experience in practicing a particular religion. But to reject therefore the idea of the existence of God is nonsense.

To those who claim to be atheists I would ask this question: "Did you grow your body from that first tiny cell?" No human being can answer that question in the affirmative, nor tell how he developed from that single cell into a human being. They might describe the science behind it, but what motivates that scientific process? There has to be some Power that caused this to take place—some Power that keeps the planets moving in orderly fashion, that causes trees and plants to grow from the remarkable pattern in little seeds. These are the miracles of a Divine Power.

One can say that he does not accept a particular concept of God, but I believe no one can logically say, "I do not accept the idea that some Power is causing all these things to happen in creation, or causing me to think and breathe and move." I have no real control over my life; an atheist has no control over his. He knows nothing about how he came here, or when he is going to die. Isn't that true?

There *is* a Power in this universe through which we exist and have the ability to reason—even to reason that we cannot accept the idea of God. It is my conviction that atheists have not thought deeply enough; otherwise they could not deny a Divine Power.

The Role of Music in the Search for God

The substance of the universe is vibration, and vibration produces sound. There are two kinds of vibration: positive or harmonious, and inharmonious. Ages ago, man had a wish to express himself, and began to produce rhythmic sounds. Today this is known as music. I must say, however, some of today's sounds are anything but musical! We are in a rather negative era, and one example of this is the lack of harmony in much of today's music; it is often an unmelodious clashing. Inspired music, painting, sculpture—all art forms—are expressions of God and His creation. Some of the greatest works of art in the world are religious, and evoke religious inspiration in man. When one goes to some of the ancient temples in India, or visits the Vatican, and sees the magnificent paintings and sculptures, so beautiful and inspiring, one cannot doubt the creative spirit of God in man. Such art forms do arouse spiritual feelings.

But one of you has asked if it is all right to listen to music while you are meditating. This individual feels that music leads him toward God. Yes, it does. In India, for example, chanting has been used for centuries in the spiritual search. In every religion, music is a part of the spiritual ritual. But it would not be correct to say that music produces the deeper realization that comes from being absolutely still and listening to the inner music.* The spiritual purpose of music—images portrayed by harmonious sounds—is to arouse devotion and inspiration; but then the devotee must go beyond external sounds, which require the use of a physical sense organ, the ear, and listen within, by deep meditation in utter silence, to the cosmic sound of the universe, the creative "Word" or "voice" of God.

Therefore you cannot *meditate* deeply while listening to or practicing music because you cannot go beyond a certain range of inspiration while dependent upon any of the senses. To a degree, as when chanting, for example, one can meditate, provided the mind dwells not on the music, but on the thought expressed by the chant. This way you are able to go within—to quiet all the senses and become utterly still; then you know what God is.

* A reference to *Aum,* the cosmic intelligent creative vibration of Spirit, an all-pervading sound perceived within through practice of Self-Realization Fellowship methods of meditation.

One of the world's greatest and best-known symphony conductors, Leopold Stokowski, told me that his experience of God was through music. He was acquainted with Guruji and these teachings, and it so happened that Master asked me to render some assistance to him while he was in Los Angeles on tour. Our conversations had often revolved around Master's teachings on meditation. On one occasion, the maestro sat down at the piano and played for me. It was quite a privilege, because I was the only audience. He played magnificently; but I was thinking, "What will I say to him? How will I explain to him that this is not enough? Inspiration is not realization."

When he had finished playing, I said, "It was beautiful!" He seemed to be expecting some further comment, so I ventured to say, "Let me ask you a question. You have told me that your meditation is when you play the piano or conduct an orchestra—that is your form of contact with God. But what would happen to that experience if suddenly you became deaf, or your hands became paralyzed so that you could no longer play or conduct?" He was thoughtfully silent. Then I said, "You are limiting your experience with God to dependence on the capabilities of the physical body."

I am not demeaning music and its value. Music has always inspired me, just as it did Guruji. I am saying there is something beyond that, which you experience only in deep meditation.

The individual who meditates does not require the physical instrumentality of his body in order to commune with God. He goes beyond dependence upon any of his organs of sense or action, except of course the higher mind or consciousness, in his communion.

Many people, because of mental restlessness, do not really want to make the effort required to meditate. They will rationalize their preference for other forms of inspiration in order to justify that inner, maybe unconscious, unwillingness. But neither music nor any other source of spiritual stimulation is an adequate substitute for meditation. All art forms can inspire, but nothing can take the place of direct God-communion.

Finding Time for God

No one ever said that the Lord was going to make life easy for any of us! It is a constant struggle, and always will be. All of creation is flowing out of God, and most of mankind is flowing with it. The individual who has turned his life towards God is in a sense moving against a tremendous tide. He is trying to go back to the Source, whereas everything else is coursing against him, in the opposite direction.

So it is difficult to find time specifically for God unless you resolutely set it aside as a part of your daily schedule. This does not mean that He will then take away all of your problems. But it does mean that from this God-contact you will gain calmness, courage, and strength with which to face whatever comes each day. Sometimes your burdens will be lighter; sometimes not so light. But those are the challenges that have to be met in life.

The happiest people are those who have a philosophy to live by. People go to pieces over problems when their minds are scattered. A devotee came to me recently and said, "I'm just torn asunder today." The reason for that kind of reaction, or emotional response, is the lack of a steadying philosophy to hold on to. Master used to tell us to make God the polestar of our lives, so that throughout all experiences the mind is revolving around Him. If you take something daily from Master's writings, and then, in the midst of activities and work, keep coming back to that thought—pulling your mind away for even just an instant—it will enable you to maintain an inner balance and strength. And it will help you to become more anchored in God.

Setting Goals for Spiritual Progress

The New Year is a favorable time to make a fresh start on the spiritual path. So many devotees say to me, "I don't know if I am moving toward God. I feel dry. I don't feel any progress." I can say only one thing to them: more effort is needed—a greater resolution to feel the presence of God, to seek Him daily in meditation.

A contributory aid to spiritual progress is to adopt one requisite quality at a time and concentrate on making it manifest in your nature. Divine qualities are already within us—humility, devotion, wisdom, compassion, cheerfulness—they are eternal attributes of our souls. It is the limited "I," the ego, that has obscured our true divinity.

Choose some quality that especially appeals to you and concentrate upon it. Dwell consciously on that virtue, probe the depths of its meaning and purpose, and seek ways to express it. Apply your determination, your continually renewed attention and zeal toward the fulfillment of your goal. When you feel some measure of accomplishment, then add to it another dimension of soul-unfoldment, until every petal of your life is a perfumed expression of God's presence.

God Is With Us Always

Our relationship with God becomes very simple and sweet when we strive to remember how close He is to us at every moment. If we seek miraculous demonstrations or phenomenal results in our quest for God, we may overlook the many ways in which He comes to us all the time. Lacking grand and glorious experiences, some devotees become discouraged, thinking that God is far away and that they are not progressing toward Him. But if we learn to be alert to the constant manifestations of His presence, as Gurudeva taught us, we quickly find assurance that God is with us *now.* I would urge you to dwell deeply on these words of Guruji:

> A common cause of spiritual discouragement is the devotee's expectation that God's response will come in a great blaze of awe-inspiring inner illumination. This erroneous notion dulls the devotee's perception of the subtle Divine responses that are present from the very beginning of one's meditative practices. God responds to the devotee's every effort, every devotional call. Even as a novice, you will realize this in your own seeking if you learn to recognize Him as the quiet, inner peace that steals over your consciousness. This peace is the first proof of God's presence within. You will know it is He who has guided and inspired you to some right decision in your life. You will feel His strength empowering you to overcome bad habits and nurture spiritual qualities. You will know Him as the ever-increasing joy

and love that surges deep within, overflowing into your everyday life and relationships.

I pray you may more and more feel His nearness and see Him in all the circumstances of your life; and that through meditation and loving Him, you may merge your heart and soul in His omnipresence.

When Will God Respond?

Guruji once said, "Through the centuries I had been seeking God, and still He did not answer me. But I said, 'Lord, someday You will come.' I didn't care how long I had to wait. I knew that through every noble desire, every good thing I had done, He was with me. And still I was calling Him, though He was so near."

One should constantly have in his heart loving demands for God's response. That is why Master taught us to continue meditating deeply after practicing Kriya, and to pray longingly: "Lord, reveal Thyself, reveal Thyself." Talk to Him persistently in the language of your soul. Feel what you say; never let your prayer become mere mechanical chanting. And do not be impatient if you feel no response. As Guruji has said, it doesn't matter how long we have to wait. Your attitude must be, "I'll go on seeking You to the end of my life"— not, "Well, I'll give you six years, Lord, but if at the end of that time You have not come, I'll turn back to the world."

Seeking God becomes a way of life, a channeling of all your energies and thoughts in one direction while still performing your duties. If you follow this, you will find, as Guruji told us, that when you least expect it— not necessarily when you are meditating, but perhaps afterward—you will receive some sign, some response from God. When that happens, do not talk about it and do not take it for granted. But inwardly say to Him, "Thank You, my Lord, thank You."

To ask when He will come to you is the wrong question, because He is already there. He has never left you. Rather it should be, "When will I be aware that You are with me?" That is what is vital. He has already come to you. What is lacking is your awareness. Meditation will sweep away the veil of *maya* that has made you feel separated from the Divine Beloved.

When Guruji said, "Someday, Lord, You will come," he was speaking in a poetic sense, for he then acknowledges, "I was calling Him, though He was already so near." What the devotee must do is to practice the presence of God—to keep his mind always centered on God. As he strives to live his life in tune with the guidance of Guru, and with what he knows to be right behavior, he suddenly comes to the awareness: "Oh! I thought You were away from me, my Lord, but I find You have been with me always."

The exercise of patience is required when we have not yet realized that He is with us. Guruji went on to say—and this is so beautiful: "If you keep shaking a glass of muddy water, it stays muddy. But if you hold the glass still, in a little while the mud settles to the bottom and the water becomes clear. The mind is like that. The little while that I sat in meditation went by so fast! Mental restlessness ceased, and my mind became crystal clear and calm." That is the purpose and value of meditation.

When we are active in the world, the mind is like the muddy water. But when we learn to sit quietly in meditation, the restlessness, or mud, settles to the bottom, and the water, or mind, becomes crystal clear.

When that happens, then in the clear, still waters of the mind we can see the reflection of the Infinite.

Do you now see why Guruji stressed again and again: meditation! meditation! Always give time to meditation; but also perform your duties conscientiously, carrying them on with the consciousness: "Lord, in whatever work I am doing, I am serving Thee."

Sharing Our Spiritual Beliefs With Others

As we grow in understanding, and in our love for God, we hasten the development of those around us: children, wife, husband. However, it is not necessarily by our words that we can best influence others. Very often, if we try to convert family members, it causes much misunderstanding. If someone in your family is not following the spiritual path, it is wrong to try to pressure that individual into accepting your beliefs. Each person must unfold, as each flower, in his or her own time. You cannot force a seed to become a flower in one day.

The search for God is an individual pursuit. I do not mean that we should hide in closets to meditate, but we should follow our spiritual routine without making family members feel guilty or uncomfortable that they are not doing the same. Otherwise, it may cause much resentment. You know, it is true that the children of ministers are often the most problematic, because the parent has consciously or unconsciously made them feel coerced. The child feels he cannot express himself, or be himself. As a result, he may turn against the religious principles his parent teaches.

The best way to change people is by the example

of our own behavior; not thinking we are better, not showing off our spiritual endeavors, but expressing the kindness, thoughtfulness, love, understanding, that begin to develop within us as a part of Self-realization. That is what touches people; and may inspire them to want to know more about the practices that enable you to behave in such an exemplary way.

Creating Harmony in Relationships With Others

Why do people quarrel? Because each one is trying to put across his point of view, and doesn't want to listen to anyone else's. We become biased in favor of our own opinions. Then, naturally, there is friction. And finally, in a family, they may get to the point where they either stop talking at all, or want to separate.

I remember once when a group of us disciples were sitting around Guruji, talking about spiritual matters; suddenly he looked at each of us and began to smile. We said, "What is it, Master?" He shook his head and replied: "I didn't draw around me any weak-minded individuals. You are all very strong-willed." Then he added: "Whenever you have difficulty, get together and talk it out." Master also used to say, "Fools argue; wise men discuss." Nobody here likes to be thought a fool, so we all sit and discuss, like wise men.

People, especially the strong-willed, need to have an agreement from the very beginning of their relationship that they will talk things out, with both sides having the opportunity to express their views. Try to communicate more with one another. The moment communication stops, the relationship gradually, totally dissolves. But if you respect the other individual's viewpoint, and give him time to express it without interruption, then perhaps he will give you the same opportunity. It is by this kind of interchange that you come to a common understanding. The purpose of marriage is not merely to produce children, but to help one another. You help, not by hitting each other with words, but by talking, sharing, communicating.

We need more understanding, and it is God, and meditation upon Him, that will give it to us. We need to include God more in our home life. "The family that prays together stays together" is a popular expression here in the West; and it is true.

"In Divine Friendship"

In many of Guruji's letters to devotees throughout the years, he closed with the words, "In divine friendship"; and he chose this phrase as the customary closing for letters from Self-Realization Fellowship to its members. He often said to us that the highest and purest relationship that can exist between souls is the spirit of friendship. There is no compulsion in it. He was not speaking of ordinary human friendship; he meant friendship that is unconditional, the kind that Christ had for his disciples and that they felt for their guru and for one another. It is impersonal, and yet is the closest of relationships. It is open in the sense that one is accepted unconditionally, as he is, with all his flaws. If differences of opinion arise, a friend is not misjudged; the friendship remains unbroken, and grows sweeter with time. Guruji used to say to those beloved devotees who were close to him: "Friendship is like wine; it grows sweeter with age."

I want to read a few thoughts of Guruji's on the ideal of universal friendship, world fellowship:

> "World fellowship" seems a very simple phrase, but in these two words is the panacea for all the individual, social, and political ills that are threatening the world's material, mental, moral, and spiritual happiness....This world belongs not to you nor to me. We are travelers, here for just a little time. This world belongs to God. He is our President, and under Him we must establish a united world, with every brother nation living in fellowship....The way is to know God; and the way to know Him is to meditate on Him....World fellowship alone can banish hatred and prevent wars. World fellowship alone can stabilize prosperity for all mankind. Therefore I say to you, bring that fellowship into your hearts by communing with God. Feel the fatherhood of God, and that every human being belongs to you. As soon as you feel God in your heart, you will contribute to world civilization as no king or politician has ever done before. Love all those with whom you come in contact. Be able to say with conviction, "He is my brother, for my God who is in me is also in him."

What our world needs so much today is that more individuals make the effort to expand their consciousness beyond the little self by giving divine love and friendship to all.

Guruji said of Mahatma Gandhi that he didn't belong to India alone. Here was a simple man—whom Guruji had met and spent some days with—a humble soul who lived in utter simplicity and dressed only in a loincloth. He was the truest Christian produced in this modern age, and yet he was a Hindu from India. He said: "Whoever loves my India, he is an Indian." In these words, he excluded no one from his love. He included all mankind in his love for God and for his own people. He recognized and exemplified the universality of the human spirit.

That is the spirit Gurudeva manifested in his life also. He knew no strangers. He met everyone with an outstretched hand—with sweet, simple, childlike trust and friendship. He gave understanding to those who understood him not. He practiced the ideal of first seeking God earnestly—we must be satisfied beyond any doubt that we are His, and that He responds to the secret call of our hearts—and then he gave the same divine love and friendship he found in God to everyone who crossed his path.

❖ ❖ ❖

To Forgive Is to Have Peace of Mind

Gurudeva used to say that as a rose gives off fragrance when crushed, so the devotee of God, when crushed by unkindness, still exudes the sweet essence of love.

Forgiveness, with its soothing vibration of divine love, neutralizes the erosive agitation of anger, guilt, and hatred. In an imperfect world where goodness inevitably meets opposition, forgiveness is an expression of God-consciousness. When we are ill-used, if, instead of condemning our offender, we grant pardon freely and wipe the slate of our consciousness clean, the result is that we earn for ourselves a blessed peace of mind.

Why is it sometimes so difficult to forgive and forget—to let go completely? The human ego demands vindication, and seeks it through vengeance or retribution; it feels superior while condemning. But this does not bring us peace. We would be far happier if we rather listened to the true Self, the soul—which is sufficient unto itself—and canceled the wrongdoer's debt, praying, "Lord, bless him." Do we not want God and others to excuse our errors? "Forgive and you shall be forgiven" is the divine law.

In the Hindu scriptures it is written: "One should forgive, under any injury....By forgiveness the universe is held together. Forgiveness is the might of the mighty; forgiveness is sacrifice; forgiveness is quiet of mind. Forgiveness and gentleness are the qualities of the Self-possessed. They represent eternal virtue." Strive to live by this ideal, offering kindness and healing love to all. Then shall you feel God's all-embracing love flowing into your own heart.

❖ ❖ ❖

Erasing Our Past Errors

Gurudeva Paramahansa Yogananda has said: "The errors of a lifetime can be corrected *today*....As soon as you give the verdict and strongly will to be a new person, you will change."

By tapping the all-conquering power of the soul, we can change instantaneously. What prevents this? We are too identified with our flaws, we accept limiting ideas about ourselves, and thereby become weighted down first with discouragement and then inertia. Having made mistakes, we carry around the "excess baggage" of remorse and defeatism.

We need to free ourselves from these dead weights. The secret in doing so is to live in the present. The past is gone; now is the time to make a sincere effort to live our lives as we know God would want us to. If we make a misstep, we should immediately correct ourselves, inwardly ask His help, and try to choose the right course. Instead of dwelling on past errors, focus on the joy the Lord feels when He sees us grow in strength and wisdom. Positive effort, with our attention focused on God, brings a sense of freedom and enthusiasm, and gives tremendous impetus to the will. Dynamic will supported by God's blessing can accomplish anything. Above all, we can become perfect lovers of God, attuned to Him, absorbed in His love, guided by His wisdom—in control of our destiny.

God's Unconditional Love for Us

What is God's nature? He is Father, Mother, Friend; love, compassion, understanding, forgiveness.

Divine incarnations such as Jesus and Krishna supremely manifested God's qualities that we might behold and know Divinity. Such examples are necessary for the encouragement of humankind, because at difficult times in our lives we need a reminder that God is loving and forgiving beyond our comprehension. Troubles too often create a perverse feeling that God has forsaken us, and the mind shuts Him out at the very moment we should be reaching out to Him in faith.

At times of weakness, it helps to dwell on some example from the scriptures showing how God, manifesting through great souls who are one with Him, views the disciple who has erred but sincerely wants to change. At the Last Supper, Jesus not only foretold that Peter would deny knowing him, but sought to comfort and protect Peter from losing heart, saying: "But I have prayed for thee, that thy faith fail not: and when thou art converted, strengthen thy brethren."* He understood that his disciple's loyalty would be overwhelmed by fear. But he saw this weakness as temporary; and it in no way altered his love for Peter or trust in his ability to accomplish God's will.

Every soul is a recipient of the unconditional love of God. Each one is His favorite, Guruji used to say. As our greatest well-wisher, the Lord is even more eager for our salvation than we are. Commune deeply with this God of endless love; He awaits you always in the temple of meditation.

"In Every Thing Give Thanks"

"Rejoice evermore," the Scripture tells us. "Pray without ceasing. In every thing give thanks."† When we gratefully acknowledge our Heavenly Father's loving-kindness, we deepen our attunement with Him. Appreciation opens the heart to the abundance of God's love in its many expressions.

There are three stages to the development of an attitude of unceasing thankfulness:

First is learning to turn immediately to God in gratitude whenever we have cause to rejoice. Any special blessing should remind us to thank sincerely the true Giver of all joys.

The second aspect involves not taking the good in our lives for granted. It is said that we rarely realize what we have until it is gone; but this need not be. Let

* Luke 22:32. † I Thessalonians 5:16–18.

us recognize and cherish the full worth of loved ones, of health, of provisions and conveniences, of the beauty in nature, of the good that abounds everywhere—all the while directing our loving attention to the Divine Provider.

Lastly, if we train our minds to thank God even in the midst of difficulties, we will discover a hidden blessing behind every adversity. Though thanking Him in these situations may require an act of will, we demonstrate thereby our trust, and automatically focus more on what is positive in that condition. Trials are but the "shade of His hand, outstretched caressingly";* thanksgiving helps to lift our gaze from the shadows to the hand of God. Our understanding opens to the valuable lessons to be learned, our spirits lift, and faith surges within. These positive feelings release healing power and strength within, and heighten our receptivity to God's transforming touch.

Thus may we "pray without ceasing," communing moment to moment with our Eternal Father and Friend. When He knows that He is first in our lives, He will clearly make known to us His everlasting, all-fulfilling love.

* From "The Hound of Heaven," by Francis Thompson.

OTHER BOOKS AND RECORDINGS BY SRI DAYA MATA

BOOKS

Only Love: Living the Spiritual Life in a Changing World

Enter the Quiet Heart:
Creating a Loving Relationship With God

Intuition: Soul-Guidance for Life's Decisions

CDs

Karma Yoga: Balancing Activity and Meditation

Moral Courage: Effecting Positive Change Through Moral and Spiritual Choices

The Way to Peace, Humility, and Love for God

AUDIOCASSETTES

Free Yourself From Tension
God First
Understanding the Soul's Need for God
Let Us Be Thankful
Anchoring Your Life in God
Is Meditation on God Compatible With Modern Life?
Living a God-Centered Life
Let Every Day Be Christmas

DVDs / VIDEOCASSETTES

Him I Shall Follow:
Remembrances of My Life With Paramahansa Yogananda

A Scripture of Love
Living in the Love of God
Security in a World of Change

The Second Coming of Christ:
Making of a Scripture—Reminiscences
by Sri Daya Mata and Sri Mrinalini Mata (DVD only)

BOOKS BY PARAMAHANSA YOGANANDA

Available at bookstores or online at www.yogananda-srf.org

Autobiography of a Yogi
Autobiography of a Yogi *(Audiobook, read by Ben Kingsley)*

God Talks With Arjuna: The Bhagavad Gita —
A New Translation and Commentary

The Second Coming of Christ: The Resurrection of the Christ Within You — A revelatory commentary on the original teachings of Jesus

The Yoga of Jesus
The Yoga of the Bhagavad Gita

The Collected Talks and Essays
Volume I: Man's Eternal Quest
Volume II: The Divine Romance
Volume III: Journey to Self-realization

Wine of the Mystic:
The Rubaiyat of Omar Khayyam — A Spiritual Interpretation

The Science of Religion
Whispers from Eternity
Songs of the Soul
Sayings of Paramahansa Yogananda
Scientific Healing Affirmations

Where There Is Light: Insight and Inspiration
for Meeting Life's Challenges

In the Sanctuary of the Soul: A Guide to Effective Prayer
Inner Peace: How to Be Calmly Active and Actively Calm
How You Can Talk With God
Metaphysical Meditations
The Law of Success
Cosmic Chants

A complete catalog of books and audio/video recordings — including rare archival recordings of Paramahansa Yogananda — is available on request or online at www.yogananda-srf.org

Self-Realization Fellowship Lessons

The scientific techniques of meditation taught by Paramahansa Yogananda, including Kriya Yoga—as well as his guidance on all aspects of balanced spiritual living—are presented in the *Self-Realization Fellowship Lessons*. For further information, please ask for the free introductory booklet, *Undreamed of Possibilities*.

SELF-REALIZATION FELLOWSHIP
3880 San Rafael Avenue • Los Angeles, California 90065-3298
TEL (323) 225-2471 • FAX (323) 225-5088
www.yogananda-srf.org

ABOUT PARAMAHANSA YOGANANDA

"The ideal of love for God and service to humanity found full expression in the life of Paramahansa Yogananda. ...Though the major part of his life was spent outside India, still he takes his place among our great saints. His work continues to grow and shine ever more brightly, drawing people everywhere on the path of the pilgrimage of the Spirit."

—from a tribute by the Government of India upon issuing a commemorative stamp in Paramahansa Yogananda's honor

Paramahansa Yogananda is widely revered as one of the preeminent spiritual figures of our time. Born in northern India in 1893, he lived and taught in the United States for more than thirty years—from 1920, when he was invited to serve as India's delegate to an international congress of religious leaders in Boston, until his passing in 1952. Through his life and teachings, he contributed in far-reaching ways to a greater awareness and appreciation in the West of the spiritual wisdom of the East.

Paramahansa Yogananda's life story, *Autobiography of a Yogi,* is at once a fascinating portrait of this beloved world teacher and a profound introduction to India's ancient science and philosophy of Yoga and its time-honored tradition of meditation. A perennial best-seller since it was first published over sixty years ago, the book has been translated into more than twenty languages and is used as a text and reference work in many colleges and universities. Considered a modern spiritual classic, it has found its way into the hearts of millions of readers around the world.

Today Paramahansa Yogananda's spiritual and humanitarian work is being carried on by Self-Realization Fellowship—the international religious society he founded in 1920—under the guidance of Sri Daya Mata. In addition to publishing his writings, lectures, and informal talks (including a comprehensive series of lessons for home study), the society oversees temples, retreats, and centers around the world; the monastic communities of the Self-Realization Order; and a Worldwide Prayer Circle.

AIMS AND IDEALS
of
Self-Realization Fellowship

As set forth by Paramahansa Yogananda, Founder
Sri Daya Mata, President

To disseminate among the nations a knowledge of definite scientific techniques for attaining direct personal experience of God.

To teach that the purpose of life is the evolution, through self-effort, of man's limited mortal consciousness into God Consciousness; and to this end to establish Self-Realization Fellowship temples for God-communion throughout the world, and to encourage the establishment of individual temples of God in the homes and in the hearts of men.

To reveal the complete harmony and basic oneness of original Christianity as taught by Jesus Christ and original Yoga as taught by Bhagavan Krishna; and to show that these principles of truth are the common scientific foundation of all true religions.

To point out the one divine highway to which all paths of true religious beliefs eventually lead: the highway of daily, scientific, devotional meditation on God.

To liberate man from his threefold suffering: physical disease, mental inharmonies, and spiritual ignorance.

To encourage "plain living and high thinking"; and to spread a spirit of brotherhood among all peoples by teaching the eternal basis of their unity: kinship with God.

To demonstrate the superiority of mind over body, of soul over mind.

To overcome evil by good, sorrow by joy, cruelty by kindness, ignorance by wisdom.

To unite science and religion through realization of the unity of their underlying principles.

To advocate cultural and spiritual understanding between East and West, and the exchange of their finest distinctive features.

To serve mankind as one's larger Self.